The MAGIC *of* TAROT

ALSO BY THE AUTHORS

The MAGIC of TAROT

LEANNA & BELETA GREENAWAY

ST. MARTIN'S
ESSENTIALS
NEW YORK

First published in the United States by St. Martin's Essentials,
an imprint of St. Martin's Publishing Group

THE MAGIC OF TAROT. Copyright © 2024 by Leanna Greenaway and Beleta Greenaway.
All rights reserved. Printed in the United States of America. For information,
address St. Martin's Publishing Group, 120 Broadway, New York, NY 10271.

www.stmartins.com

Designed by Steven Seighman

The Library of Congress Cataloging-in-Publication Data is available upon request.

ISBN 978-1-250-90273-3 (trade paperback)
ISBN 978-1-250-90274-0 (ebook)

Our books may be purchased in bulk for promotional, educational, or business use.
Please contact your local bookseller or the Macmillan Corporate and Premium
Sales Department at 1-800-221-7945, extension 5442, or by email at
MacmillanSpecialMarkets@macmillan.com.

First Edition: 2024

10 9 8 7 6 5 4 3 2 1

To all those who choose to explore the magical mysteries of Tarot,
this book is for you

Contents

Preface

Together, we have amassed over seventy years of Tarot knowledge. When we decided to write this book, we wanted to give our readers the most comprehensive information to become proficient Tarot practitioners. We regard this as a teaching manual, and even if you are already skilled in using Tarot, we are sure you will find alternative aspects to consider. Throughout the pages, we've given detailed descriptions on each card, offering traditional and modern meanings so that you can choose the interpretation you prefer. We also provide tips on memorizing the cards, grouping them to make the readings unique, and have included some case studies that might help you understand what to expect if you pursue the Tarot as a career.

Suppose you have already studied the Tarot and know the cards well; in that case, you will find that some books you read will probably be different and offer alternative interpretations. It's a fact that although many traditional aspects of the Tarot have been passed down through the ages, the interpretations in modern decks can all differ somewhat. In truth, there are no right or wrong descriptions; it's an individual choice. Some readers will simply use the cards as a crutch and take from their psychic inspiration, whereas others might read the cards by the book and implement everything they have learned. No two Tarot readers are the same; we all have unique and personal styles.

You might prefer the old-fashioned interpretations. Reading old-style Tarot is fine, but because these meanings date back hundreds of years, you may struggle to decipher the descriptions for the modern client. We offer a section on the traditional definitions based on decks like the Rider-Waite and the Morgan-Greer, but we advise you to study the section on the modern interpretations, too; in our opinion, this is a better route to follow. Here we present more realistic situations that your clients might identify with, including love, sex, drugs, alcohol, marriage, divorce, children, finances, and a wide range of other topics. You will also find them easier to learn because each card will be more relevant to the issues that present themselves in the lives of people today.

We have learned a lot through reading countless Tarot books over the years and included information that we psychically channeled from our spirit helpers and guides of others. Tarot is a complex and enigmatic subject to study, but once you grasp it, the cards will always guide you when you are unsure of the future. Don't worry if it takes you time to absorb the meanings. Everyone is different, and you will learn at your own pace.

The MAGIC of
TAROT

1

A Brief History

Another term for Tarot or card reading is "cartomancy," and a practitioner is referred to as a cartomancer. We don't hear these phrases much today as we tend to identify more as Tarot readers, fortune tellers, clairvoyants, and psychics. Tarot, through the ages, has been an aid for divination and stimuli for psychic information. It can help to make decisions and cast light on complex problems. According to many, the cards remind the soul of its ancient wisdom and possess knowledge of the universe. The history of Tarot is sketchy, but we know it has Italian roots. Based on the illustrations from the Middle Ages, it was initially developed as a game that the Europeans adopted. It has been said that the earliest Tarot deck consisted of seventeen cards and was discovered in Italy in 1392. Thirty years later, Bonifacio Bembo was commissioned by the duke of Milan to paint the full deck. It was called the Visconti deck, after the duke's family name. As their popularity grew, the cards appeared in different parts of Europe, and the travelers and Roma made them famous by using them for fortune-telling to earn a little money.

Do I Have to Be Psychic to Read the Cards?

We believe that every person on the planet possesses a sixth sense. Some people may be in tune with their psychic side, whereas others have yet to make that connection. We all primarily rely on our five senses, but our sixth sense is just as vital and is frequently overlooked. Most of us lead busy lives and have little free time to meditate or reflect on spiritual matters. Our ancient ancestors were far more connected to the earth and their mystical beliefs, but they had had more time to be still. Animals also possess a sixth sense, seeing or feeling otherworldly presences. They will move to higher ground before a storm strikes because they have an innate sense of when danger is coming. Humans have gradually lost this natural feeling, but by regaining it, you can connect with your inner self and go on to receive communications from the spirit world.

Learning the Tarot, or any other form of divination, is a perfect way to unleash your psychic abilities. The more you do it, the better you will get. Of course, even the best readers don't wake up feeling psychic every morning, yet the Tarot will never let you down. Your reading can still be accurate since it will always provide you with the details you need to foretell the future for your clients. People have often asked us how the cards work; in all honesty, no one is really sure. It's our opinion that the cards awaken upon shuffling and tune into the client's psyche while being handled. Magically, with the spirit world's help, the cards are positioned precisely so the reader can decipher them. In truth, we think it's safe to say that the mysteries of Tarot are shrouded in secrecy, but if you are open to their magic, they will give you a wealth of information. It is incredible to turn over a card in front of a stranger and tell them everything about themselves, their likes, dislikes, and how their journey in life is progressing.

Does the Tarot Bring Bad Luck?

Some folks are so superstitious, they even believe keeping a deck of Tarot cards in the house will bring them ill fortune. In times gone by, when religion ruled the thoughts and actions of humanity, this stigma was unfairly placed upon the Tarot cards. Rumor said they represented the work of the Devil, and because of this, the Tarot was forced underground and used secretly by seers, witches, and Roma. Its popularity started to blossom in the nineteenth and twentieth centuries, and it has become one of the most used forms of divination today. As with most things, people fear what they don't understand, so rest assured that your Tarot cards are not unlucky, and they will not bring bad luck or misfortune. If anything, they will become your trusted companion.

Choosing Your Tarot

Choosing a Tarot deck can be mind-boggling, to say the least, with thousands of packs in circulation today and endless books that can sometimes contradict one another. With all these choices, those who become adept at Tarot are sure to find at least one or two decks that they fall in love with and, over time, will probably end up with a vast collection to suit their every mood. Some people collect them purely for the artwork, which can often be stunning.

Before experimenting with specialized packs, it's best to learn the basics with traditional Tarot decks such as the Rider-Waite (Arthur Edward Waite), Morgan-Greer (Lloyd Morgan and Bill F. Greer), 1JJ Swiss Tarot (Stuart Kaplan), and Hanson-Roberts (Mary Hanson-Roberts). Studying the meanings of these will make for good groundwork. Once you have mastered them and have an insight into the traditional interpretations, you can then go on to explore more specialized cards, like the Tarot of the Old Path (Howard Rodway), the Tarot of Dreams (Ciro Marchetti), the Mythic Tarot (Juliet Sharman-Burke and Liz Greene), or more faith-inspired decks like the Tarot of the Witches (Fergus Hall) or the Druid Craft Tarot (Philip Carr-Gomm). One of our absolute favorites is the Gilded Tarot Royale by Ciro Marchetti, which has exquisite illustrations.

There will undoubtedly be other interesting decks you might be drawn to, as there are hundreds of esoteric and holistic packs as well as Wiccan and New Age decks.

In this book, we chose the Rider-Waite deck to offer a traditional approach and the One World Tarot, a lovely contemporary deck illustrated by Alexandra Filipek, for modern interpretations.

Whichever decks of Tarot become your favorite, you can rest assured that using the interpretations from this book's traditional and modern teachings will apply to almost any that you decide to use. We advise that while you are learning, stick to one deck only, and when you are entirely confident with the cards' meanings, you can go on to explore different ones.

Welcoming Your Tarot

The Tarot is steeped in magical mystery, and if you want to get the best out of the cards, you must treat them with great respect. Every time we buy a new deck, we like to give the cards a small blessing; this harmonizes the Tarot's energy with ours and serves as a type of introduction, similar to when you meet someone for the first time. So many people will purchase a new set and neglect to prepare them for use, so if you follow the steps below with each pack you acquire, you won't go far wrong.

Preparing Your Cards

Step 1: Remove any plastic wrapping and take your cards out of their box. Sit quietly, holding them for at least five minutes. Close your eyes, and in your mind, imagine light radiating from the center of your forehead, projecting toward your Tarot. Next, visualize the glow radiating back from the cards to your forehead. This process should take about ten minutes, and don't be surprised if you feel a little lightheaded afterward; this is nothing to worry about. You are simply receiving the Tarot's energy, which will open the third eye chakra, located between your eyebrows.

Slowly begin to take each card, studying every image thoroughly. While you are doing this, repeat this chant with each one:

"Magical Tarot, I bless thee, unite with me, predict for me."

This verse should be spoken seventy-eight times, once for each card. We know it sounds tedious, but you will be working with these cards for many years to come, and you need to make a connection with them if they are to give you accurate predictions.

Step 2: Place the cards on a table and smudge them with either a white sage bundle or a sage incense stick. Light the sage and blow out the flames until the embers are red; this will settle down after a few seconds until it is just smoking. White sage will spiritually disinfect any unwanted energy left over from anyone who might have handled the cards when they were packaged and sealed.

Next, take a small handbell or some Tibetan bells and ring them over the cards; this will attune them, a bit like tuning a musical instrument.

Place a clear quartz crystal on top of the Tarot pack for a few hours. Quartz is an amplifying stone and will increase the deck's power radiating throughout.

Sleeping with the cards under your pillow for a night is beneficial, as it improves your ability to connect with their energy.

Finally, wrap the cards in a silken scarf. If you believe in the magical properties of colors, choose a shade that resonates with you.

✳ White scarves represent all that is pure and angelic; this is important for those who believe in angels and use them to channel their energy into a reading.

✳ Deep purple or indigo is the highest mystical color. It would be perfect for those who prefer to do more spiritual readings.

* Pale blue enhances psychic ability and will help you fine-tune your client's vibration.
* Yellow is a healing color, representing sunshine, which will work toward bringing positivity and hope into a reading.
* Orange will remove any psychic blocks, allowing you to understand your predictions clearly.
* Red is a great color if you have a special deck used solely for predictions relating to love and passion.
* Pink is also used for love but is gentler and more compassionate and will bring balance and harmony.
* Green is more nature-based, so witches might like to wrap their cards in this color to channel their psychic flow and tune into the meridian levels of the planet.
* Black: We believe this is an unfavorable color and inappropriate for Tarot readings. It is well known that some who experiment with the dark side may accept this, but we categorically reject it. In the wrong hands, Tarot can open sinister portals similar to that of the Ouija board.

When you have selected a scarf in which to wrap your new set of Tarot, you can also purchase a drawstring bag or a fancy box to house the cards; this is entirely your choice. We know many readers prefer to make their own bags, and some witches and Wiccans like to have a pentagram image on their box or pouch, which gives added protection.

One important thing to remember is that these are your Tarot cards, so don't allow others to do readings with them or let children play around with them; if you do, future readings could be muddled and confusing.

Energizing Your Tarot in the Moonlight

Sometimes your cards will feel lackluster, or if you've done a lot of readings, they may be drained of energy. You can tell when this is happening, as they won't be as accurate, or the cards might appear jumbled and hard to read. Having more than one deck is a good idea; you can rest and recharge one while using another.

A Moon Blessing

This part is optional but is something Leanna likes to do. On a dry night of a full moon phase, take the cards outside, place them on a table, and weigh them down with a large piece of moonstone. If you don't have a garden or yard, you can position the cards inside the house on a window ledge. Leave them overnight to soak up the moon's rays. This procedure can be done at any time and will charge and empower your cards, awakening their magic and leaving them ready to work.

Once you have engaged with your pack of Tarot cards and energized and blessed them, you are now ready to forge ahead and let the magic begin.

Your journey starts here.

2

Your Tarot Toolbox

When we began our Tarot journey years ago, it wasn't always straightforward to find the required supplies. Many readers would only have one pack of Tarot cards if they were lucky, and if they couldn't easily source them, they would use playing cards as a substitute. Today, we have the internet at our fingertips and are so fortunate to be able to purchase everything we need.

Around the world, countless vibrant Tarot decks are for sale, complete with booklets describing the mysticism in each card: We tend to take internet tutorials and direct answers from search engines for granted, and we don't rely on word of mouth anymore, though we should. For those who are keen to learn, there are online courses and even chat rooms where you can meet like-minded people, and these folks love to help and are happy to share their knowledge.

Whatever you decide to collect in your Tarot toolbox is entirely up to you, but you will need a few fundamentals. The most important is a table large enough to seat two people with enough space on the surface to lay out your cards. There is no right or wrong way to set up your reading table; you have to do what feels right and surround yourself with items you love or are comfortable with. One other necessary item is a candle of your choice. The size isn't important. You might prefer a white tealight or something a little fancier. Candles will clear away leftover energy and set the right scene for your readings.

Below we have listed a few other things you might find helpful.

A Glass Circle

If you choose to have a cloth on your table, you might find that the cards are not easy to maneuver, and when you move them around, they can ruck the material. It is a good idea to have a large glass circle that you can place in the middle over the fabric. You can then deal your cards onto this, and they will easily slide around.

Crystals

The magic of crystals can work for you in so many ways. Some stones, like clear quartz, will amplify the power of the cards to give you more precise and accurate predictions. Then there are those crystals you might place on your table to protect you from unwanted negative energies. These include amethyst, fluorite, black tourmaline, and black obsidian. Moldavite is an extraterrestrial stone that, when worn as jewelry, homes into the reader's psychic ability, helping them tune into the client. Moldavite is so powerful that the wearer may occasionally feel queasy or lightheaded; therefore, it does come with caution. It might be best to wear it around the house for a few weeks so you can attune to it and get used to its energy before you use it during a reading. Some readers will even wear it to bed to receive prophetic dreams.

Over time, you may have a collection of gemstones that you dot around your reading room. Like a battery, crystals often go flat and need regular recharging. Although they emit positive energy, they can also act like a sponge and soak up negative vibes; this can happen if you have read for clients who are unhappy or crying. We always suggest you cleanse and charge them at least once a month, and some Tarot readers will go one step further and cleanse them after every reading.

Charging Your Crystals

A safe way to cleanse and charge your stones is to leave the crystal outside overnight to soak up the moon's rays. You might also like to light a sage incense stick or a white sage smudging bundle and trail it around the stone. Other ways include submerging the stone in water or salt, but you must be careful because some crystals are porous, and this method might make the color fade. It's best to do some research beforehand to make sure.

Here is a cleansing ritual we use with our crystals: Light a white sage smudging stick and waft it all around the room where the crystals are housed. Play some soft meditation music, and then, standing before the stones, ring some Tibetan bells. Say this mantra three times.

> *"Crystals of beauty, I empower thee,*
> *Generate your force so you can help me,*
> *Convey only good and positive energy."*

It's a good idea to purchase a varied selection of crystal tumble stones for all different situations; you might like to give one to the client to take home. You can buy some pretty, small drawstring bags relatively cheaply online to place them in. The customer now has a reminder of their reading with this thoughtful gesture.

For more information on crystals and their magical correspondences, you can purchase the book *The Crystal Witch: The Magickal Way to Calm and Heal the Body, Mind, and Spirit* by Leanna Greenaway and Shawn Robbins, or *The Little Book of Crystals: An Inspiring Introduction to Everything You Need to Know to Enhance Your Life Using Crystals* by Beleta Greenaway.

A Pendulum

Sometimes when the cards are being stubborn or your psychic juices refuse to flow, a pendulum can give quick results, especially if you need a yes or no answer. If you shop online, you will find an array of different kinds, and some have crystals fixed to the chain so you can use the appropriate stone pendulum for particular situations. For instance, if you need the answer to a romantic question, rose quartz would be suitable. If someone were worried for their health, then an amethyst would suffice. Between us, we own about seven or eight different crystal pendulums that we use from time to time in our readings.

How to Use the Pendulum

Rest your elbow on the table to keep your hand steady and hold the chain between your thumb and forefinger. Hover this over the Tarot card representing the question that requires answering. The pendulum will mostly move in a clockwise circular motion for "yes" and counterclockwise for "no." Focus on the swinging crystal and ask the question in your mind. You should receive the answer in no time. If the chain refuses to move, it is not correctly tuned in or doesn't know the outcome.

As we have mentioned for crystals, make sure pendulums are cleansed regularly.

Candles and Oils

We've briefly mentioned candles above, and they are wonderful in creating the right ambience or warding off any negative vibes that may be lurking around. We usually have about two or three burning in the reading room, mainly white or purple, as these are the dominant spiritual colors.

If you like to use an oil burner, you can burn specific essential oils that enhance your psychic ability. These include cedar, frankincense, lavender, peppermint, sandalwood, rose, and jasmine. It's best to ensure that you get a good quality essential oil from a reputable seller, as some cheaper versions can be watered down.

Protective Salt and Symbols

Because you will be reading for people you don't know, keep a container of salt nearby as a source of protection. It's excellent for warding off negative spirits and will act as a sanitizer in the room. Even a small bowl with a few teaspoons of salt will work just fine. You can place it on your reading table or a shelf somewhere in the room.

Witches like to have the pentagram symbol close, as this is also a powerful protective emblem. Often the witchy reader will wear a pentagram necklace or ring and might even hang garlic by the door to ward off evil spirits.

Angel Cards

Having a pack of angel cards nearby is a nice idea to use alongside the reading. There are numerous, beautiful angel decks to purchase, usually consisting of around forty-four cards, and they have a little message of inspiration on each one. When the reading ends, you can ask the client to choose one or two angel cards and use them as the client's final communication from the spirit world. The messages are so accurate and often very moving.

Hand Gel

Since the COVID-19 pandemic, many readers are asking their clients to use hand sanitizer before touching the Tarot cards. This is a good idea because if you read for three or four people in a day, germs can linger on the cards, and any viruses can be passed on. If the client can't use the hand gel for whatever reason, ask them to wash their hands before they touch the cards.

Kleenex

As we mention later in the book, many clients will become overwhelmed during a reading and cry. This can happen for several reasons: Perhaps they are struggling with life in general, a partnership or relationship might have ended, or they may have lost someone close to them. Having a box of Kleenex on the table is a good idea, as is keeping a stash in reserve because you'll be replacing them often.

Helpful Phone Numbers

If you choose Tarot as a career, you will meet an array of different people over the years. Some might be healers, acupuncturists, reflexologists, nutritionists, counselors, or hypnotherapists; the list is endless. It's a nice idea to have their cards on display to direct your client to a suitable person once your consultation is over. Another set of important numbers to have at hand are those for family services, shelters, and charity organizations. You won't be able to fix someone in sixty minutes, so you will need to direct them toward those who can offer additional support when they leave you. If you can, try to promote only those who come from recommendations, or, better still, visit them yourself so you can be confident in their respectable reputation for their work.

You will find that not all Tarot readers are mediums, so if you have a client interested in communicating with a loved one in spirit, find a reputable medium in your area you can recommend.

3

The Major Arcana

When you begin your Tarot journey, it is imperative to learn the meanings of each card. A perfect way to start is to memorize the key points of one upright card each day. It's not necessary to remember every single word in the card descriptions, so to begin with, aim for two or three quick triggers.

Example—for the Fool, you might focus on the following:

A new path ahead, but be patient. New people to enter the client's life. Don't over-think things.

Even if you memorize the first two points on each card—say, a new job and the birth of a child—it will help. Look closely at the details on each card and familiarize yourself with them. Usually, a part of the image will jump out at you or make you feel emotional or empathetic. You might see or feel things that others can't see. Gradually, you will link with your deck and what it's trying to communicate.

Once you have learned a few meanings, it's a good idea to ask someone to test you.

Many Tarot readers dislike reading the reverse meanings—when the cards are upside down—because they can appear too negative. Because there is a trend to sanitize Tarot decks, some readers will go for the easy option of only reading them in the upright position. We believe you should use both positions if you wish to be truly proficient at this skill. If you don't, you will miss out on predictions you would otherwise have. When you feel comfortable mastering all seventy-eight cards upright, move on to learning their reverse meanings. In many cases, the reverse is the opposite of the upright meaning, which proves very helpful.

It will probably take a good year of study to understand the meanings completely, but once they are ingrained in your mind, you shouldn't forget them.

If you can, continue practicing daily to create a clear memory. After a while, you'll gain sufficient experience to glance at a card and immediately know its meaning.

We have included our channeled inspirations in each card description as another way to help you remember. These lyrics are lovely to learn and can get you out of a tight spot if you have a memory lapse.

Example: the Two of Wands—*A choice to make with business plans. Accept the challenge with both hands.* Straightaway, you'll remember that all twos in Tarot represent choices and decisions, so you are halfway to remembering the other critical points about the card.

Finally, if you are still a student, the most important thing is to work with one Tarot deck and stick with it. Other packs have unique visual styles; some are more conventional, while others could be themed and exotic. When you have passed your apprenticeship, you can cherry-pick whatever style appeals to you as long as it has seventy-eight cards and you feel a connection to it. Collectively, we have at least sixty decks, and over the years, you will probably accumulate many yourself, but nothing compares to that first deck that helped you find your calling.

When purchasing a new set of Tarot cards, you will note they often come with a small booklet offering denotations and interpretations. Don't feel daunted about this as their slant could be very useful, but remember the card descriptions you trained with. The definitions in this book will work for any pack of Tarot with seventy-eight cards. Yes, specialized decks have different interpretations, but Tarot is usually generic.

The Twelve Birth Signs for the Major Arcana

Twelve of the Major Arcana cards have a birth sign associated with them, and so by learning these dates, you can use the times to predict when an event might likely occur. For instance, if the Hierophant (Taurus) is in the spread, it could mean the situations appearing in the reading could occur in either April or May. Another example would be if the Hierophant were placed somewhere around the Hermit (Virgo); the prediction could happen between April (Hierophant) and September (Hermit). Let's say the Emperor (Aries) is next to the King of Swords in a spread; you might ask the client if there is an Aries man around her—this is an example of associating the cards with a person's star sign. A good thing to remember is that you can use one of these twelve cards to predict a situation and use it again in the same spread to represent the time scale.

Example: the Hierophant (a house move), the Six of Swords (a move out of the area), the Sun (happiness).

Answer: The client will move house (Hierophant), probably to a different town (Six of Swords), around Taurus time (Hierophant) in April or May. It will be an easy move, and the client will be happy about it (the Sun).

The Emperor, Aries, March 21–April 19

The Hierophant, Taurus, April 20–May 20

The Lovers, Gemini, May 21–June 20

The Chariot, Cancer, June 21–July 22

Strength, Leo, July 23–August 22

The Hermit, Virgo, August 23–September 22

Justice, Libra, September 23–October 22

Death, Scorpio, October 23–November 21

Temperance, Sagittarius, November 22–December 21

The Devil, Capricorn, December 22–January 19

The Star, Aquarius, January 20–February 18

The Moon, Pisces, February 19–March 20

Using the Major Arcana Only

It is purported that nineteenth-century French occultist Jean-Baptiste Pitois first named the twenty-two trump cards the Major Arcana. He believed the cards symbolized mystical knowledge, and if they were used on their own for readings, it would give the predictions more impact.

Some people will prefer to use only the Major Arcana in their readings, possibly when they first discover the Tarot and find the Minor Arcana overwhelming. There are no hard and fast rules, as we all explore our own decks the way we wish. We always look at the Minor cards as the talkative cards that pack out the meanings of the spread. Using just the Major Arcana, we will get detailed meanings that are straight to the point. The purist might disagree and say these are just the headlines, not the whole story. As the Major Arcana connects to the universal energy, it can portray an in-depth spiritual meaning of our life.

For a past, present, future prediction spread, shuffle the cards and lay out three rows of five cards.

Rider-Waite Tarot   One World Tarot

The Fool

Fate now leads you where you tread. An unexpected path ahead.

CARD NUMBER: 0 or 22 **CRYSTALS:** tourmaline and turquoise
HERBS: cedar and rose geranium **KEYWORDS:** new paths ahead

Rider-Waite Interpretation

Traditionally, in many decks, the Fool is a juggler or a beggar in rags, without shoes upon his feet. He represents numbers 0 or 22 in the Tarot deck, 0 being the first card and 22 being the last, symbolizing the unceasing cycle of life, birth, and death. Here we see an innocent young man setting out on a journey of discovery. He has no idea where he is heading, but he is prepared to take risks and trusts that the universe will care for him. Warmly the sun shines down on him and his little dog; he hasn't a care in the world, for all he wants is freedom from any base desires. He is an optimistic dreamer, and his journey is full of excitement, wonderment, and challenge. A beautiful white rose is held in his hand, depicting his innocence and naivety, and he carries a modest bundle with his scant possessions tied around a stick and placed over his shoulder. His faithful white dog at his feet encourages him to forge ahead but warns him not to step blithely over the cliff.

One World Interpretation

The Fool is a genuinely positive card with the number 0 representing a period of time before something is about to happen. The client faces a new path ahead, but they must be patient because their journey on it won't happen right away. They are bewildered by the sudden unconventional twists and turns in their life, but the result could be gratifying, too. Suddenly the rules are thrown out the window as fate makes them look at everything differently. Instead of jumping in with both feet, they should consider their actions and take time to contemplate.

Bizarre and entertaining new people explode into the seeker's space. Everything is so mind-blowing; the client will have to watch their nerves and try not to overthink things.

MEMORIZE

A time before something happens ✳ A new path ahead, but be patient ✳ New people to enter the client's life ✳ Don't overthink things

Associated Cards with Upright Fool

✳ If the Lovers card (upright) is in the same spread, the client's sex life could become amazing as a new partner urges them to try different techniques.

✳ If the card appears with the Ace of Wands (upright), someone will introduce them to a fascinating new job.

✳ If the Sun (upright) is close, the client should forge ahead without worry, as their new path will lead them to success.

✳ If the Fool (reversed) is present with the Empress (upright) and a Page (upright or reversed), the seeker must take care of an unwanted pregnancy. If the Three of Swords (upright or reversed) is also present, the pregnancy might be linked to a person who is already married.

Rider-Waite Interpretation

New projects are in the making, but now isn't the right time to act. Something is stopping the client from proceeding; perhaps they lack self-confidence and don't believe their ideas will work.

Another interpretation is that they are taking unnecessary risks and not thinking about the consequences of their actions and how they could impact others.

One World Interpretation

Double check, you must make sure, or very bad luck you will endure.

KEYWORD: *disorder*

The Fool's luck is, at last, running out; will there be anything he can salvage at the end of the day? This card in the reverse position does not bode well. It signifies a time for the client to grow up and take responsibility for their own actions. They need a plan for the future and to go over details carefully, or they will invite disorder into their life. Their finances could be in dire straits, or someone close to them might be gambling. Don't step over the cliff into oblivion.

MEMORIZE

⟶ · ·•· · ⟵

Luck is running out ✳ Grow up and take responsibility ✳ Make a plan for the future ✳ Poor finances ✳ Someone gambling

Rider-Waite Tarot

One World Tarot

The Magician

Your psychic ability can be found; magic and power are all around.

CARD NUMBER: 1 **CRYSTALS:** opal and goldstone **HERB:** rosemary **KEYWORD:** magic
OTHER NAMES: the Magus, the Juggler, the Trickster, the Wizard, the Shaman

---

Rider-Waite Interpretation

One of the Magician's hands points to the sky and the other to the ground, showing his magical connection between heaven and earth. The Magician controls his environment and uses his willpower to overcome obstacles. Above his head is a nimbus or a lemniscate, which in modern terms is described as the figure-eight symbol on its side, depicting life everlasting, into eternity. The snake eating its tail is wrapped tightly around his waist to represent infinity. The robe he wears is snow white for purity, the crimson cloak for his experiences in life and the dynamic ability to gain strength from them. In the Rider-Waite deck he stands before an altar, and the items before him symbolize the four suits of the Minor Arcana—Swords, Pentacles, Wands, and Cups; these also represent air, earth, fire, and water. This is the vital allegory representing the secret knowledge to aid his journey. The Magician can mediate between this world and the next; this he does freely, adding to his already vast knowledge. He is also known as the Juggler or the Trickster because of his complex and unpredictable nature, often using magic to spellbind his audience.

As time passed, his role changed, and he now assists people using his incredible insight and psychic abilities. His role is to help others reach their life goals and fulfill the challenges to improve their karmic lessons and soul growth.

One World Interpretation

Over the centuries, the Magician has become a dynamic spiritual guide; if he comes into the querent's cards, it is a good omen of protection. Sometimes he urges a bold step forward, a leap of faith, to diversify and try something that one has never done before, perhaps a new business, a journey of adventure, or a feat of bravery.

This card can also appear if the client has a psychic ability. They could be having unusual dreams or experiencing something supernatural. Always encourage them to open the door to their psychic capacities, pay attention to their dreams, and not brush off any strange feelings. The seeker will be able to weave magic or even predict the future and perhaps have success with affirmations or casting spells.

The Magician will gently guide the person through the psychic process and awaken their senses.

Memorize

Powerful male guide, protecting and guiding ✶ Take a leap of faith ✶ Client could be psychic ✶ Pay attention to dreams and feelings ✶ Affirmations and spells

Associated Cards with Upright Magician

* If the Magician appears with a group of Wands (upright or reversed), the person will be stressed out at work and must juggle their time to fit in everything.
* If the Four of Swords (upright) is nearby, the Magician advises rest and recuperation. Meditation is needed so that he can use his powerful healing magic to improve the situation.
* If Strength (upright) is in situ, help and support will be given to the person to find the right solutions.
* The Magician (reversed) together with the Four of Swords (upright) can indicate trouble with respiratory ailments such as chest infections, influenza, or bronchitis.

Rider-Waite Interpretation

The querent will be struggling to fulfill their ambitions and might face obstacles wherever they turn. With this card depicted as the trickster, one must think before manipulating a situation, and seek not to harm others. The client is talented in many things but has failed to use their potential so far. Something needs to change before they can reach their goals because there is much more to give.

One World Interpretation

Discipline is what you need. Make a plan to sow the seeds.

KEYWORDS: *Grinding halt*

A lack of energy and stamina could be holding the person back, so projects might come to a grinding halt. Some interference from others will block the flow, and a way out is hard to find. The client is not focusing on the problems and only wishes for a quick fix, but there is a need to look deeper into situations and regain some control. Connect with the Magician and trust yourself to find the answers that he will provide. Self-discipline is a must; although it could be easy to push problems out of the way, it will only bring more difficulties in the end. With patience and perseverance the solutions will come, and harmony will be restored.

MEMORIZE

Lack of stamina ✶ Not focusing on problems ✶ Connect with the Magician ✶ Patience and perseverance ✶ Harmony restored

Rider-Waite Tarot   *One World Tarot*

The High Priestess

Healing from your lives past will free you from the pain at last.

CARD NUMBER: 2 **CRYSTALS:** labradorite and moonstone **HERBS:** sandalwood and lemongrass
KEYWORD: guide **OTHER NAMES:** the Female Pope, La Papessa, Goddess of the Moon, Daughter of the Moon, Temple Virgin, Witch, Triple-Faced Goddess, Egyptian Goddess Isis

---

Rider-Waite Interpretation

The history of the High Priestess likens her to Persephone, the queen of the underworld and the goddess of grain, nature, and spring. Her robes are blue, and she holds the scroll of universal knowledge in her lap. Traditionally, the High Priestess is virginal and does not empathize or want to be with the male sex. She is powerful in understanding all people's sexuality and moods, menstruation, and sensitivity. Her feet are placed on a sickle moon representing her understanding of the tides and water. The crown signifies the cow horns of the Egyptian goddess Isis, which depicts abundance and the knowledge of the cosmos. In other traditional decks, behind her is a veil to different dimensions, suspended between the two pillars of Solomon.

She represents mystery and the secrets of the universe, and in times gone by, a whole religion was based upon her power and wisdom. She was known to guard the gateways to the mind and the deepest recesses of the soul.

One World Interpretation

Today, the High Priestess is acknowledged as a beautiful female guide who completely understands feminine energy. As she is magical, she will help others hone their sixth sense and appear when the time is precisely right, assisting them on their new journey. If someone is struggling with past life trauma, she can be called upon to balance and heal the soul. This card can often appear when one is reading for different genders, and she will help all LGBTQ+ people appreciate themselves, nurture any concerns or fears, and offer heterosexual men support in discovering more about their feminine side.

The client must pay attention to dream sleep, as this card indicates that they could be receiving messages from the spirit world to better help them in the future. After connecting with the High Priestess, the client's psychic abilities could be awakened, leading them on a mystical voyage. She is more likely to make a spiritual connection with the querent between the hours of 2 A.M. and 5 A.M. Encourage them to keep a pad and pen near the bed to write down any strange dreams. Her messages might make sense later.

> ### MEMORIZE
> ⌒⸳⸳⸳⸳⸳⸳⌒
>
> Wonderful spirit guide ✳ Helps LGBTQ+ people to appreciate themselves ✳ Past life trauma ✳ Awakens psychic abilities ✳ Receives messages in dream sleep

Associated Cards with Upright High Priestess

✳ If the High Priestess appears with the Nine of Swords (upright or reversed), the client might suffer from their digestive system.

✳ If the High Priestess is around the King of Swords (upright or reversed), a man in the client's life will lack spiritual understanding.

✳ If the card appears next to the Four of Cups (upright), there will be tears and regrets of the past and a feeling of utter loneliness.

✳ When the High Priestess sits next to the Seven of Cups (upright), strange predictive dreams will be coming into the seeker's life, which could be mind-blowing.

✳ If she presents herself in the reversed position next to a court mentor (upright or reversed), her message is to put the court mentor's needs first.

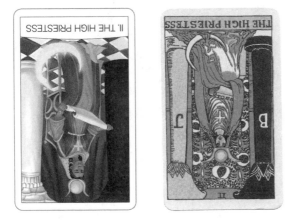

Rider-Waite Interpretation

Don't be influenced by others' ideas or drawn into someone else's drama. The client must focus on their own path and put their desires first. The time is right for some quiet reflection, to delve into the soul and psychoanalyze oneself. The High Priestess will always be available to help, and because she expresses the truth, she will speak to the client's subconscious, so it's time for them to trust their intuition.

One World Interpretation

The goddess of the moon draws near. Dry your eyes and have no fear.
KEYWORD: *confusion*

If the High Priestess is reversed, it signifies a confusing time ahead, especially if the client is dealing with female relationships. Gossip could be widespread, and a catty group of females will upset the seeker, making them feel isolated. This situation could arise both at work or in the family environment. It's a time for them to rely on their sixth sense and ask for a feminine perspective from the High Priestess. Suggest to the querent to go to bed an hour early, take a moonstone crystal to hold, and ask the High Priestess for guidance when meditating. Family life could be difficult, and some members will feel like strangers. A lack of communication might never be resolved until someone finally backs down.

MEMORIZE

❡ ·•· ❡

Confusing time ✳ Problems with female relationships ✳ Gossips and catty women ✳ Meditate with a moonstone crystal ✳ Family members feeling like strangers

Rider-Waite Tarot   *One World Tarot*

The Empress

Motherhood and business good. Harvest your benefits as you should.

CARD NUMBER: 3 **CRYSTALS:** rose quartz and aventurine **HERB:** red clover **KEYWORDS:** mother goddess **OTHER NAMES:** Mother Goddess, Ishtar, Eostre, Easter, Astarte, Adelaide

Rider-Waite Interpretation

The Empress has a crown of twelve stars to represent the planet Venus; the symbol is also shown on a shield nearby. Venus symbolizes beauty and harmony but mostly love. The crown also depicts the twelve signs of the zodiac and the twelve months of the year.

The Empress is seated in a stunning garden, which is fertile and verdant. Usually, there will be some water nearby or a fountain splashing.

Ears of corn are growing at her feet, and in her right hand, she holds a scepter, which denotes the embodiment of her power and authority. The Empress is seen wearing a snow-white gown decorated with red pomegranates, the fruit of fertility and abundance. Looking closely at the card, you will see she is heavily pregnant and ready to give birth.

One World Interpretation

The Empress depicts all that is powerful in its feminine form and reminds us to thank Mother Earth for all she has provided. A popular trend for the Empress is representing her as one's mother or grandmother. She also signifies pregnancy, especially if a Page is present, so if your client is of childbearing age, she may soon find that she's expecting a child. If you are reading for a more mature person, news of pregnancy will occur in the client's family or close circle of friends.

The Empress also signifies creativity, so new projects could impact the seeker's life. Perhaps they might be refurbishing a house or starting an art class or a dressmaking course. Another meaning could be the birth of a brand-new business venture that should grow into abundance. The garden will come under focus, too, and those around the querent might begin to take an interest in gardening or try their hand at growing produce. If there is a new relationship, it will show harmony and a happy sex life.

> **MEMORIZE**
>
> ⌐••••⌐
>
> A pregnancy ✳ A mother or grandmother ✳ Creativity ✳ New projects or business ✳ New relationship

Associated Cards with Upright Empress

✳ When the World (upright or reversed) is in the same spread, the message is that our planet is a school, where we come to learn our karmic lessons in creativity, expansion, and knowledge.

✳ An excellent job or new opportunity could bring much happiness if the Empress is situated next to the Ace of Pentacles (upright).

✳ A pregnancy might soon be announced when a Page (upright or reversed) is next to the Empress. If these cards come out with either the Nine or Ten of Swords (upright or reversed) alongside the Death card (upright), the client will hear of a miscarriage.

✳ If the Empress has Justice (upright or reversed) in situ, legal situations must be attended to.

✳ When the Empress is next to the Ace of Pentacles (reversed), a business could topple, with disappearing funds, leading to panic.

Rider-Waite Interpretation

The querent must look after themselves, and then they will have the energy to care for others. Take time to feel an affinity with Mother Nature and perhaps spend time walking in the countryside or the garden. The client may not be content with their self-image, so they need to love themselves, lumps, bumps, and all. The Empress (reversed) can also indicate that the person is taking their mothering skills too far by being too controlling with a child and not allowing them any freedom.

One World Interpretation

Family fights and many tears. Will it mend, is what you fear.

KEYWORD: *infertility*

Fertility problems bring about unhappiness and frustration. A much-wanted child will be lacking in their life, and monthly disappointment could bring tears. Other sexual difficulties could present themselves to those in long-term relationships. Perhaps one partner has a higher sex drive than the other.

The client could lack trust in a particular family member, which could cause mayhem and quarrels. As the Empress represents the home and safety, a disturbance will spoil what has been. Troublesome new neighbors could move in next door, or a rowdy family could ruin the harmony of the neighborhood.

MEMORIZE

Not being able to conceive ✳ Sexual problems in a relationship ✳ Lacking trust in a family member ✳ Arguments and quarrels ✳ Troublesome neighbors

Rider-Waite Tarot

One World Tarot

The Emperor

A powerful man, full of control. An entrepreneur is his role.

CARD NUMBER: 4 **BIRTH SIGN:** Aries, March 21–April 19 **CRYSTALS:** red jasper and carnelian **HERBS:** parsley and coriander **KEYWORD:** authority

Rider-Waite Interpretation

The Emperor sits on his throne, with a ram's head visible on either side. This card is associated with the first sign of the zodiac, Aries. Its ruler is Mars, the planet of war, which gives us a dynamic representation of a man who gets what he wants. He demonstrates power, presence, and masculinity. His crimson robe indicates strength, authority, and dominance, and he holds a golden scepter, a masculine phallic symbol. His white hair and beard depict wisdom and knowledge, and the crown on his head portrays an elite man with the influence to change people's lives.

The Emperor is an entrepreneur and, more often than not, a boss. He is not the sort to be told by others what to do as he thinks his ways are the best, and on the whole, this assumption is valid. He may have built up multiple businesses and may own more than one property, perhaps a string of them. In some readings, he might be considered a millionaire with investments worldwide. As he represents structure, to see him in a reading is a good omen, especially if he is around the money cards.

through the ranks. As a boss, he will be fair, but his employees won't see his true nature as he looks down on emotion as a sign of weakness. "Have a stiff upper lip" will be his motto. This man will have friends, but they will have been carefully selected to boost his ego and make him feel superior. He is quite old-fashioned in his mannerisms and will always speak his mind, which might make him unpopular sometimes, but he's not fazed by criticism as he believes he must always protect his property and those around him.

You can also use the Emperor as a timing card, predicting that things might happen in the spring from March to April.

One World Interpretation

The Emperor represents a man who seeks power, money, and respect. He is uncomfortable falling in love because he always has control of his emotions. If he does marry, he'll hold the reigns in the relationship, and his partner will undoubtedly have to be the submissive type. If he is single, this man is keen on sex but without commitment. As a father, he cannot be faulted as he will invest wholeheartedly in his children's future and will be the type to buy them their first house. However, his children must follow the structures and guidelines already set in place to enjoy what the Emperor has created.

He can sometimes symbolize a person in the armed forces who will have climbed up

> ### MEMORIZE
> c—···—ɔ
>
> A controlled man ✳ Seeks power, money, and respect ✳ Always showing the stiff upper lip ✳ Old-fashioned in his manner ✳ A good father ✳ Seeks a submissive partner ✳ Timing: March–April

Other Meanings

When the Emperor appears in a reading, it is a good omen for security and new jobs. The client might have connections with a fast-growing company that has some excellent benefits, which will help them climb the ladder to success.

Associated Cards with Upright Emperor

* When the Emperor is placed with the Sun (upright), this will bring excellent financial benefits for the querent. Something good is about to happen, which could change their life.
* If the Fool (upright) is around, a big mistake is pending, which could cause ruination, especially if the Five of Wands (upright or reversed) is also nearby. Discipline will be required, so don't be too hasty. Take time and plan carefully for the future.
* When the Chariot (reversed) is in the reading, it might be wise to delay a new venture for a while and keep with a well-tested format.
* If a Sword (upright or reversed) or the Death (upright) card is present, a funeral in the family could be imminent for the seeker.
* If the Lovers (upright) appear, the Emperor could find himself alone when his partner finds a warmer and more loving replacement.

Rider-Waite Interpretation

The Emperor, in the reversed position, represents a controlling man who will abuse his power to satisfy his ego. If the querent is in business, a younger, more forceful man could rock the boat, questioning the structure of what has always been traditional. This guy has modern ideas that could get the backing of others on the team. The client may feel vulnerable for a time because they are losing authority with those around them.

One World Interpretation

You always sow what you'll reap. Lonely in your bed you'll sleep.

KEYWORD: *alone*

The Emperor will be cold and unloving as a father, not showing his children affection. Later in life, they will come to resent him. He may also be so unpopular that he needs to buy people around him; perhaps his partner is only with him for his money. If the client is married to the Emperor (reversed), they will find that the relationship is unequal, so they will need to assert more power and not allow him to dominate; this will cause disruptions. As the family grows and moves away, he will find himself lonely and without friends.

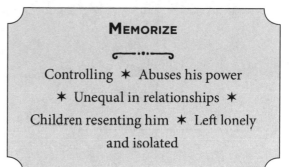

MEMORIZE

Controlling ✶ Abuses his power ✶ Unequal in relationships ✶ Children resenting him ✶ Left lonely and isolated

Rider-Waite Tarot

One World Tarot

The Hierophant

Should you go or should you stay? Take a chance to move away.

CARD NUMBER: 5 **EARTH SIGN:** Taurus, April 20–May 20 **CRYSTALS:** citrine, sunstone, and selenite **HERBS:** mint and basil **KEYWORDS:** spiritual teacher
OTHER NAMES FOR THE HIEROPHANT: the Pope, Lapape, the High Priest, the Pontiff

---

Rider-Waite Interpretation

In the past, the Hierophant signified the head of the church and was characterized as the Pope or Pontiff, meaning the bridge between Earth and Heaven. Behind the Hierophant are stone-gray pillars that, unlike the High Priestess, have no veil; this indicates free spiritual knowledge to all those who seek it. Over time, the symbols at the top of the pillars have caused controversy. Some say they are pine cones or acorns; others have suggested a uterus, a connection that links the Hierophant to the High Priestess.

The Hierophant's crown represents a "camelaucum," a triple diadem, recognized as a sign of his elite social standing. The monks at his feet show deference to him, and their tunics are covered in roses and lilies, a blending of psychic integrity and human desire. The yellow or white palliums on the robe depict erudite gifts and knowledge. The crossed keys at the Hierophant's feet link to St. Peter, the guardian of the keys to the Gates of Heaven.

One World Interpretation

In the One World Tarot, we see the priest welcoming his congregation from all walks of life and nationalities. His role is to understand and help them all.

As this is a card of learning, the client might be ready to commence study or enter a university or college.

The Hierophant today can represent the client's male guide who is elevated in his status and offers protection throughout their life. When this card is in the seeker's spread, they must keep an open mind and be ready to change their opinions. They lead a busy lifestyle but must be encouraged to invite spirituality into their heart. It's time to look at the bigger picture and try hard to become more spiritual.

A house move could be on the horizon, and there might be more than one property on offer. The client must listen carefully to their in-

ner truth when choosing. It could be that their new dwelling is not far from a church or chapel.

Financially, their careful nature will mean money is in the bank, and they will make sure they are "saving for a rainy day."

Sometimes when the Hierophant is present in a spread, a special person will enter the client's life and offer advice that could be life-changing. You can also use Taurus for timing: April–May.

MEMORIZE

A high-status guide ✷ Seek all things spiritual to raise vibrations ✷ A house move, perhaps two properties to choose from ✷ Money and savings in the bank ✷ Timing: April–May

---

Associated Cards with Upright Hierophant

* If the Hierophant is next to the Nine of Cups (upright), there will be a wonderful wedding with lifelong happiness. It could even be soul mates tying the knot and later producing spiritually minded children.
* When the Ace of Pentacles (upright) is placed nearby, the seeker will consider buying a large house with lots of land. Now is a good time to do it.

✳ When the Judgement card (upright) is
in situ, the person will have to examine
how they are doing on their spiritual
journey and try to improve the structure
of their karma. The Hierophant will
guide them to the best way forward;
the help could also come from a wise
advisor who points them in the right
direction.

✳ If other cards of spiritual protection are
around (upright or reversed), the seeker
will have more than one spirit guide.

✳ If the Hierophant is in the reversed
position alongside the Eight of Pentacles
(upright), an excellent fresh start is
predicted and perhaps a new job.

Rider-Waite Interpretation

The client will no longer seek the approval
of others and will forge ahead without outside interference. For a while, they may
feel claustrophobic and tired of following
authoritative leaders. Now is the time for
them to implement their own rules. They
may have a brush with the law or find
themselves standing up for others.

One World Interpretation

*Perception comes from deep within. Your
guide is here, so let him in.*

KEYWORD: *transformation*

The client may suddenly change their faith
to something that rings truer to their soul,
dismissing everything their elders have
taught. It will mean a massive upheaval in
their life, leading them to have intense feelings of having to get away from it all. They
need to be still and retreat to a place where

they can think things through for a while. Within the workplace, the seeker will feel disrespect for colleagues and bosses who are stuck in a draconian rut. New beginnings are afoot, and help will come from the spirit world as the chrysalis is about to transform into a butterfly. A house purchase might suddenly fall through.

MEMORIZE

Changing faith ✳ Time alone to reflect ✳ Disrespect for colleagues and bosses ✳ New beginnings ✳ A house move falls through

Rider-Waite Tarot | *One World Tarot*

The Lovers

Will you choose love, or will you choose lust? Take care to find the one you trust.

CARD NUMBER: 6 **AIR SIGN:** Gemini, approx. May 21–June 20 **CRYSTALS:** rose quartz and tanzanite
HERBS: lemon balm and valerian **KEYWORD:** love **OTHER NAME FOR THE LOVERS:** the Twins

Rider-Waite Interpretation

The Lovers, also known as the Twins, are standing in the garden of Eden; the female, Eve, is gazing up to the sky where the magnificent archangel Raphael (the angel of healing and air) looks down upon them. He reminds the couple of their allegiance to God, their creator, and all that is divine within them. On the right-hand side of the male, Adam, there is a tree with twelve flames; these represent the twelve signs of the zodiac. On the left-hand side, next to Eve, is the tree of knowledge with the forbidden apple hanging from it, tempting her to eat it. The serpent is wrapped around the tree, symbolizing life's bodily pleasures that entice them away from the divine.

The Lovers have each found their partner and want to live together in harmony for the rest of their lives. The union portrays romantic and physical love and doing what is best for each other. The marriage vows will be taken in front of a priest, in a church, with the blessings of God. The couple will live just for each other, unable to bear being apart because of the intensity of the relationship.

One World Interpretation

The Lovers is a choice card; it can involve choosing a partner or even a work situation. The modern version of the Lovers will tell the person to trust their instincts and go with their heart, especially in matters relating to love. There will soon be a serious choice to make; perhaps the person is already with another, and the twin flame suddenly makes an appearance. Often, the card can mean that the client or someone close to them will meet their soul mate. As twin flames rarely meet in reincarnation (see page 299), this will cause a real dichotomy, which could bring havoc to both sides. Usually, the temptation is too powerful, and something in their lives will be given up if they choose to be together. Family and friends will try to talk sense to them, but it will be a hopeless task. The karmic pull will be in action, and there will be no way back from it. You can use Gemini for timing: May–June.

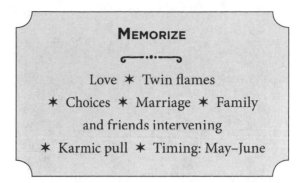

MEMORIZE

Love ✳ Twin flames ✳ Choices ✳ Marriage ✳ Family and friends intervening ✳ Karmic pull ✳ Timing: May–June

Associated Cards with Upright Lovers

* If the Three of Swords (upright or reversed) is in the same spread, it always foretells an adulterous affair.
* When the Eight of Pentacles (upright) is present, the seeker might have to decide whether to continue in their steady job or engage in an apprenticeship that will lead to self-employment.
* A flirtation could develop with a work colleague if the Ace of Wands (upright) is in situ. The client must let their heart lead them to what is best.
* If the Lovers is in the reversed position around the Tower (upright or reversed), an explosive argument will occur within a relationship, and one person will walk away for good.

Rider-Waite Interpretation

The client may realize that they have grown apart from their partner or spouse and feel the need to part ways. It could be time to end the relationship if arguments and a lack of respect for one another continue to plague the union. The couple must do what's best for each other and work hard to maintain their integrity.

One World Interpretation

Separation, tears, and strife. Creating havoc in your life.

KEYWORD: *cheating*

In reverse, the Lovers can predict infidelity in a relationship simply because there is a lack of sex. If one person in the relationship is tired, working, or doing the lion's share of the childcare, their libido will run low. The other will seek sexual gratification outside of the relationship without committing anything emotionally to their lover. Lust is chosen over love, and as a result, they will lose everything.

Also, the reversed Lovers can signify that the client is fighting and arguing with their partner; this doesn't bode well for the future.

MEMORIZE

⌐ ·••· ¬

Infidelity ✶ A lack of sex ✶
Choosing lust over love ✶
Losing everything ✶
Fighting with a partner

Rider-Waite Tarot   One World Tarot

The Chariot

Harness your energy to move ahead when this card is in the spread.

CARD NUMBER: 7 **WATER SIGN:** Cancer, June 21–July 22 **CRYSTALS:** orange calcite and amber
HERBS: turmeric and comfrey **KEYWORD:** action

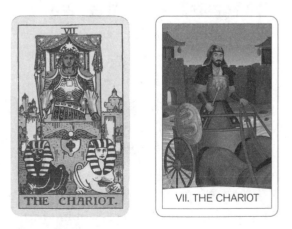

Rider-Waite Interpretation

Here we see the charioteer resplendent in his uniform. Upon his head are the stars of destiny, which connect him to the spirit world, and a pale blue canopy above his head signifies that everything is written in the stars. Beneath the crown are the laurel leaves of triumph. His battle has been won, and he returns victorious. The shoulder armor is represented by two lunar moons related to the birth sign of Cancer.

The belt is said to characterize the twelve zodiac signs, and the wings below offer inspiration and knowledge. A red lingam sits underneath the wings, pointing out the yin and yang principles. Beneath are the two sphinxes, meaning night and day; they hold their tails between their paws, reminding us of the serpent eating its tail to signify life everlasting.

The Chariot relates to tuning in to the cosmic cycles to gain more information about what is hidden. There has been a battle to conquer nature and tame Mother Earth, but the tide is turning against humanity. If we don't respect our planet, our world will fight back with a vengeance. After a spell of hard work, the seeker will reap the rewards; it's been a long and tedious business, but all the effort has paid off. They've achieved their goals. Others will say, "Lucky you!" But hard graft has won the day, not luck. The Chariot means pushing on through every obstacle and not giving in, and if it doesn't work today, then have another go tomorrow, until a solution can be found. In some teachings, the charioteer is the son of the Emperor and Empress. His strength and prowess come from his father, and his blessings from his mother.

One World Interpretation

Today, the Chariot can represent an automobile, so its appearance in a spread can mean a journey ahead for the seeker. You will have to look at the surrounding cards to establish where the client might be going, but it can depict their journey in life, work, or love. They must maintain discipline and avoid becoming sidetracked by the trivialities of life if they are to achieve their goals and aspirations. A clear message is "Get on with it and stop putting things off."

The client needs to clear the cobwebs away and take another look at any unfinished projects from the past. The Chariot brings inspiration, so it is a great time to move forward. Encourage them to take hold of the reigns in life and steer themselves in the right direction.

MEMORIZE

An automobile ✴ A journey ✴ Discipline is needed ✴ Stop putting things off ✴ Son of the Emperor or Empress

---

Associated Cards with Upright Chariot

✴ If the Chariot is situated next to the Wheel of Fortune (upright), fantastic news and a change of lifestyle could be on the way.

✴ If the Tower (upright or reversed) appears, a car crash or accident may be on the horizon for someone close to the querent. Look at the surrounding cards for an outcome.

✴ If the Emperor (upright or reversed), Empress (upright or reversed), and Chariot (upright or reversed) appear together, this could represent mother, father, and son.

* With the Lovers (upright or reversed) in situ, a sudden red-hot romance will make the client throw caution to the wind.
* If the Chariot appears with the Eight of Wands (upright) or Six of Swords (upright), a journey will take the seeker out of the country.
* A huge family quarrel will occur when the Chariot (reversed) is in the same spread as the Four of Wands (reversed).

Rider-Waite Interpretation

Obstacles surround the seeker, and nothing is going to plan. Despite their desire to forge ahead, they have hit a brick wall. Perhaps it's time to change direction and focus their attention on something else. The client might be burying their head in the sand and not facing what is right in front of them. A change of attitude is needed, and fresh ideas will flow more smoothly.

One World Interpretation

Your life must alter, this cannot be. The need to change is plain to see.

KEYWORDS: *unpleasant attitudes*

The Chariot card in some decks can warn of an addiction or unpleasant attitude toward others, bringing unpopularity. Someone around the client has suddenly developed an ego because of their past successes and thinks they know better than others. But the querent is in danger of straying away from their spiritual values, so gently encourage them to delve deeper and invite some form of spirituality into their life. Those in relationships could be treated callously and driven away because of their partner's negative attitude. Like the crab, the charioteer hangs on to past glories, refusing to change.

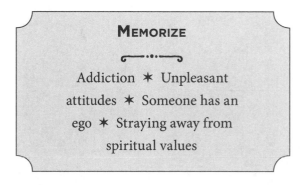

MEMORIZE

Addiction ✳ Unpleasant attitudes ✳ Someone has an ego ✳ Straying away from spiritual values

Rider-Waite Tarot   *One World Tarot*

Strength

Use your strength to win the day. Weakness will make for disarray.

CARD NUMBER: 8 **BIRTH SIGN:** Leo, July 23–August 22
CRYSTALS: unakite and bloodstone **HERBS:** sage and ginseng **KEYWORD:** courage

---

Rider-Waite Interpretation

We see a beautiful maiden calming a furious lion upon the Strength card. She sees no fear; her sole aim is to quiet him with the power of her mind. In many traditional decks, she wears a pure white gown adorned with blooms and a crown of flowers in her hair; this tells us that she is connected to nature, loving and appreciating the world around her. Above the maiden's head is a lemniscate (the figure eight on its side), representing the energy of thought that spans into eternity. You might see her wearing a wide-brimmed hat in other decks, mimicking the lemniscate. Many would try to use power over the lion, to dominate him with cruelty and violence, but that is not her way. She connects on a higher level to its mysterious, instinctive feline behavior, and he understands her thoughts and actions, becoming calm and receptive. So, the two shift together where humans and animals blend to become one.

Strength must be used quietly and subtly, because if one throws their weight around, it won't solve the problem. Brute force and ignorance will only create friction and even more upset, so it is best to go along at a leisurely pace.

If others around you are having temper tantrums, it's a good idea to walk away and leave them to their histrionics. Someone close to the client may feel out of sorts, perhaps as they recover from a long illness or an operation. Kind words and support could make all the difference in bringing their strength back to normal. This Leo card can also depict self-discipline and the need to get life back on track; if there is a lack of self-esteem, work must be done to restore the client's balance.

One World Interpretation

If a person loves an animal, the soul is wise; if a person dislikes an animal, the soul is young and unawakened.

When an argument or a dispute has occurred, the client should be able to resolve the situation quickly and even become friends with the perpetrator(s). Because they have kept a cool head, there is no blame to be put upon them. They will need strength in the future to deal with any issues that may arise, but by being stronger than they realize, they can conquer their fears and win the day.

We all know how an animal can touch the soul; they make no judgements on us and will care for us, warts and all. In Tarot, very few cards pertain to animal predictions, so this card represents all pets and wildlife. Perhaps the client is feeding a stray cat or contemplating adopting an animal from a shelter.

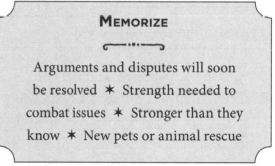

MEMORIZE

Arguments and disputes will soon be resolved ✳ Strength needed to combat issues ✳ Stronger than they know ✳ New pets or animal rescue

Associated Cards with Upright Strength

✳ When Justice (upright) is situated next to Strength, a legal battle will have to be fought. It might feel as if there is no hope, but if the Wheel of Fortune (upright) turns up, fate and destiny will have a very different view and step in to throw the cat among the pigeons.

✳ The Three of Swords (upright) next to

Strength indicates the need to look after an animal's health. Look at their teeth or gums, maybe their nails need a clip, or take them to the vet for a checkup.

* If the Seven of Swords (upright or reversed) is present, an animal could be ill-treated, and the client may report this to the authorities.

* When Strength is around cards such as the Nine of Swords (upright or reversed) and Ten of Swords (upright or reversed), the client or someone close to them will have to muster all of their strength to overcome an illness. Look at surrounding cards for the outcome.

* If Death (upright) is near Strength with the Ten of Swords (upright or reversed), this could represent a loss or separation that is hard to bear, or even the death of a beloved pet.

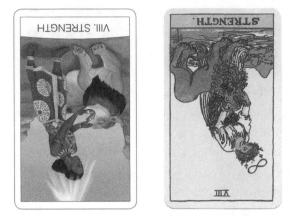

Rider-Waite Interpretation

The client is feeling despondent and worn out, and their energy is at an all-time low. They have been pushing too hard and may be working longer hours than usual.

The person should take a step back and rejuvenate their energies; otherwise, they can be left vulnerable. Someone around them could have an explosive temper and show signs of unpredictability.

One World Interpretation

Stand up straight and don't fall down. Lift yourself from off the ground.

KEYWORDS: *giving in*

When the Strength card is reversed, it can have quite a few meanings. One is a lack of confidence and feelings of utter rejection. The client might give in and have no fighting spirit left. Life and people have been too cruel, and they have received one blow after another. Fear and failure are all around. Look at the other cards that are present, as this will indicate which ways the disasters have struck. The only way out of this dilemma is the person's inner strength; it has got to be restored, and only they can surmount the obstacles. A telling time indeed.

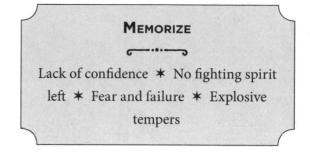

MEMORIZE

Lack of confidence ✳ No fighting spirit left ✳ Fear and failure ✳ Explosive tempers

Rider-Waite Tarot

One World Tarot

The Hermit

Knowledge from dreams feeds the soul. Your guide will help you reach your goals.

CARD NUMBER: 9 **BIRTH SIGN:** Virgo, August 23–September 22 **CRYSTALS:** peridot and smoky quartz **HERBS:** nettle and chamomile **KEYWORD:** meditation

Rider-Waite Interpretation

The Hermit's habit is similar to that of a monk's, long and pale gray. The hood keeps him warm from the winter snow as he climbs to the top of a mountain range. The wooden staff gives him stability on the slippery ice and helps him get to the safety of his cave, where he lives. In his hand, he holds a lantern with a six-pointed star encased inside. It represents the Seal of Solomon, a symbol of knowledge, wisdom, and the light that, although limited, helps him to proceed on his journey of inner discovery and awareness. He has no company to distract him, as he knows he must purify his soul from arrogance and deceit.

It's a time to get out of the rat race, focus on oneself, and do what is best. Listening to others and what they want won't be the right solution. The client may do some walking, join a retreat, or delve deeper into the meaning of life. The material achievements through hard work have been met, but the soul longs for new knowledge that can only be gained by isolation and deep thinking. The last piece of the jigsaw must be put into place.

One World Interpretation

The Hermit is a sage, guide, or teacher, and when we see this wonderful card in a person's Tarot reading, we know they are loved and blessed by the spirit realms. Often the undeveloped client won't pay any importance to spiritual matters. Instead, they will want to know about work, affairs, children, and family. The Hermit encourages them to grow their soul and begin to focus on the bigger picture and their place in the cosmos. In modern Tarot, we class him as a male guide who is gentle and loving; he will usually appear in dream sleep to aid the client in some way, especially if they are experiencing difficulties in their life. Everything will have to be analyzed very carefully, and their karma will be under intense scrutiny. Suggest to them that they switch off their cell phone, lock the door, and have a candle meditation in a warm, scented bath.

As this is the Virgo card, many things could start developing in and around August and September.

> ### MEMORIZE
> ꜱ━━ ·••· ━━ꜱ
> A spirit guide ✳ Loved and blessed from above ✳ Karma under scrutiny ✳ Timing: August–September

Associated Cards with Upright Hermit

✳ When the Nine of Cups (upright) is present in a spread, it's a blessing to see, as the client will be guided in all they do.

✳ If the Hermit is linked with the Four of Swords (upright or reversed), this represents hurt and betrayal. It's a time to be still and maybe recover from someone's cruel words.

✳ If the Sun (upright) is nearby, the client will be privy to wonderful revelations and knowledge not usually given to others. The person is gaining in their karmic knowledge, meaning that their soul will need fewer reincarnations on earth.

✳ If the Hanged Man (upright) is in the reading, there will be feelings of being stuck, and the answers will not be available at this time. Meditating could help, and calling on one's guide should do the trick.

Rider-Waite Interpretation

The time has come for the client to do some soul-searching and delve deep into a journey of self-discovery. In relationships, one party becomes distant and craves to be alone, leaving the other feeling isolated. The querent must take time to understand what their partner needs and compromise to keep the relationship strong. The Hermit urges them to look at life in a more nonphysical way, setting aside the practical and reaching deep within themselves to find the truth.

One World Interpretation

Time on your own needs to be found, for you to see what's all around.

KEYWORDS: *fear of being alone*

The client will go through a phase where they will fear being left alone. As soon as they venture into their home, they will turn on the TV or the radio to mask the silence. They are scared of looking within themselves because they don't like what they might find. The Hermit encourages self-analysis and an honest appraisal of one's desires and intentions. If this message doesn't get through, the universe can often enforce inactivity for the seeker, such as an accident or a minor illness that grounds them. Those who love sport could find themselves on crutches, or a dancer might have to rest a sprained tendon; they'll be forced to contemplate. The Hermit will step in and help with this process of *inner* learning.

MEMORIZE

☞ • ·•· • ☜

Fear of being alone ✳ Self-analysis ✳ Universe forcing inactivity ✳ Minor illness or accident ✳ One partner needing time away from a relationship

Rider-Waite Tarot

One World Tarot

Wheel of Fortune

Trust in magic and the laws of fate. Changes come that cannot wait.

CARD NUMBER: 10 **CRYSTALS:** lapis lazuli and black opal
HERBS: lavender and oregano **KEYWORD:** fate

Rider-Waite Interpretation

This card holds immense complexity and significance in the Tarot, symbolizing the cycle of death and rebirth. The sphinx sits on the top of the wheel, his sword in his hand, representing strength and knowledge. He's also privy to the secrets of time. Having been in existence for thousands of years, the sphinx has repeatedly experienced and seen the circle of life.

In each corner of the card, one of four

symbols appears. On the top left, the angel to Aquarius; top right, the eagle to Scorpio. At the base, to the left, the bull to Taurus, and right, the lion to Leo. A snake slithers down on the wheel's left, indicating the life force gaining access to the material world. The Egyptian god of the dead, Anubis, who welcomes souls to the underworld, emerges on the right side of the Wheel of Fortune. The inner wheel, which signifies seminal power, features the alchemical symbols for mercury, sulfur, water, and salt, the four essential ingredients of life.

The Wheel of Fortune has no boundaries and will either bring joy or trauma to unsuspecting humans. Destiny will challenge free will to try to bring out the best within all of us. What we like or what we want isn't necessarily what we are going to get. Humans are like chess pieces on a board; the gods are in charge of our movements. The Wheel of Fortune is turning, heralding a new life cycle; it can be exciting and challenging. Those brave souls will embrace the new learning time, but others who fear could fall at the first hurdle. It's best not to fight when destiny turns up; after the trials and tribulations, a whole new world will be presented to the client.

One World Interpretation

We've all said it at one time or another: "Wait until I tell you this!" or "Guess what?" New information comes to light when the Wheel of Fortune appears in a reading. The client could meet a long-lost friend out of the blue, or someone might casually remark that a new job in their workplace is up for

grabs; suddenly, the seeker has been promoted and is loving everything about it. A new social circle with interesting friends opens up, and invitations and travel appear out of nowhere. Life will be good with all of this new variety to experience. Little coincidences will occur, too; the client might be thinking of someone, and the next day that person will call them for a chat, but is it just a coincidence? Perhaps not! Above all, their life is steered by fate and destiny, so encourage them to accept all new opportunities.

MEMORIZE

New situations appearing out of the blue ✷ Meeting old friends ✷ Small coincidences ✷ Life is ruled by fate and destiny ✷ Accept all opportunities

---

Associated Cards with Upright Wheel of Fortune

* If the Tower (upright or reversed) is placed directly beside the Wheel of Fortune, we can expect some horror story. It might portray a fatal accident or a suicide, damage to the head, or a car crash with serious injuries.
* If the Wheel of Fortune appears with the Sun (upright) or the Ten of Pentacles (upright), great joy and happiness will come.

✱ If Temperance (upright) is in the same spread, fate and destiny are in charge, so take a deep breath and embrace all that is coming; none of it will be a mistake!

✱ When negative Sword cards (upright or reversed) appear in the spread, such as the Five, Seven, Nine, or Ten of Swords, the client could be stuck in a never-ending cycle of doom and gloom with no resolutions to problems.

Rider-Waite Interpretation

Everything is topsy-turvy, and bad luck seems to surround the client. They can either accept it and decide to do nothing or take fate into their own hands and try to improve things. The seeker must take a long, hard look at how their actions have played a part in this negative phase. Owning one's faults and admitting they were wrong leads one halfway to changing the situation. The Wheel of Fortune reversed can also signify fluctuations in the seeker's life that happen by chance. These changes can leave the client feeling stressed and overwhelmed.

One World Interpretation

Fate is in charge of all you do. Trust your guide to see you through.

KEYWORDS: *bad omens*

Readers never like to see the Wheel of Fortune in reverse, as it's considered a bad omen. Bad luck can follow the client around, and it might be tough to shake off. A black cloud hangs over them, and everything seems to go wrong. The cat may go missing, or they'll take a tumble down the stairs, or a colleague will get the promotion that they really wanted. It would be best not to try new projects as there will be a strong likelihood of failure. Wait until this destructive cycle is over, and things will gradually calm down and return to normal. On a lighter side, the client's guides will bring about something beneficial in the forthcoming months to lighten the storm.

> **MEMORIZE**
>
> ┏━━ ·•· ━━┓
>
> Bad luck ✱ Bad omens ✱ Everything going wrong ✱ Be patient and wait it out ✱ Guides bringing about a positive outcome

Rider-Waite Tarot

One World Tarot

Justice

Balance the scales in all you do, and a peaceful path is ahead of you.

CARD NUMBER: 11 **BIRTH SIGN:** Libra, September 23–October 22
CRYSTALS: jade and carnelian **HERBS:** garlic and honeysuckle **KEYWORD:** decision

Rider-Waite Interpretation

A female figure stares ahead in a purposeful way, showing her supreme authority. Her resplendent gown is crimson, and the mantle golden and green. Upon her head is a crown with a small golden square in its center, which portrays her wisdom. She is trustworthy, astute, and fair. A purple veil hangs behind her and is attached to two gray stone pillars representing balance, law, and structure. The double-edged sword reminds us that all our actions carry consequences. One white shoe peeps out from the hem of her gown, depicting her spiritual purity. On the right-hand side of the picture, she holds the scales of justice used in ancient times by the goddess Maat to weigh the souls of the dead against the feather of truth.

This card can signify the laws of karma; what has been sown must be reaped. Justice will finally be done as the cause-and-effect laws are now set in place. This card represents the Libra sign and is linked with harmony and balance. A logical decision will have to be made, and trusting one's truth will be necessary. It won't be a time to rush things, so list the pros and cons and set out a plan, as it will benefit the client later.

Imposing legal documents must be dealt with, and it may be a good idea to employ a lawyer to help cut through the red tape.

One World Interpretation

Primarily, this card represents all that is lawful, so the client must scour the fine print of any legal documents they encounter. It can mean taking out a new insurance policy, filing for divorce, or even making a will. Conversations and emails between accountants, lawyers, or the police force will be on the agenda or a brush with the law could be expected. The client may speak to law enforcement officers or, in rarer cases, even observe a crime and have to attend court as a witness.

It is a time to balance everything if they want to create a peaceful life, weighing the pros and the cons and striving to improve

things. This card says that the client may have done something they regret, but they will be treated fairly if they own up to their mistakes and accept responsibility. Important decisions will have to be made, but they must make sure their choices don't upset or impact other people. Use Libra for timing: September–October.

> ### MEMORIZE
> ⌐••••⌐
>
> Legal dealings, accountants, or lawyers ✳ Insurance policies, divorce legalities, and wills ✳ Doing something they regret ✳ Owning up to mistakes ✳ Important decisions ✳ Timing: September–October

Associated Cards with Upright Justice

✳ When the Justice card is next to the Six of Wands (upright), a victory for the client will bring good news, especially if they have been fighting a legal battle.

✳ If Justice is next to the Nine of Pentacles (upright), long-awaited cash will finally arrive after a series of holdups.

✳ If the Ace of Wands (upright or reversed) is present, the client will be signing contracts, or a mortgage will finally be paid off.

✳ When the Hermit (upright or reversed) is in situ, the client will have to consider their karma and try to resolve bad habits that will hold them back. More work is needed to improve the personality and eliminate bad habits such as smoking or drinking.

✳ The seeker will find themselves on the wrong side of the law with problematic cards, such as the Tower (upright or reversed) or the Nine or Ten of Swords (upright). They might get a fine or even a prison sentence.

✳ If the Chariot (upright or reversed) is in the same spread, watch out for traffic violations and fines.

Rider-Waite Interpretation

The client will be battling with their conscience as they know they have misbehaved. They have a choice as to whether they own up to their misdemeanors or bury their head in the sand, hoping no one will notice. Alternatively, they might be scrutinizing their past actions and coming down extra hard on themselves. They must learn to forgive themselves before expecting others to absolve them. Encourage the client to be helpful to others so their karma can make up for their wrongdoings in the past.

One World Interpretation

Battle your conscience; do the right thing. Your karma is calling; search for your sins.

KEYWORD: *acrimony*

When the Justice card is in reverse, it does not augur well. The law and order the client had in the past could suddenly come crashing down around them, bringing mayhem. They may feel like their life is out of control, as a court case could unfairly represent them. A divorce might become very acrimonious, leaving the client without savings and security. Getting justice will take a long time, and money won't be there to help ease the situation. The seeker's house of cards is scattered everywhere with no hope in sight. Connecting to higher beings or one's god could improve the problems, as miracles can and do happen.

MEMORIZE

Out of control ✳ Acrimonious divorce ✳ Justice takes a long time ✳ Connect to the god force

Rider-Waite Tarot

One World Tarot

The Hanged Man

Feeling stuck; which way to go? Keep your faith and then you'll know.

CARD NUMBER: 12 **CRYSTALS:** aquamarine and sodalite
HERB: calathea **KEYWORD:** restrictions

Rider-Waite Interpretation

As soon as one perceives the Hanged Man, the sense of doom from this disturbing image will instinctively say that it's a depressing and troublesome card. Its origins are mostly pagan, and the man on the card appears to be hung in a peculiar way. The right foot is strapped to a living tree, but the other leg is free, and both arms are secured firmly behind his back, forming an upturned triangle. The whole observation lacks any joy. The red hose on his legs depict his human passion, and the blue doublet denotes hard-earned knowledge. A golden halo shines around his head; although his body is inert, he still has the faculties for insight and alertness.

The sense of strength emanating from the Hanged Man's ominous appearance will immediately cause one to assume that the card is dismal and unpleasant.

The Hanged Man is well and truly stuck. His life will feel like the film *Groundhog Day*, as nothing seems to change; there are no new pathways ahead for him, just deadlock. This enforced interruption in the client's life is frustrating, but there will be a reason for it, and they must hang in there. The karmic laws ask the seeker to make a change, especially with their personality, so it's a time to let go of old habits and childish ways. Once this is done, the situations around them will resolve themselves, and a new time will unfold.

One World Interpretation

The client is stuck in a rut, left hanging in limbo with no sign of change. They must be patient and not give up because there is a spiritual reason why they can't move forward. Later, when they look back, they will understand why they were grounded. The querent may also be refusing to change mentally, which can, in turn, cause the holdups. Maybe they are bored with their job but frightened to move on, or they remain in a rut because they fear change. Ideas will have to be reformed, and a new approach is needed. Find another way, especially in rela-

tionships with family members and marriage. Although time is suspended for a little while, it will resolve itself eventually, and out of the ashes will come a brand-new start. One key factor is that this card represents change, but it will take twelve months before the way becomes clear.

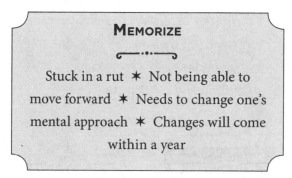

MEMORIZE

Stuck in a rut ✳ Not being able to move forward ✳ Needs to change one's mental approach ✳ Changes will come within a year

Associated Cards with Upright Hanged Man

✳ If the Hanged Man is next to the Ten of Swords (upright or reversed), someone around the client may have died, and the overwhelming grief may prevent the client from moving on.

✳ When the Hanged Man is next to the Ace of Wands (upright), there could be losses in the business world, and bad investments and unwise advice could throw a wrench in the works. Lots of money could be lost and never recovered, so bankruptcy might be expected.

✳ If the Devil (upright or reversed) is present, then manipulation from others could ruin someone's life. It takes courage, but the client will have to stand up for themselves, or they will stay trapped in the situation, sinking themselves deeper and deeper into the quagmire.

✴ If the Hanged Man is reversed and in the same spread as the Five of Pentacles (upright or reversed), the client could be jeopardizing their health by indulging in bad habits such as smoking, drinking, and overeating.

Rider-Waite Interpretation

The reversed Hanged Man is now pictured upright and can perceive much more around him. There has been a time of reflection, but now an active phase has started; soon, the client will regain good spirits, but has to keep a positive outlook for this to be achieved. Others could try to tempt them back to bad habits, because changing takes courage, but this can be

accomplished. Although busy with new work and projects, they must slow down, or they could burn themselves out.

One World Interpretation

Change your lifestyle, steer from strife, or it will impact you later in life.

KEYWORDS: *kick bad habits*

When the Hanged Man is in reverse, there is a real need for the client to address any bad habits and seek a lifestyle change because they will bring massive restrictions and health issues later in life. The old ways need reinventing, and when at last that new opportunity presents itself, the seeker must grab it with both hands. In relationships, the seeker could be waiting around to see if their partner will commit to them. They will only delay for a certain period before they pack up and move on.

MEMORIZE

Being alert, seeing all around ✴ Kicking bad habits ✴ Waiting for a partner to commit ✴ Busy with work, slowing down

Rider-Waite Tarot

One World Tarot

Death

Off with the old and on with the new. Your life is changing right on cue.

CARD NUMBER: 13 **BIRTH SIGN:** Scorpio, October 23–November 21 **CRYSTALS:** black obsidian and black tourmaline **HERBS:** motherwort and peppermint **KEYWORD:** transition

Rider-Waite Interpretation

Here we see the Grim Reaper, or a skeleton encased in black armor, the color of mourning. His beautiful white stallion represents purity and wisdom. The Reaper holds a black flag with a five-petaled rose emblazoned on its background. The number five symbolizes enforced change; who can stop the process of death? At the horse's feet, a mother and a young child, the bishop, and a crucified noble all beg for their lives to be spared. Astrologically, the Death card represents Scorpio, which is number thirteen in the Tarot deck and, in medieval times, was seen as an unfortunate number linked with the thirteen witches in a coven.

As Death is connected with the Scorpio sign, this card signifies the secrecy of Scorpio and the mystery of death. When it turns up in a reading, a client will usually be quite frightened, especially with its harrowing imagery. Death is a mystery for most of us, but this can also be very positive, especially with certain cards around it. One thing is for sure; this card is the end of one phase and the beginning of another. The laws of karma are stringent, and the client will now find themselves in a new schoolroom of learning; it could be wonderful or somewhat daunting.

One World Interpretation

In modern Tarot, the Death card only ever means the death of a person when it is in the same spread as either the Tower or the Nine or Ten of Swords. On its own, it simply means a time of change and transition from one phase in life to another.

However you perceive it, the Death card is always severe. Even if a death is not predicted, the changes that come will be significant to the seeker. What was before will no longer be. If Death does arrive in a spread alongside the cards above, the matter must be dealt with sensitively and even softened or played down. The reader must not cause the client worry or concern. Perhaps inform them they could be attending a

funeral in the future, but it's more likely they could simply pay their respects to someone who has passed. If they go on to lose someone close, they will remember that Death came up in the reading and forgive you for not divulging all. After a death, a baby is usually to be born, so the client will hear news of a pregnancy or birth.

You can also use Scorpio (October–November) as a time reference for when changes might occur.

MEMORIZE

———••••———

Only means the death of a person with the Tower or the Nine or Ten of Swords ✳ Big changes ahead ✳ Off with the old and on with the new ✳ A birth or pregnancy ✳ The birth of something new ✳ Timing: October–November

Associated Cards with Upright Death

✳ If Death is in the same spread as the Sun (upright), a beautiful and rewarding new phase will take place for the client. They may have struggled over the years, but now that is over; they are going onward and upward for a fresh start.

✳ When Death is in situ with the Chariot (upright or reversed) and the Nine of Pentacles (upright or reversed), a sweeping change will present itself. Perhaps a move to a different country.

* With the Tower (upright or reversed) and the Nine or Ten of Swords (upright), death could be the result of an accident.
* If Death, Strength (upright), and the Ten of Swords (upright) appear together, it might be time to say goodbye to a beloved pet.
* If Death appears around Kings and Knights (upright or reversed) or the Nine or Ten of Swords (upright), a man around the client will pass away. Around Queens (upright or reversed), a woman. Around Pages (upright or reversed), a child.
* If Death is placed next to the Empress (upright), news of pregnancy or birth. If the Nine or Ten of Swords (upright) is present, a miscarriage or stillbirth.

Rider-Waite Interpretation

The client must let go of the past and start something new; their life has been plodding along in the same direction for so long that changes need to happen quickly. It can sometimes mean that the person has been on the brink of change for some time but they have resisted it because they are scared of a challenge. Please encourage them to venture forth because they cannot fail.

One World Interpretation

Hands are tied, you cannot move out. Look for new goals to think about.

KEYWORD: *unwell*

Death in reverse implies the client could feel under the weather or have no life energy. Are they working too hard or not getting the correct amount of sleep? One thing is for sure; they will feel worn out and not be motivated at all. There will be a desire to drag the duvet over their head and stay in bed. Others in their circle could be demanding and ask too much of them when they already have a long list of things to do. Sometimes this can mean being trapped in a toxic relationship with no money to set the person free. There is nowhere to go, so stalemate situations seem to last forever. Encourage the client to pursue new goals and keep their faith.

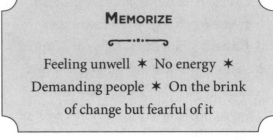

MEMORIZE

Feeling unwell ✶ No energy ✶ Demanding people ✶ On the brink of change but fearful of it

Rider-Waite Tarot   One World Tarot

Temperance

Patience brings many rewards. Your angel awaits with your awards.

CARD NUMBER: 14 **BIRTH SIGN:** Sagittarius, November 22–December 21
CRYSTALS: amethyst and kunzite **HERBS:** catnip and clover **KEYWORDS:** the flow of life

Rider-Waite Interpretation

The central figure is an angel; some say it's the angel Gabriel, a messenger of God. Other representations portray a female or an androgynous angel. One foot is placed in the water, showing the ebb and flow of life; the other foot stands on a small rock, indicating stability and grounding. Two vessels are held with water flowing between the goblets, displaying harmony and balance. In the foliage behind the angel, two golden irises are linked to the goddess Isis, who can visit any part of the world she wants with no restrictions. The crown has a square to indicate how humans are bound to the earth's energies, and the golden light on the left of the picture foretells a higher pathway for all of us.

Temperance is a card of balance and harmony, and the client will be wise as they can see both sides of the story. Perhaps they have reincarnated many times and have tremendous empathy for specific problems. They may be called upon to settle a dispute or play devil's advocate, or to shine a light for others to move on.

One World Interpretation

Many modern readers look at this card as the client's guardian angel, helping them learn patience and bringing balance to their lives. The seeker might be given new work, perhaps setting up a team of organizers; their managerial skills of understanding different personalities will put them in good stead. The message is to stay calm and be centered in all aspects of their life, gently going with the flow.

Temperare is a Latin word for moderation and blending, so today, we interpret Temperance as a card of abstention from alcohol. The card signifies that the client has an artistic ability that could be encouraged by a guide or a muse in dream sleep. They might decide to change their image or dream up some fantastic ideas to improve the interior of their house. Creativity is a gift from above, so it might be

an idea for them to start a new hobby, such as painting, pottery, or sculpting; with patience, the rewards will be pleasing. Use Sagittarius (November–December) for timing.

> ## MEMORIZE
> ⌐━ **·•·** ━⌐
>
> A guardian angel ✴ Balance and harmony ✴ New work ✴ Creative projects ✴ Changing their image ✴ Timing: November–December

Associated Cards with Upright Temperance

✴ The Temperance angel is also a protector or guide; if placed next to sinister cards (upright or reversed), it will assist the person in warding off negativity.

✴ If Temperance appears next to the Sun (upright), a wonderful surprise is about to happen for the client, which makes them believe in the good things in life, especially if they have been having a rough time.

✴ Temperance with the Lovers (upright) predicts a romantic love match: Perhaps they will meet their soul mate. A dynamic time is coming.

✴ When any Page (upright or reversed) and the Empress (upright) sit together with this card, a wonderful child will come into the querent's life. This particular soul is reincarnating to help others.

✳ If Temperance appears next to any court mentors in the reversed position, someone will try to manipulate the client.

Rider-Waite Interpretation

A negative cycle is coming in for the querent, and they must restore balance and harmony to succeed. Someone could be overindulging in life's pleasures, taking everything too far; this could be a family member who consumes excessive amounts of alcohol or whose eating is out of control. They could be warring with a parent or quarrelling with a partner. Self-healing is needed, so everything in the client's life should be reevaluated.

One World Interpretation

Your energies are very scattered. Take care, lest your dreams be shattered.

KEYWORDS: *bogged down*

An upset in routine could throw a wrench in the works; balance and harmony will no longer be present, and tempers will be hard to control. Without warning, the client could find themselves competing with a more assertive person at work, which could undermine their confidence.

As they get bogged down with more pressure, the workload will grow, and they will not have enough hours in the day to sort it all out. The person will take their stress home and vent their anger on the family. Arguments with a spouse could get out of hand, or the client may lack patience with their children. There has to be a way to restore the balance, or it might be too late.

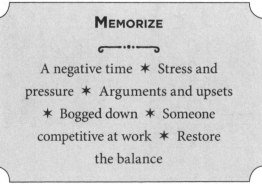

MEMORIZE

A negative time ✳ Stress and pressure ✳ Arguments and upsets ✳ Bogged down ✳ Someone competitive at work ✳ Restore the balance

Rider-Waite Tarot

One World Tarot

The Devil

Bad habits bring trouble and strife. Make amends now for a better life.

CARD NUMBER: 15 **BIRTH SIGN:** Capricorn, December 22–January 19 **CRYSTALS:** black diamond, jet, obsidian **HERBS:** garlic, mugwort, and bergamot **KEYWORD:** materialism

Rider-Waite Interpretation

At a glance, the Devil card is quite frightening, and it is a challenging card. In history, he was depicted as Pan, the half-human and half-goat son of the god Hermes. Pan's feet were cloven, and he had animal horns on his head. His main aim was to get drunk, fornicate, and be merry. Dancing was on the agenda, too, and he embraced revelry of any kind with enthusiasm. Around the Middle Ages, Pan was replaced by the Devil, and because Satan was purported to be evil, the merrymaker Pan was then regarded as wicked. Below the Devil stands an unfortunate couple chained to a block, and they will do his bidding for eternity.

First and foremost, this is not a card to be feared; it doesn't suggest possession, haunting, or the evil eye. Its main link is to money or the material, which has its place in society for good and evil. Money is a powerful energy; if a person has very little, it can restrict their life. If the client is trapped in a job or a bad relationship, a lack of cash will keep them tethered to the people they wish to move away from. Money does bring freedom, but it will sometimes bring out the worst in humanity. Families may dispute an inheritance, or a person might try to buy friendship or sex; on the darker side, someone could even use blackmail to exert control.

One World Interpretation

The client may find themselves around someone sly or cunning and be tempted to do something they wouldn't ordinarily do. The Devil represents man's depravity, especially anything that "takes them out of it." It's a sexual card, too, and can be linked to those who are obsessed with it. The person might have sexual fetishes, visit pornography sites, and perhaps even enjoy the idea of sex with multiple people. So, it's easy to see that any relationship won't last long, especially if their habits are twinned with alcohol or drug abuse. Because of these situations, the person's higher self can't surface, and they may collect negative karma. The

whole point of reincarnation is to dispel the negative karma accumulated from past lives, not to add more to it. The client must try to climb out of the damaging hole they're in and steer toward the positive.

The Devil can also signify problems with headaches or mental illness and cruelty, both physical and psychological.

For timing, this represents the wintertime, so the reader can use Capricorn (December–January).

MEMORIZE

Materialism ✳ Cruelty and control ✳ Lack of cash ✳ Sexual fetishes ✳ One's negative needs ✳ Headaches or mental illness ✳ Timing: December–January

---

Associated Cards with Upright Devil

* If the Tower (upright or reversed) is around the Devil, someone could be sexually harassing the client. With other negative cards (upright or reversed) it could even signify rape.
* When the Devil is near the Five or Seven of Swords (upright), there could be sinister events with younger men or gang warfare.

* When a Page (upright or reversed) is close, a child could be bullied at school or blackmailed to steal money.
* If the Lovers (upright) appears, a red-hot love affair could ruin a steady marriage or relationship. This will impact the family, especially the children.
* If the Devil is present with one or more court mentor cards (upright or reversed), the client could be around an unsavory person and must watch their back.
* When the Devil appears with the Tower (upright or reversed), someone violent or abusive could be in the seeker's life.

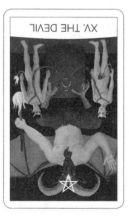 

Rider-Waite Interpretation

The Devil reversed encourages the client to confront inner fears and conquer addictions such as smoking, drug use, or alcohol dependence. This is a time for them to look closely at their lifestyle and eat healthier.

They must also delve deep and try to correct any personality flaws. Instead of focusing so much time on themselves, they must work hard at family relationships and put others first. Encourage them to bring a positive change into their life and face those inner demons.

One World Interpretation

Drinking, sex, and drug abuse; this waste of life is just no use.

KEYWORD: *obsession*

The Devil, in reverse, is a little more serious for the client, who may be drinking heavily or taking drugs. The noose is tightening around their neck because they lack funds to pay for their vice. Money will become an obsession, and all other values could come crashing down around them, as their focus will be solely on themselves and their needs, much to the detriment of others. They might also become obsessed with a friend or a potential love interest, needing to know where they are at all times or pestering someone relentlessly. As their palate becomes more jaded, they look for other distractions to amuse themselves, which could be played out in new sexual experiences. The client could be thinking of traveling to different countries to experiment and mix with others who are as decadent as themselves.

MEMORIZE

Obsessive nature ✳ Obsessed over money ✳ Alcohol and drug abuse ✳ New negative sexual experiences

Rider-Waite Tarot

One World Tarot

The Tower

Karmic forces change things forever. Accept what's come; old links are severed.

CARD NUMBER: 16 **CRYSTALS:** garnet and hematite **HERBS:** yarrow and honeysuckle
KEYWORD: turmoil **OTHER NAMES FOR THE TOWER:** the House of God,
Tower of Babel Blasted, the Lightning-Struck Tower, the Tower of Destruction

---

Rider-Waite Interpretation

Over the years, many authors of Tarot books and readers have tried to sanitize the denotation of the Tower by watering down the true meaning of this explosive card. We have thought long and hard about how to represent it in our book and decided to maintain the traditional connotations. You may feel uncomfortable using the meanings in this book as the Tower presents itself as an extremely negative card. Instead, you may use a gentler approach. It is for you to decide.

The Tower is considered one of the most disruptive cards in the Tarot deck, so the surrounding cards must be studied carefully. The tall tower is perched precariously above the gray rocks, and although it is solid in its composition, the substandard foundation bodes trouble. Lightning represents masculine energies, as does aggressive Mars, which is linked to this card. Here we see two unfortunate people being blasted out of the top of the tower by a thunderbolt. They leap into the unknown without warning about where they will end up. The twelve flames around the left-hand character depict the twelve signs of the zodiac, and the ten points of the Tree of Life, spewing out from the crown of the building, foretell utter chaos.

A white-knuckle ride is about to disrupt the seeker's life but in the end, it might be a change for the better. The client could be shell-shocked by the way their life has completely transformed. Fate and destiny have thrown a wrench in the works, and there isn't a thing to be done to change it. Acceptance is the prime reason not to feel judged or cursed, as *out of the ashes, the phoenix is reborn.*

One World Interpretation

This card is probably the worst in Tarot, so something awful is bound to occur when it appears in a reading. Surrounding cards must be studied to see where the chaos is coming from.

One thing to remember is the speed at which one's life can change. Suddenly the client could be redundant after working in the same place for years, or a friendship since childhood will be blown apart by a huge fight. If the person is stressed, their temper will be hard to control, and others will retaliate accordingly. A fed-up spouse might pack their bags and move out, never to return, and although there will be opposition from their partner, many benefits can follow.

The unexpected will rock others to their foundations, and so on. The worst-case scenario is damage to a house or even a fire.

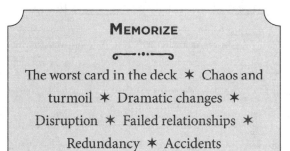

MEMORIZE

The worst card in the deck ✳ Chaos and turmoil ✳ Dramatic changes ✳ Disruption ✳ Failed relationships ✳ Redundancy ✳ Accidents

Associated Cards with Upright Tower

* If the Eight of Pentacles (upright) shows up, it is worth going through the upheaval to build a more robust structure for the future.
* When the King of Swords (upright or reversed) comes next to the Tower, the death of an older man could be imminent.

* The Chariot (reversed) could signify a car crash. This can be a small bump or a more significant accident.
* With the Ace of Cups (upright) or the Sun (upright) in the same spread, the upheaval won't be too bad, and the client will come out unscathed.
* If the Tower appears with the Five or Nine of Swords (upright), someone faces imprisonment and might go to jail.
* Alongside the Five of Pentacles (upright) or the Four of Swords (upright) in the same spread, the Tower can sometimes predict brain tumors or blows to the head.

WARNING: *If the Devil is sitting next to the Tower, there could be a danger of rape.*

If the Devil, the Tower, and any Page are in the same spread, this could signify child cruelty.

Rider-Waite Interpretation

Changes are coming, but the client is in denial and refuses to accept them. Because something significant is about to happen, they must accept it as inevitable instead of resisting it. It could also mean it's time to alter their course and embrace a new spiritual belief. People will force their ideas and opinions on the client, and they will feel suffocated, not knowing which way to turn. Someone close is suffering from depression and is miserable all the time. Encourage them to seek medical advice, or their thoughts could turn suicidal.

One World Interpretation

Look to your guide to find the light. Use your strength and prepare to fight.

KEYWORD: *collapse*

Sadly, this card in reverse is just as bad as when it sits upright. The Tower is well known as a card for accidents and mobility problems, making the seeker feel trapped or incapacitated. The client, or someone close by, might get the sack, and it could be an unfair dismissal, which creates a court case to plow through. Everything will collapse around them overnight. A relationship could suddenly end, or they will be facing financial ruin. Sometimes bad things happen as a way of enforcing change, so later, when this negative phase has passed, they will understand why it had to happen.

MEMORIZE

Changes ahead ✳ Being in denial ✳ Accidents and mobility issues ✳ Getting the sack ✳ Relationships ending ✳ Financial ruin

Rider-Waite Tarot   *One World Tarot*

The Star

Inspiration from those above, sending you eternal love.

CARD NUMBER: 17 **BIRTH SIGN:** Aquarius, January 20–February 18 **CRYSTALS:** turquoise, moldavite, and angelite **HERBS:** peppermint and angelica **KEYWORD:** hope

Rider-Waite Interpretation

With the Star, we see a naked female portraying her link to nature. Her purity and vulnerability don't hold her back, as she has gained the knowledge of universal wisdom and thought. To maintain the earth's fertility, she pours water from an urn into a pool and runs the water over the ground with another pot in her other hand.

In the sky, eight stars shine down; some say the smaller ones are the stars that depict the seven sisters of the constellation Pleiades. The larger star has been said to indicate divine existence and the human ability to ascend to a higher level.

As the Star represents the sign of Aquarius, this card encourages the union of reason and intuition. Humanitarian principles must be implemented, especially for one's ideals and wishes to manifest. Seventeen is classed as a significant number and deemed lucky; it brings beneficial extras into the client's life. If difficult situations have caused upset to the seeker, this card in readings brings hope and raised spirits. Life can be good and also hold new surprises of joy and attainment.

One World Interpretation

This card is one of the loveliest in the Tarot deck and has many meanings.

Some readers consider this the most spiritual card in the deck, which offers the client the ultimate in spiritual protection. The Star can predict a challenging journey, but the traveler will be shielded from any misfortune. It would be beneficial to return to nature and the understanding of the seasons, so the seeker might feel compelled to grow plants, flowers, or even produce. Leaving the city and suburbia behind for a while will be therapeutic, especially if they can venture somewhere to connect with animals and birds. The client's work and love life will be more positive, and there will be plenty of time for relaxation and meditation. As new horizons open up, there will be an increase in energy and inspiration, which will help lift others' spirits.

Today, many modern Tarot readers consider this card highly spiritual and use it to represent the client's female guide or guardian angel. This spirit helper holds great power and has an elevated status. She will help the client understand the process of reincarnation and karma.

MEMORIZE

Getting back to nature ✳ A challenging journey ✳ Love life ✳ Increased psychic energy ✳ Ideas from a muse

Associated Cards with Upright Star

* When there are two or more Wands (upright or reversed) around the Star, there will be a need to focus on another career. The Star represents Aquarius, an air sign. Therefore, employment might be connected with green subjects, the environment, or humanitarian issues. Social work and helping the sick could be different branches to consider.
* If the Nine or Ten of Cups (upright) makes an appearance, a new and long-lasting relationship, which could be karmically linked to the client, will bring joy into their life.

✳ If the High Priestess (upright) is next to the Star, universal understanding and revelations are given, which only a few people will be privy to.

Rider-Waite Interpretation

The spiritual side of the client could be tired as they focus only on the material side of their life. It's now a time to reconnect and get back on the right pathway. Old habits might surface as they give in to an easy life, so suggest to the client that there is no gain without pain. Sometimes the Star in reverse can depict exhaustion from trying to please everyone. Their pessimism can blur the real picture. The Star still hopes for good things in the future, but self-discipline will be important in bringing balance and harmony back into place.

One World Interpretation

Universal knowledge is yours to take. Seek the truth; stay wide awake.

KEYWORD: *learning*

The client may have lost their faith and feel abandoned by their deity. However hard they pray for a better outcome, nothing is forthcoming. They are entering a time of learning and are being spiritually tested to show their resolve. The person must trust in the universe and let go of any cynicism. Relationship problems will surface, which are a result of trust issues. One partner is not letting go of the past, leaving the other feeling unloved. The seeker or someone close to them may suffer from insomnia. It would be beneficial to meditate to avoid feelings of weariness.

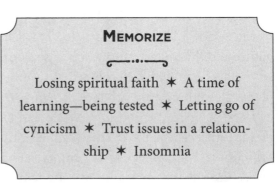

MEMORIZE

Losing spiritual faith ✳ A time of learning—being tested ✳ Letting go of cynicism ✳ Trust issues in a relationship ✳ Insomnia

Rider-Waite Tarot

One World Tarot

The Moon

Mysterious Moon connects to you. Now trust the truth in all you do.

CARD NUMBER: 18 **BIRTH SIGN:** Pisces, February 19–March 20 **CRYSTALS:** moonstone, moldavite, and selenite **HERBS:** eucalyptus and sandalwood **KEYWORD:** mystery

Rider-Waite Interpretation

A full moon is suspended in the night sky, and the landscape beneath looks eerie and otherworldly.

Two white towers beckon, daring us to pass through them to seek new knowledge and enlightenment. In the central part of the card, two canines lift their heads and bay sinisterly at the moon. In times gone by, this would predict that death was on its way. Behind them is a menacing crayfish lurking in the pool of unconsciousness, ready to scuttle out and nip their ankles. This reminds us of our earliest stages of growth and how we must now become prepared and be made aware of what is hidden.

The Moon had a bad reputation in olden times, and superstition portrayed it as a card of evil or ill intent. This complex card pertains to the tides and dream sleep. Around the client, there is someone who has a colorful imagination. Dreams could appear with strange symbols and vivid pictures that make no sense. There may be rows of numbers or mathematical equations waiting to be solved by the dreamer. As this is a watery card, don't let these strange cyphers throw you; go with the flow.

One World Interpretation

The Moon can characterize lies and deceit; if a court mentor is next to it, the querent has secrets and subterfuge around them, which could harm the seeker. Within relationships, someone is refusing to see what is right in front of their eyes because they are scared of the truth. Healthwise, the Moon can indicate that the client or a family member might suffer from water retention or gynecological upsets, such as menstruation pain, issues with the ovaries, or bladder infections. Reminding the client to drink more water because of dehydration might be a wise thing to do. Pisces is considered one of the more psychic signs in the zodiac, so it might be the case that the seeker possesses a psychic gift or has healing abilities.

Encourage them to delve a little deeper into this. Use Pisces (February–March) for timing.

MEMORIZE

Lies and deceit ✳ Gynecological problems ✳ Bladder infections ✳ Psychic or healing abilities ✳ Being scared of the truth ✳ Timing: February–March

---

Associated Cards with Upright Moon

✳ If the Moon appears next to a creative court mentor (upright or reversed), the client might suddenly become inspired to start a small business linked to art, pottery, or music. In dream sleep, the connection can come from inspiration through a guide or spiritual muse.

✳ If the Hermit (upright) is present, healing energy is manifesting to either help others or the client become healthier.

✳ One of the most well-known predictions in Tarot is when the Moon card is placed next to the Four of Swords (upright), indicating insomnia, nightmares, and broken sleep.

✳ When the Five of Pentacles (upright or reversed) is present with the Moon, the client or someone close to them might need a hysterectomy.

✳ If the Devil (upright or reversed) is around a King, Queen, or Knight (upright or reversed) and the Eight of Cups, the client's partner could have kept a secret for a long time.

✳ If this card comes next to the Devil (upright) and the Four of Cups (upright), booze or drugs could be wrecking someone's life, and it will be hard for them to get back on the straight and narrow.

Rider-Waite Interpretation

Dishonest people surround the client, and they must be careful not to get drawn into situations they can't control. Trust one's instincts, and if the inner voice is screaming a warning, take heed. Job offers or new opportunities might be delayed or may not come to fruition. It's a time to work through any anxieties; if not, depression could take hold, and it will be hard to climb out of it.

One World Interpretation

Hidden doubts, uncertain days. Stay strong and silent in your ways.

KEYWORD: *instincts*

People close by live in a web of lies, and they will want to draw the client into it because they believe to be the truth. There will be a struggle to know what is normal and what is not. The client will need great strength to walk away and start afresh. When starting a new business, keep the plans secret, as others might steal them and claim them as their work. Warn the person not to get too embroiled, as someone could grab them by the ankle and pull them down.

MEMORIZE

Lies and dishonesty ✳ Someone dragging you down ✳ Walking away, fresh start ✳ Trusting instincts

Rider-Waite Tarot   One World Tarot

The Sun

Happiness, hope, and health. Blessings are showered to give you wealth.

CARD NUMBER: 19   **CRYSTALS:** amber and tiger's eye
HERBS: fennel and rosemary   **KEYWORD:** happiness

Rider-Waite Interpretation

Here we see a golden sun in a cloudless blue sky; the naked child sits astride a snow-white horse representing purity. The animal has no dark thoughts and knows only love. The infant holds a red banner depicting the regeneration of the life force, bringing vitality, energy, and achievement. Behind the child, sunflowers grow in abundance and are also present in the garland clasped around his head. These striking flowers represent the creator's love and understanding.

This glorious happy card can change any negativity you see in a reading. Happiness will be on its way, and if someone has been ill for a long time, their recovery will accelerate the return to health and vitality.

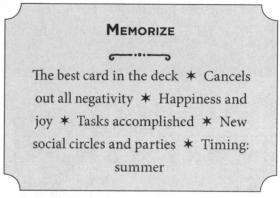

MEMORIZE

The best card in the deck ✳ Cancels out all negativity ✳ Happiness and joy ✳ Tasks accomplished ✳ New social circles and parties ✳ Timing: summer

One World Interpretation

The Sun card is considered the best Tarot card of all. In the modern world, the Sun card brings joy, peace, and happiness, which can be found even in the smallest things in life. Should any negative cards be in a spread, the Sun will cancel them out and foretell a happy ending, however dire the reading might be. Tasks the client has set aside for themselves have been accomplished, and there will be strong feelings of achievement, progress, and order. Travel might be on the agenda to a warm, sunny place, perhaps near the coast or a stunning lake. From the journey, there will be real moments of joy and treasured memories to take back home. New social circles could open up, and invitations will come flooding in. Expect things like happy, lazy barbeques and fun parties with joyous children running around. These get-togethers will lift the spirits and bring back optimism and laughter. When the Sun appears, it can represent the summer months, so if the reader wants to predict future events, summer timings are usually very accurate.

Associated Cards with Upright Sun

✳ If the Sun appears next to the Empress (upright) and a Page (upright or reversed), healthy children will be making an entrance into the world, and there might even be news of twins.

✳ If the Sun is placed with the Two of Cups (upright), an engagement or wedding invitation will be given to the client.

✳ A happy windfall or inheritance is coming when the Wheel of Fortune (upright) turns up. This will bring joy, and the client will share it with other family members.

✳ If the Sun appears in the same spread as the Ace of Cups (upright), something extraordinarily wonderful will happen for the querent. Look at surrounding cards.

✳ If the Sun (upright) appears with the Ace of Cups (upright), the Nine of Pentacles (upright), or the Ace of Pentacles (upright), the client might win the lottery or come first in a competition.

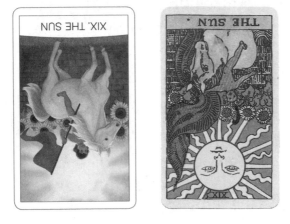

Rider-Waite Interpretation

The seeker might have trouble looking on the bright side and be bogged down with work and responsibility. At home, they are taken for granted and feel like they are doing the lion's share of mundane tasks, or they might be concerned about a child in the family. They could suffer some setbacks and obstacles, which will be frustrating, especially when all they want to do is forge ahead. Because the Sun, in general, is a positive card, any problems that present themselves will be short-lived. It's time to let out the inner child and have some fun.

One World Interpretation

Don't aim for the sky, it could fall down. Check that all is safe and sound.

KEYWORD: *double-check*

The Sun card in reverse is not sinister; it is more likely an annoyance. Children might be rude, hyperactive, or naughty and will need plenty of strict discipline. Where romance is concerned, the client should focus more on their partner's requirements. They may be lazy and neglect the other person in the relationship who, in effect, really loves them. Being too optimistic is not good, and aiming for the sky might bring acute disappointment. It will be essential to check and then double-check that silly mistakes are not repeated.

MEMORIZE

Rude children need discipline ✳ Not paying attention to relationships ✳ Bogged down with work ✳ Obstacles and setbacks ✳ Problems are short-lived

Rider-Waite Tarot

One World Tarot

Judgement

The karmic ties are stripped away to make for sunny, happy days.

CARD NUMBER: 20 **CRYSTALS:** malachite and fluorite
HERBS: rosemary and thyme **KEYWORD:** atonement

Rider-Waite Interpretation

A huge angel fills the sky and, with his golden trumpet, blows a warning to herald the end of days. Most teachings say it's Raphael, some say Gabriel, and in other decks, it is thought to be the archangel Michael. This tradition isn't only present in Christianity; it's also known in many ancient cultures, such as Persian, Norse, and Hindu. People are seen on the card rising from their graves, calling out to the angel so he can help them reach a higher awareness. Judgement Day is upon them, and rebirth or resurrection awaits them.

This card asks the seeker to transform their thinking, improve their personality, and turn over a new leaf. Time is running out for them as a new challenge lies ahead, which could change everything forever. A big decision is on the agenda, and with the right choices, some fantastic things could transpire. Morally and ethically, something will have to be scrutinized as the client's actions will go under the microscope with the angels of karma watching. Opportunities will come to correct past mistakes, especially with friends or family. These new bridges that are being built will form for the client the foundations of wisdom and soul growth.

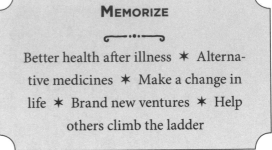

MEMORIZE

Better health after illness ✳ Alternative medicines ✳ Make a change in life ✳ Brand new ventures ✳ Help others climb the ladder

One World Interpretation

When the Judgement card is drawn, it is a good sign of renewed health, so if the seeker or someone close to them has been ill, they will recover soon. Someone might seek a spiritual healer or try alternative medicines. Things may have been flat for a while in the client's work or career, so they are encouraged to take a bold step forward and perhaps ask for a raise or promotion. This move will bring more financial rewards and a successful outcome. Brand-new business ventures are highly starred, so for those seeking self-employment, now is the time to implement plans. Helping others up the social ladder or giving them a job will pay dividends as they could be a real asset to the business.

Associated Cards with Upright Judgement

✳ If the Lovers card (upright) is present, a twin flame might appear in the seeker's life.

✳ With the Ace of Wands (upright) in the spread, a great and successful business is on the horizon, which might provide inroads into foreign countries.

✳ If Judgement is placed next to the Moon (upright or reversed), a dream could be spiritually given that could foretell the death of someone close to the client. If the Star (upright) is also present, the information could come from an alien or extraterrestrial source.

✳ When Judgement is reversed and sitting beside the Hierophant (upright), the client will stall moving house.

✳ If Judgement appears with any spirit guide cards, the client is undergoing a spiritual transformation.

Rider-Waite Interpretation

The client is not listening to the spirit world's messages and is ignoring what they are meant to do. They will repeatedly push it out of their mind, not wanting to face change and growth. The angel's call will continue to ring out. Eventually, the client will have to face their future head-on. The querent lacks self-worth and has no confidence in their decisions. Their actions are causing delays. Fear of death or someone dying could consume them for a while. Trust in the angel, and all will be well.

KEYWORD: *indecision*

It's a time to stop dithering and make a decision. It's better to do something rather than let things stagnate. Relationships will be complex, especially in marriage. There is still a lot to be saved, but the client needs personal space first.

Many people fear this card as it does represent death and resurrection. Because it has a mystical and powerful message, the fear of the unknown can be the stuff of nightmares. Karma is at work, so encourage the client to do their best. It is all the angel asks of them.

> **MEMORIZE**
>
> Stop dithering and make a decision ✳ Fear of death or dying ✳ Not listening to their intuition ✳ Relationship problems ✳ Karma

One World Interpretation

Your soul is fearful and can't be lifted. Take heart, for change will be gifted.

Rider-Waite Tarot

One World Tarot

The World

Freedom comes to you at last to break the ties from the past.

CARD NUMBER: 21 **CRYSTALS:** opal and onyx
HERBS: bay, basil, and mugwort **KEYWORD:** accomplishment

Rider-Waite Interpretation

A dancing maiden at the center of the card stands on one leg inside a cosmic oval. She is surrounded by laurel leaves, symbolizing victory. Her deep purple robe represents her spiritual qualities and understanding of the earth and all its mysteries. In each hand, she holds a baton, again implying universal knowledge and advancement. In the corners of the card are four characters that depict the four elements: earth, air, fire, and water. In the top left of the card, we see humanity, represented by the air sign of Aquarius. In the top right, the Eagle is portrayed; this is the water sign of Scorpio. In the bottom left, the bull represents the Earth sign Taurus, and lastly, at the bottom right, a lion is present, indicative of the fire sign Leo.

A door is shutting, and a renewal is in place. After much hard work and dedication, the client can breathe a sigh of relief as past problems will seem to fade, leaving a space for something else. The seeker has grown spiritually, and their soul is wiser and more patient. This new understanding has created fresh layers of strength where before there was weakness. The World is accomplished and recognized.

One World Interpretation

This card is one of the best in Tarot, and it has numerous positive meanings. The past may have been challenging, but now it is over, so the client awaits better things. Older children might have flown the coop, or perhaps tedious work or study routine has been completed, allowing for more leisure time. If the seeker is younger, they may think about leaving the single life behind and starting a family. Travel to far-flung places is on the horizon; maybe a cruise or snorkeling holiday. It's exciting and refreshing now to enjoy the world and explore new countries. An opportunity could present itself to change homes or move abroad; more choices will be available now. Victory is all around.

MEMORIZE

One of the great cards * Better times to come * The end of a phase in life * Holidays or moves abroad * Starting a family * Older children leaving the nest

---

Associated Cards with Upright World

* The Chariot (reversed) depicts a canceled holiday plan, or an accident in the car may cause an upset.
* When the World (upright) is with the Seven of Cups (upright), the client might decide to go on a spiritual retreat, to a monastery or perhaps a transcendental meditation course.
* If a court mentor (upright or reversed) is in place, the seeker might meet someone new who could live abroad, and a holiday romance could be likely. Look closely at the cards around it to see if they will be positive or negative.
* The client will get through life's problems and emerge victorious when the World is next to the Tower (upright).
* The World in reverse alongside relationship cards (upright or reversed) signifies that the client can't let go of a

past love, which thwarts any new relationships.

Rider-Waite Interpretation

The client must accept what has happened and let go of the past. They may still cling to a love or harbor long-held grudges against someone. The seeker must accede to where they are and make the most of what they have throughout this acceptance period. Someone around them is not achieving their goals; this has nothing to do with their ability, they just haven't taken the first steps yet. Once they get into gear, they will be proud of their success.

One World Interpretation

Let the past fade right away. The future's where you want to stay.

KEYWORD: *postponements*

The World in reverse mainly represents slow going of some sort; things won't be happening quickly enough for the client, but patience has to be learned, and then the rewards will eventually come. There could be possible delays around a house move, with everything on hold. It could be a holiday that gets canceled and rebooked, or someone might fall ill on vacation. The main lesson of the World in reverse is that the client will have to let something go that they have been hanging on to for a long time. It might be resentment toward a person or an old argument or feud. It's time to bury the hatchet.

MEMORIZE

◦—··•··—◦

Delays around house moves ✳ Patience is needed ✳ Canceled holiday or illness abroad ✳ Holding resentment toward another ✳ Clinging on to a past love

4

The Minor Arcana

———

The Suit of Wands

BIRTH SIGNS: Aries, Leo, Sagittarius

SEASON: spring

ALSO KNOWN AS: Clubs, Rods, Staffs, Staves, and Batons

**REPRESENTS: jobs, the workplace, business, money, social standing,
intelligence, creativity, and emotions**

Wands are a dynamic and powerful suit in Tarot; with this energy is born creativity and mental awareness. This suit represents anything to do with work and business, so when a selection of Wands is present in a reading, you will know immediately that the cards will pertain to the client's employment.

The court mentors are lively, cheery, and amusing. Their world is always slightly bizarre, and they love to take chances. Animals and pets will play an essential role in their lives, and they are generally very kind and loving people.

Rider-Waite Tarot   One World Tarot

Ace of Wands

A brand-new start of work is here. You must move forward, that is clear.

CARD NUMBER: 23 **KEYWORD:** work

Rider-Waite Interpretation

Held by the hand of God bearing gifts, one rod sits proudly in the center of the card. In many decks, branches are growing out of the staff, representing new growth and rebirth. This card depicts fresh beginnings and success in everything. From little acorns, great oaks grow. The client will be inspired to start something new and be advised to follow their dreams. It can also characterize spiritual growth and awareness.

One World Interpretation

This is an optimistic card, which is always good to see in a spread, and promises better things to come. Something different is about to emerge. Because Wands represent all things relating to work, the likelihood of a new job, career, or business is on the horizon. This innovative venture will flourish and bring positivity and tremendous headway for the seeker.

There may be a birth in the family, or someone close to the seeker will be announcing a pregnancy. There could also be vital letters in the mail, or a phone call with good news about a property or house move. In general, all Aces are positive.

> **MEMORIZE**
>
> ⌒—•••—⌒
>
> New job, career, business ✳ Birth of a child ✳ Moving house ✳ An important letter or phone call

Associated Cards with Upright Ace of Wands

✳ With the Ace of Wands around the Tower (upright), a sudden disaster could bring ruination and destruction to the job front.

✳ With the Devil (upright or reversed) in the same spread, someone will hide their emotions, staying silent about how they truly feel. Watch others who want to secretively control what is not theirs.

✳ Happy times are around the corner near the Nine of Cups (upright).

✳ With the Ace of Wands next to the Ace of Pentacles (upright), the client or someone around them will receive a large lump sum of money.

✳ If the card appears around the Five of Pentacles (upright or reversed), any financial issues will soon be over as money flows more freely.

Rider-Waite Interpretation

Delays are dominating the client's life, and nothing is moving. This is frustrating because every time they try to make changes, they face obstacles. The questioner could feel like they are wading through treacle. A series of events must happen before the blocks are lifted. Their energy factor is low, leaving them unmotivated and pessimistic about the future. As hard as it is to believe, changes will come in time. Patience is a must.

One World Interpretation

A pause has come; you'll have to wait. Just be patient; all is great.

KEYWORD: *delays*

The person will be looking to change their job, but after many interviews, they will find they still haven't had a break. If they are employed, setbacks will occur, and their position might hang in the balance.

The end results will come after a long period of waiting. Tell the seeker they must not give up and keep trying. Look at the surrounding cards to see if any Major Arcana could be used as a time frame. This card reversed can also signify a delay in plans or even the cancellation of a vacation or journey.

MEMORIZE

⌐ · ·•· · ¬

Stuck in a rut, nothing changing ✳ Patience ✳ Delay in plans and canceling vacations ✳ Job hanging in the balance ✳ Stay positive

Rider-Waite Tarot

One World Tarot

Two of Wands

A choice to make with business plans. Accept the challenge with both hands.

CARD NUMBER: 24 **KEYWORD:** choice

Rider-Waite Interpretation

A man stands gazing out at the land before him; one hand is placed on a rod and the other is at his side. The rod represents decision-making and opportunities to come. The globe in his hand offers the wisdom he needs to make the correct choices. The client isn't yet ready to put their ideas into practice; instead, they are waiting for changes or a positive sign that they should move forward.

One World Interpretation

All twos in Tarot signify choices, and this suit is mainly connected to the workplace or one's career. Soon the client will have to make decisions about their work and employment. New opportunities lie ahead, but the seeker must decide whether to pursue them. If they are self-employed, an innovative business partnership could come their way with a chance to sign contracts. The future looks good, so encourage them to forge ahead.

This card can also indicate an expensive purchase, such as a gift for someone or a new car.

> ### MEMORIZE
> ⸻ ·••· ⸻
> Making decisions about work or business ✳ New opportunities ✳ Signing contracts ✳ Expensive purchases

Associated Cards with Upright Two of Wands

* If the Two of Wands appears around the Empress card (upright), brand new prospects will present themselves quickly. With the Emperor (upright) in situ, an important contact could be mind-blowing, and the client's life will thrust them in a positive direction.
* The Seven of Swords (reversed) in proximity signifies disruption in the workplace. Someone at work could be stealing; investigations will follow.
* With the Seven of Cups (upright) in the spread, the client may be unsure whether they are making the right choices, but soon things will become clear to them, and they will embark on the right path.

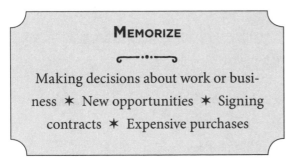

Rider-Waite Interpretation

A strong individual will try to dominate the questioner's thinking, so urge them not to be influenced and to stand their ground. It would be best to trust one's instincts for a better result, and more organization is needed to create harmony in their life. This can also mean that the person or someone close to them will have a fantastic idea about something but won't be sure how to implement their concepts. Because of this, great opportunities could be lost.

One World Interpretation

In a rut, the future's on hold; stand your ground, be strong and bold.

KEYWORD: *obstacles*

The seeker will have made firm plans for the future, but nothing is happening, and they are blocked by many obstacles. Tell them to have patience, and things will move when they are ready. A phase is ahead where their work grinds to a halt, and boredom plays a big part in their daily life, about which they can do little to change the circumstances. The wrong decision has been made, and they are now living to regret it.

MEMORIZE

Plans for the future thwarted ✳ Things will change eventually ✳ A strong person is trying to influence ✳ More organization is needed in life ✳ Making the wrong decision

Rider-Waite Tarot

One World Tarot

Three of Wands

Reach out and get the help you need; good advice you will receive.

CARD NUMBER: 25 **KEYWORD:** advice

Rider-Waite Interpretation

The card depicts a man standing above the shoreline, looking at the passing ships. Three rods are planted next to him, representing his commitment to his responsibilities. From where he stands, he has a good view of all that life offers and can see possible issues he may encounter in the future. Traditionally, he has great wisdom and will be relied upon to help others.

One World Interpretation

Listen to others, and take any advice that is offered. The querent can either be giving advice, receiving it, or even going into a profession where they will be helping others. Look at the surrounding cards to provide an indication. Seeds can now be planted for any new business venture that will flourish in the coming years. Someone at work will approve an assignment, bringing more money and success. A person around the client can be very needy and demand attention and reassurance, leaving them feeling drained and exhausted.

MEMORIZE

New business ventures ✳ Giving or receiving advice ✳ Someone is enhancing a project at work ✳ Needy and demanding people ✳ Feeling exhausted

---

Associated Cards with Upright Three of Wands

* With the Three of Wands around any of the four Knights (upright or reversed), the client will be guiding a young man in his up-and-coming career.
* With the Two of Pentacles (upright) in the spread, the client will be seeking the help of a financial advisor and getting their assets in order.
* With the card placed next to the Wheel of Fortune (upright), approach work with a more positive attitude, and you will have a change in fortune.
* When the Three of Wands appears with the King or Queen of Pentacles (upright or reversed), this could represent a teacher or a head of education that could open new doors.

 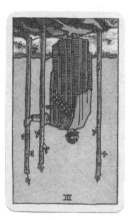

Rider-Waite Interpretation

This card can represent studying, but because it's reversed, the client could be struggling to perform. They have tried many times to accomplish their goals but failed. Encourage them to read the small print on any documents they might be signing in the future, or do a little research to ensure that all is ethical and aboveboard.

The seeker may not be using their full potential and wasting their talents on trivia.

One World Interpretation

Egos must be put away, or from your pathway you will stray.

KEYWORD: *egotistical*

Either the querent or someone close to them will be full of self-importance. This could be their ruination, and the negativity could impact their work life. They may be slapdash when making plans for the future, and their hasty decisions will be full of loopholes. Someone around them is giving bad advice, so they must err on the side of caution, as things could start to tumble around them.

MEMORIZE

Having an ego is not a good thing ✳ Rushing decisions ✳ Receiving bad advice ✳ Reading the small print ✳ Not using one's full potential

Rider-Waite Tarot   *One World Tarot*

Four of Wands

Reap the good in what you've done. Time to relax and have some fun.

CARD NUMBER: 26 **KEYWORD:** family

Rider-Waite Interpretation

Four wands are standing erect, depicting the four solid walls of a home. This is a card of contentment and happiness. In some ancient Tarot decks, a blossomed wreath is present on the card, but this deck displays the flowers in the trees, indicating prosperity, abundance, and contentment.

The castle behind the happy couple signifies their home life and harmony within the family. The client has many blessings and is surrounded by people who love them dearly.

One World Interpretation

This is a lovely card; the seeker will have a very settled family life at some point in the future. Someone in the household might be planning a wedding, but for those already married, it will represent stability. Because all Wands in the Tarot signify work, the seeker will have to put in more effort to keep their relationship sweet and balance the finances. They may have also gone through a rough time in their relationship, but because the right foundations are in place, they have managed to work it out. This card can sometimes depict the client's struggle with past relationships.

> ### MEMORIZE
> ↩ • ·•· • ↪
>
> Happy family ✳ Planning a wedding ✳ Happy marriage, but it must be worked at ✳ Keeping finances balanced ✳ Bad relationships in the past

Associated Cards with Upright Four of Wands

✳ With the Two of Swords (upright), the divorce card, appearing in the spread, the seeker will have experienced a bad marriage in the past but will go on to have a very joyful one in the future.

✳ Around the High Priestess (upright), the Four of Wands indicates spiritual awareness is escalating, and the client's guide will be close.

✳ With the World (upright) in the spread, a fantastic opportunity will present itself; this could be in conjunction with a key job.

✳ With the card around the Two of Cups (upright), the seeker will meet their soul mate after a string of bad relationships.

✳ When the Four of Wands is reversed and around the Chariot, family arguments could result in someone moving out of the home.

Rider-Waite Interpretation

The client will be involved in family disagreements, and there is a complete breakdown of communication. Look at surrounding cards to see who is being difficult. The arguments may not necessarily be related to the couple, as others can cause mayhem around them. If a Page or Knight is present in the spread, it could indicate that the seeker or someone close by will be clashing with a child or teenager.

One World Interpretation

Success is here, but do recall: Your family matters most of all.

KEYWORD: *neglect*

Someone in the relationship will be selfish, not paying their partner or children attention. If they continue to behave this way, the marriage/partnership could fail. Work and success have become more important. This card can also signify that the client is overspending and needs to tighten their purse strings. A colossal argument will occur with a family member, and there's no coming back from it. Advise them to think before speaking, or they could upset someone.

> ### Memorize
>
> ⌐—··—⌐
>
> Someone in the marriage has a careless attitude ✻ Family arguments and quarrels ✻ If Pages and Knights are present, problems with youngsters ✻ Overspending ✻ Thinking before you speak

Rider-Waite Tarot

One World Tarot

Five of Wands

Competition pulls you down. Those at work will make you frown.

CARD NUMBER: 27 **KEYWORD:** conflict

Rider-Waite Interpretation

Five men are wielding rods above their heads in battle, all wearing different colors, portraying their diverse backgrounds. Conflict is all around, and poor communication makes life difficult. Since everyone wants to be the boss, the seeker could become overly preoccupied with the rivalry and impede their own advancement. Because Wands represent work, there will be tension and trouble in the workplace.

One World Interpretation

Problems and skirmishes occur at work, with colleagues unhappy with how things are being run. No peace or harmony exists, leaving the questioner hassled and hopeless.

The company they work for will be highly competitive, creating a bad vibe with their teammates. Communication between the bosses and the people on the ground is poor, and no one wants to listen. Because of this disharmony, employees will be worried about their future.

> ### MEMORIZE
> ⌒–·••·–⌒
>
> People taking umbrage at work ✷ Conflict and poor communication ✷ Company restructuring ✷ Employees worried about the future

Associated Cards with Upright Five of Wands

* With Justice (reversed) in situ, the querent will encounter groups of aggressive men.
* With the Five of Wands near the Tower (upright or reversed), confrontations become physical, and someone could be hurt or badly injured.
* With one or more Kings (upright or reversed) in the same spread, a father may be jealous of a highly successful son with modern ideas and a bright new future.
* When the Five of Wands is placed near the Hermit (upright), one must not rely on others. Anything that needs doing can be achieved by the client, who will have to rely on their instincts.
* With the card placed around the Devil (upright or reversed), a controlling bully at work holds a managerial position.

Rider-Waite Interpretation

Leaving one job and starting a better one. People will be kind and generous, bestowing gifts and blessings. Encourage the querent to take care of their health; a good diet and exercise are advised, so perhaps encourage yoga or some mindful meditation. After the fresh beginning, the person experiences a sense of fulfillment, and they can finally accomplish their goals.

One World Interpretation

All the stress is finally gone; with a smile, you carry on.

KEYWORD: *generosity*

After a troubled time, new opportunities will fall at the client's feet, and things will finally look up. It may take time to get used to a problem-free life, but don't be pessimistic; relax and enjoy the ambience. The seeker will be generous and share their good fortune with those around them. A time is near when they can finally complete any unfinished tasks.

Success is ahead, and a happy time is on the horizon.

MEMORIZE

◦—·⋯·—◦

After hardship, things are looking up ✳ New opportunities ✳ Leaving a job and starting another ✳ Taking care of health ✳ Generous people

Rider-Waite Tarot   One World Tarot

Six of Wands

After troubles and unrest, victory follows, from bad to best.

CARD NUMBER: 28 **KEYWORD:** improvement

Rider-Waite Interpretation

A man sits astride a white horse and is surrounded by men holding rods. This image represents victory after a time of hardship. He has a pole with a wreath of laurel leaves in his hand, entwined with a red ribbon, symbolizing virtue and success. Sometimes the laurel leaves will be upon the head of the victor. This is the card of success; finally, the client will have achieved everything they dreamed of.

One World Interpretation

The person will endure a time of trouble where nothing seems to go right for them. However, this card represents victory following hardship, so they will triumph in the end.

Relationships will begin to improve both in the work field and in love, so the seeker will soon feel contented once again. Reassure them by telling them to keep pushing on and not to give up. Look at surrounding cards to see which part of life this applies to.

There could be someone with a scientific mind around the querent who will bring them success in the future. All goals have now been reached, and someone at work could pat the client on the back.

> ### MEMORIZE
> ⌐ • ⋅ ⋅ • ¬
> Victory and success follow a hard time ✴ Relationships improve in work and love ✴ Don't give up ✴ Congratulations at work

Associated Cards with Upright Six of Wands

✴ With the Chariot (upright) in the spread, the querent will be purchasing a car, and if around two or more Swords (upright or reversed), there will be a problem with a vehicle.

✴ A lengthy legal battle will be won with the Justice card (upright) in the spread.

✴ Next to the Sun (upright) or the Ace of Cups (upright), the Six of Wands portends good news on the way, and the client will be punching the air in joy.

✴ With Death (upright) in situ, a new beginning with work will present itself around Scorpio time.

Rider-Waite Interpretation

This card in reverse can show the seeker being full of self-importance and sporting an ego, making them unpopular with work colleagues.

Around the work field, someone could be devious by taking all the credit for a project the client has done. Will they be believed when the complaint is brought to the boss's attention? Sometimes, this card can represent a fall from grace. This might occur because the seeker is overly confident, and someone will take pleasure in causing their downfall.

One World Interpretation

Someone close could be a cheat. Stand your ground for their defeat.

KEYWORD: *embarrassment*

At work, the client or someone around them could fall from grace or not get the recognition they deserve. Through lack of concentration, the seeker can make huge mistakes in the workplace, which could be embarrassing for them. For a while, they will struggle with self-confidence and pre-fer not to stand out in the crowd. Becoming envious of others does them no favors, because the grass may not actually be greener on the other side. The equine on the card can represent a mode of transport in the reading. Look at surrounding cards to see if this is positive or negative.

MEMORIZE

⌐—·ıı·—⌐

Making a mistake that causes embarrassment ✳ Struggling with self-confidence ✳ Full of self-importance, egotistical ✳ Unpopular with colleagues ✳ Someone is taking the credit for a job the seeker has done ✳ A vehicle

| Rider-Waite Tarot | One World Tarot |

Seven of Wands

Be courageous, and fight to win. To lose it now would be a sin.

CARD NUMBER: 29 **KEYWORDS:** promotion, redundancy

Rider-Waite Interpretation

A man stands firmly with a rod in his hand, fighting off the other six rods rising from the ground. This card is about defending one's territory and fighting hard for recognition. The man depicted on the card represents a person with strength of mind but who is under pressure in the workplace. They might be challenged by others who want to take their job.

One World Interpretation

The client will be unhappy in the work field and must protect their position as others muscle in to do it their way. However, there will be one of two scenarios to dwell on; either they will be made redundant from their job, or, on a more positive note, they will enjoy a promotion within the same spectrum. You will need to study the surrounding cards to see if they bring negative or positive influences. Even if the cards spell redundancy, the person will have a new job on the horizon that pays a far better salary.

This Wand card can represent the querent teaching or training others in some decks.

> **MEMORIZE**
>
> ⟶ ··· ⟵
>
> Redundancy or promotion ✳ Protecting one's territory ✳ A new job soon ✳ Teaching and training others

Associated Cards with Upright Seven of Wands

✳ With the Seven of Wands around the Ace of Wands (upright), the client can expect to begin a different job for a brand-new company.

✳ With the Nine or Ten of Swords (upright or reversed) in the spread, time off work due to illness.

✳ With the Five of Pentacles (upright or reversed) in situ, worry and hopelessness, not earning enough money.

✳ If the Seven of Wands appears around the Hanged Man (upright), wait for twelve months before changes occur.

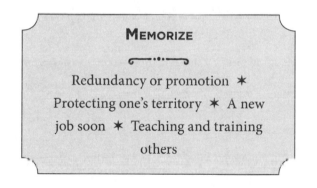

Rider-Waite Interpretation

The client feels overwhelmed, and no matter how hard they strive to achieve, they keep hitting a brick wall. Encourage them to keep fighting because they will win in the end. They need to defend their territory at home, as spats with the neighbors could be an issue. The client has made too many commitments and feels stressed with their workload. This card can also mean the person is not standing up for themselves and will be beaten down by others.

One World Interpretation

Adjust your thoughts to bring success. Rash decisions cause distress.

KEYWORD: *stress*

The seeker is in continuous opposition at work, feeling very stressed and worried about the future. The pressure could result in taking time off for mental health issues.

Think about decisions before jumping in headfirst. Mull things over for a while, as there's no rush. Someone could undermine or make the client feel small in front of a group. This embarrassment will leave them in an unstable position.

MEMORIZE

◦—···—◦

Opposition at work ✳ Worried about the future ✳ Taking time off work with stress ✳ Keep fighting on until the battle is won ✳ Think carefully before making decisions ✳ Being undermined or belittled

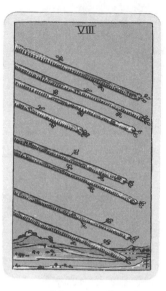

Rider-Waite Tarot

EIGHT OF WANDS

One World Tarot

Eight of Wands

A journey comes, prepare for haste. An opportunity you cannot waste.

CARD NUMBER: 30 **KEYWORD:** journeys

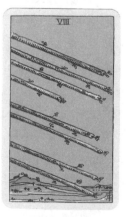

EIGHT OF WANDS

Rider-Waite Interpretation

The eight rods in this card hang high in the clouds, representing flight, freedom, and travel. The sky is blue and clear, and the seeker will have boundless energy to grab opportunities that will turn out to be victorious. As all eights in Tarot symbolize good luck and good fortune, any goals the querent wishes to pursue must be taken up now.

Encourage them to clear away any distractions and set their mind to completing their goals.

One World Interpretation

Within twelve months, journeys will be planned, and because the Wands are suspended in the sky, this portrays air travel and flights. This journey could be for business or pleasure, so study the surrounding cards to see which one it refers to.

Since the eight is the card of movement, it frequently indicates a house move, so the client will consider relocating within twelve months. Positive shifts at work may start out slowly before accelerating later.

MEMORIZE

Travel by air ✳ A change of address ✳ Positive changes with work ✳ New projects

---

Associated Cards with Upright Eight of Wands

✳ A business trip is predicted if there is an abundance of Wands (upright or reversed) in the same spread.

✳ With many Cups (upright) present, a family vacation could be expected.

✳ The client will be separating from their partner if any relationship cards are placed next to the Three of Swords (upright or reversed).

✳ With the Eight of Wands around negative cards, the journey could be held up or the trip could be difficult, and they'll be pleased to get home.

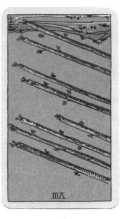

Rider-Waite Interpretation

The querent is clear about their ideas, and is forging ahead to complete their ambitions, but someone or something is holding them back. This is frustrating because they have a clear vision of what they want to do, but they are being delayed and distracted from every angle. Sometimes this card can signify cancellations, especially with travel.

One World Interpretation

Don't rush by and spoil the plot, or else you'll lose all you've got.

KEYWORD: *postponements*

Journeys and travel are delayed. The client needs to get a grip on their emotions. Advise them to stop and think about their choices and not rush into anything. A jealous person is around, so the client must look closely to establish who it is and detach them from their radar. The sale of a property might fall through at the last minute, and the client may lose money. Never count your chickens before they hatch, and expect the unexpected.

MEMORIZE

❮ —•••— ❯

Travel delays ✳ Manage emotions ✳ Stop and think about choices ✳ A jealous person ✳ House sales fall through ✳ Expect the unexpected

Rider-Waite Tarot

One World Tarot

Nine of Wands

Your strength must come in these challenging times. To give up now would be a crime.

CARD NUMBER: 31 **KEYWORD:** dejected

Rider-Waite Interpretation

A man clutches a single staff, with eight other rods looming over him. He must find his strength to complete life's tests. In some decks, the staff he is holding is positioned across his chest in a defensive position, and in other packs, the eight vertical rods are symbols of protection. Other decks portray the hurdles that must be surmounted. Today, it warns one to be on their guard and not to trust everything that's seen or heard.

One World Interpretation

The client could be really frustrated and feel overcome with anxiety. They might not be in good health, or they may struggle with minor ailments because of the stress buildup. This card also holds a message to be on guard and weigh everything before making decisions.

A devious person is around the querent, so they must look closer at friends and colleagues who might not be as agreeable as they appear. At work, small groups of individuals could gossip, trying to bring the querent down. Even though the seeker may not feel strong, they can deal with all the challenges before them.

> ### MEMORIZE
> ⸻•••⸻
> Overwhelmed and unwell ✳ Be on guard ✳ A devious person around ✳ Small groups bring the client down ✳ They can face their challengers

Associated Cards with Upright Nine of Wands

✳ The Nine next to the Ten of Wands (upright) signifies purchasing property or starting a new business venture.

✳ With the Magician (upright) in the spread, the client must not be scared to open the mind and work on their psychic ability.

✳ If one or more court mentors are present (upright or reversed), a horrible person will try to invade their space. Tell them to seek out the individual and gain back their power.

✳ If the Nine of Wands appears around the Lovers (upright), the querent will be wary of entering into a relationship. They must trust their instincts.

✳ With the Five of Swords (upright or reversed) in the spread, someone around the client will suffer from paranoia, and lies will be revealed.

Rider-Waite Interpretation

A time of great courage as the karmic laws are set in place. Will the person stay strong or fall at the first hurdle? There is no one to help, as only they can achieve this. Pain from rheumatism, creaking bones, or an achy back will make the seeker feel old and worn-out, and someone around them could have a knee injury.

One World Interpretation

Brick walls appear in front of you. No way forward; you're in a queue.

KEYWORD: *freeloaders*

The client is surrounded by people who offer no support. If they are in a relationship, they might feel like a one-man band, working full-time, caring for the children, and doing all the household chores without help. At work, others could be slacking, and the querent will be doing someone else's job as well as their own.

Every time they try to move forward, they will be beaten back, with one obstacle after another. Determination is a must, and things will start to move eventually.

Poor health will affect the client or someone close to them.

> **MEMORIZE**
>
> Having no support at work or at home ✳ Obstacles and blocks ✳ Patience, things will change ✳ Poor health ✳ Aches and pains

Rider-Waite Tarot

TEN OF WANDS

One World Tarot

Ten of Wands

Life is harsh, and morale is down. Keep both feet planted on the ground.

CARD NUMBER: 32 **KEYWORD:** responsibility

Rider-Waite Interpretation

This card illustrates a person traveling toward a nearby town while hauling a sizable bundle of sticks. The burden that is being carried pulls them down, yet soon they will reach their destination and be able to let go of the bundle, feeling enlightened and refreshed. This can sometimes mean that the client has too many responsibilities. They could be caring for someone sick while trying to look after the children and go to work. The stress will become too much in the end.

One World Interpretation

This card can often mean that the client is in a dead-end job with a boss constantly adding more and more responsibilities. This could get to be too much for the seeker, and they will want to leave their employment. If you establish that they are happy with their job, they will face tricky challenges over the coming months that will change their mindset to one of negativity. They are being pulled in every direction and will have no time for themselves. The client must delegate jobs both at work and around the home in order to stay sane. This card can also indicate back or knee problems resulting from lifting something too heavy. Warn the person to take care; they might stumble and fall.

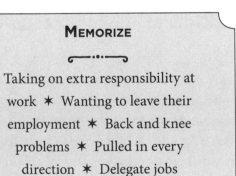

MEMORIZE

⸺ ·•·· ⸺

Taking on extra responsibility at work ✳ Wanting to leave their employment ✳ Back and knee problems ✳ Pulled in every direction ✳ Delegate jobs

Associated Cards with Upright Ten of Wands

* With the Ten of Wands appearing around the Star (upright), positive changes at work are coming soon.
* With this card appearing around the Six of Swords (upright), a job offer might mean a change of location.
* If the Ten of Wands appears next to the Moon (upright), someone is lying and gossiping at work.
* Around Knights or young Queens (upright or reversed), they'll feel overwhelmed and hopeless with courses and failed exams.

Rider-Waite Interpretation

This card is quite dismal when reversed. A tired body has to work harder than others as they are taken advantage of. When leaving the workplace, chores await them at home. There seems to be no escape from it all, so stress and depression will step in. Clients must stand up for themselves and not allow others to abuse their kindness.

One World Interpretation

Past mistakes take their toll. Stand up straight, lest you should fall.

KEYWORD: *mistakes*

Because the client is overworked and unable to concentrate on multiple activities, they will make silly mistakes. They desperately want a promotion or to better themselves at work, but sadly, no such advancement is predicted. The client could also break a bone or be around someone who has an accident or ends up in the ER.

Support the person in an understanding way to stand firm, and all will be well.

MEMORIZE

Mistakes are made, but tasks are completed in the end ✳ Wanting a promotion ✳ Breaking bones or injuries ✳ Being treated unfairly

The Court Mentors: Wands

King of Wands, Queen of Wands,
Knight of Wands, Page of Wands

BIRTH SIGNS: Aries, Leo, and Sagittarius

CAREERS FOR ARIES FIRE SIGN: entrepreneurs and business owners; authoritative roles such as managers, bosses, supervisors, personal assistants, armed forces, HR roles, magistrates, and lawyers

CAREERS FOR LEO FIRE SIGN: theatrical work, film directors, drama teachers, public relations, sculptors, public speakers, lecturers, CEOs, and decision-makers

CAREERS FOR SAGITTARIUS FIRE SIGN: self-employed, sporty roles, PE teachers, salespeople, technical sales, engineers, builders, plasterers, laborers, carpentry, bodybuilding, and overseas work

Rider-Waite Tarot

One World Tarot

Page of Wands

News has come of someone young. Get ready now for lots of fun.

CARD NUMBER: 33 **KEYWORDS:** sweet youngster
Child, boy or girl, aged birth–16

Rider-Waite Interpretation

In most decks, this fire sign child stands holding a staff and is engrossed with the emerging leaves. This symbolizes creative growth and the belief that his path can travel in any direction. He is seeking inspiration and has not yet made his decision. In his hat, the feathers represent his achievements and tributes.

One World Interpretation

Like all Pages, this card depicts a youngster with an attractive disposition, and in some decks, it may be seen as a boy. The child will be multitalented with a vibrant nature and easy to bring up. They will have a flair for anything creative and might later work with their hands. The Page of Wands is usually more practical than academic, but makes logical choices.

MEMORIZE

Young child, boy or girl ✳ Sweet disposition and creativity ✳ Good news is on the way ✳ Important letters or phone calls

---

Other Meanings

This could be a time when creativity is blocked, so embrace new projects and test out ideas. The client may feel like exploring the more spiritual aspects of life, so encourage them to open their mind to more important information. This card can also mean that good news is on the way, and they could receive an important letter or phone call.

Associated Cards with Upright Page of Wands

✳ If the Page of Wands is around court mentors (upright or reversed), this child will be in the family, usually a son, daughter, or grandchild.

✳ If the child is well-behaved and the Page is shown in a spread with disruptive cards, you can reassure the client that any bad behavior is just a phase.

✳ If the Page of Wands appears around Judgement (upright), lots of necessary paperwork will need to be addressed.

✳ With the Ace of Wands (upright) in the spread, a new job brings lots of administration.

Reversed Meaning

A child is crying and feeling lost, as into the storm they are tossed.

KEYWORD: *upset*

The worried child keeps their fears to themselves but doesn't have the life skills to solve the problem. In the hustle and bustle of life, they could become overlooked. An adult must take them to one side and help soothe their fears. Bad news may come to the client, or someone in the family could suffer from ill health. Visits to doctors, dentists, or specialists may be necessary. Inspiration is blocked, so they must rest for a while and wait for the creative juices to start flowing again.

MEMORIZE

A child in the family is upset ✳ Get to the bottom of what is wrong ✳ Bad news ✳ Illness ✳ Creative blocks

Rider-Waite Tarot　　　　　*One World Tarot*

Knight of Wands

A new start now with journeys waiting. A move of house will need debating.

CARD NUMBER: 34 **KEYWORDS:** positive attitudes
Young man, aged 16–29

Rider-Waite Interpretation

This fire sign Knight is seated on his horse, holding a rod over his right shoulder. The horse is rearing up, symbolizing that the young man is enthusiastic and ready to leap into action. He is full of new ideas and has a clear vision of where he wants to go.

One World Interpretation

This young man is happy-go-lucky and will have a positive attitude about life. In his youth, he can be somewhat erratic, taking time to grow up, but his traditional thinking will enable him to grow into a fine man. In his early adult life, he will flit from job to job, never settling down, and might have a string of girlfriends without committing to any one of them. He's a good communicator and has a charming personality.

MEMORIZE

Nice young man ✳ Good communicator ✳ Job hop and bed hop ✳ International travel ✳ Good business ✳ House move

---

Other Meanings

It's time to put ideas into action, and once the client makes a big move, they will almost certainly succeed. Everything is possible because self-confidence is blooming. All will be good, so aim high. This card can denote international travel and professional achievement, depending on the situation. It might also be indicative of a house move.

Associated Cards with Upright Knight of Wands

* With the World (upright) or the Eight of Wands (upright or reversed), the Knight may take a gap year and travel abroad.
* Next to the Four of Cups (upright) and Five of Cups (upright or reversed), this Knight could be overindulging in alcohol or drugs.
* If around the Tower (upright or reversed) and the Chariot (upright or reversed), the young Knight needs to be careful when driving to avoid having an accident.
* If next to the Judgement card (upright), he will embrace his spiritual side early and have a belief in otherworldly beings like aliens and UFOs.
* Around the Empress (upright) and the Lovers (upright), he must take care not to get a girl pregnant.

Reversed Meaning

Rivalry with young men fighting. Family feuds as quick as lightning.

KEYWORD: *fighting*

A self-centered individual. A typical example would be a young man spending hours in his room, playing video games and not engaging with family members. He will be uncommunicative and even demonstrate signs of jealousy with a sibling. He'll need a firm hand and strong direction to get him out of bad habits.

He may live with his parents and lack energy, showing signs of being lazy. Make him walk the straight and narrow; he needs to grow up. If around other Knights, he might be physically fighting or have an aggressive nature. There could be discord within the family if Kings and Queens are present.

MEMORIZE

Living at home with parents ✳ Lazy, lacking in energy, and uncommunicative ✳ Jealousy ✳ Fighting and aggression

Rider-Waite Tarot   One World Tarot

Queen of Wands

Fire sign queen helps with guidance. She brings forth wisdom, love, and balance.

CARD NUMBER: 35 **KEYWORDS:** pleasant woman
Woman, aged 16 onward

Rider-Waite Interpretation

This Queen represents courage and self-assurance. She is determined to take risks and implement all of her ideas. In older decks, like the Rider-Waite, she is positioned between two lions that stand for strength and fire. A black cat sits at her feet, showing us that she has a more mysterious side to her nature.

One World Interpretation

In today's Tarot readings, this pleasant, charming woman loves nature and animals. She is wise and sensible and will give good, sound advice when needed. She adores her home, so she will make an effort with the interior design and keep her house orderly and clean. She provides her family with love and support, making her the ideal wife and mother. Because she is a romantic type, her husband or partner must be attentive. If he fails and she becomes bored, she could flirt and get the attention she seeks elsewhere.

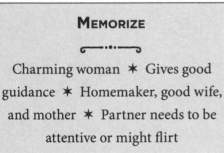

MEMORIZE

Charming woman ✳ Gives good guidance ✳ Homemaker, good wife, and mother ✳ Partner needs to be attentive or might flirt

Other Meanings

Don't be afraid to embrace self-confidence and make a conscious effort to fill life with fun. It's a time to become a social butterfly and make new friends and acquaintances.

Associated Cards with Upright Queen of Wands

✳ With the Queen next to another court mentor (upright), the client will work with a kind and fair boss.
✳ If the Queen of Wands appears around other Queens (upright or reversed), the client may have a sister or a large social circle of girlfriends.
✳ (Reverse Queen) With the Devil and Seven of Swords present, a violent woman will show signs of physical aggression.
✳ (Reverse Queen) If around two or more Wand cards relating to work, there could be a demanding boss or colleague.

Reversed Meaning

A fickle lady, her soul is hard. Don't be trusting; be on your guard.

KEYWORD: *henpecked*

She can be hard-hearted and think nothing of having a string of affairs; however, it is wise to only predict this if the Lovers card is in the same spread. Her personality is captivating, so she is used to getting her own way with charm and flattery, but if you cross her, it's a very different story, and the client could find themselves in a catfight that they won't win.

This Queen is narrow-minded, fickle, and, if riled, a force to be reckoned with. She lacks love and sympathy and is an extremely strict parent.

Her partner may be henpecked and not able to think for himself, and her children fear her temper tantrums.

Memorize

Narrow-minded ✳ Strict with children ✳ Bossy wife, henpecked husband ✳ The type to have affairs

Rider-Waite Tarot

One World Tarot

King of Wands

This fire sign man has a heart of gold. He creates wealth and privilege untold.

CARD NUMBER: 36 **KEYWORDS:** honest man
Man, aged 29 onward

Rider-Waite Interpretation

A king sits proudly on his throne, in front of a gold panel with lions. He is different from the other court mentors of this suit; he doesn't focus so much on creativity.

Instead, he assumes the position of a visionary leader, prepared to guide his followers toward a single objective.

One World Interpretation

A king sits proudly on his throne, adorned with two golden lions depicting courage and strength. In many deck descriptions, he is the most likeable king in the Tarot, and in the upright position, he possesses many admirable qualities. He is popular, honest, and reliable, with a sweet character. He is devoted and faithful in relationships and will put his partner's needs first. He is also a wonderful parent, raising his kids with solid morals and high standards, even though he may occasionally be a bit soft. He is intelligent and will be a good employer or employee, able to make logical decisions.

> **MEMORIZE**
> ⌐—··⦁··—⌐
> Great guy, nicest of all kings ✳ Devoted, honest, and faithful ✳ Good father, employer, or employee

Other Meanings

The client will accomplish a lot because they are confident about their future. The advice is to avoid spending time on things or people who are pointless; instead, keep a vision in mind and venture forth to complete it.

Associated Cards with Upright King of Wands

✳ Next to the World (upright), he may have a job where he works away.
✳ Around other Kings (upright or reversed), the man may have brothers or enjoy the company of men.
✳ (Reversed King) With the Three of Swords (upright), this indicates that his actions could hurt others, and they will eventually detach themselves from his life.
✳ (Reversed King) Around the Eight of Cups (upright), this represents the king feeling deep regret for his past actions.

Reversed Meaning

A lack of tolerance makes you sad. In the workplace, all is mad.

KEYWORD: *unloving*

He is usually divorced at least once because previous partners wouldn't put up with him. As a father, he is likely to be unloving and disinterested. Having the mind of a butterfly, he will flit from one project to another, soon getting bored and achieving little.

He exhibits arrogance, particularly at work, is unpopular with his coworkers, tends to talk without thinking, and is intolerant of those around him. In relationships, he leans toward being sexist, believing a woman's place is in the home. He might show signs of being verbally aggressive and lazy around the house.

> **MEMORIZE**
>
> ⌐—··—⌐
>
> Arrogant and unpopular ✳ Usually divorced ✳ A disinterested, unloving father ✳ Lazy and verbally aggressive

The Suit of Cups

BIRTH SIGNS: Cancer, Scorpio, Pisces

SEASON: summer

ALSO KNOWN AS: Hearts, Chalices, Coups, and Goblets

REPRESENTS: emotions, the home, mindfulness, family, children and relationships, marriages, love and affection

Cups represent the water signs of Pisces, Cancer, and Scorpio. This watery suit governs the client's emotions and is linked with matters of the heart, such as family, children, love, sex, and marriage, which can be complex cards to read. Most Cups are pleasant, but the interpretations can paint a different picture when blended with more challenging cards, like the Swords. The court mentors are likable individuals and often graced with creative gifts. They can be charming and witty, are good problem solvers, and rarely enter into conflict, preferring a quieter life. Many see this suit as having psychic abilities, especially those born under the Scorpio and Pisces signs.

Rider-Waite Tarot

One World Tarot

Ace of Cups

Magic and joy within your heart. This card will bring a brand-new start.

CARD NUMBER: 37 **KEYWORD:** brilliance

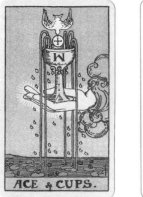

Rider-Waite Interpretation

The Ace of Cups represents relationships, emotion, love, and compassion, and the profound link between those on earth and loved ones in the spirit realms.

Here we see the hand of the creator emerging from a snowy white cloud. In a bright blue sky, the Ace of Cups is held aloft with five rivulets of water cascading down into a pool below, depicting the five senses of spiritual energy we all have within us. They also remind us of our spiritual sustenance from the divine force. The white dove hovers over the chalice with the hope and promise of peace to come.

This first card in the suit of Cups depicts joy and new beginnings, leaving the past behind and embarking on a journey of discovery, bringing love and fulfillment.

One World Interpretation

Wedding bells ring in tune, celebrations are coming soon.

KEYWORD: *Love*

The Ace of Cups is one of the best cards in the deck of Tarot and is truly remarkable in many ways. The cup of life overflows with love and peace, leaving the querent happy and looking forward to a positive future. There might be an announcement of a wedding, engagement, or news of a pregnancy. Often, the querent will embark on a romantic love affair, or their social circle will expand with many new friendships about to take place.

If lots of Swords or problematic cards are present, this Ace can foretell a happy outcome. You need to look at the other cards in the spread to determine where this good fortune is coming from.

MEMORIZE

One of the best cards in the deck ✳ If around negative cards, a happy outcome ✳ Weddings, engagements, and news of a pregnancy ✳ A new home

---

Associated Cards with Upright Ace of Cups

* If the Ace of Cups (upright) is in the same spread as the Sun (upright), then something truly wonderful is predicted for the querent.
* When more than two Aces appear in the spread, dramatic changes will come.
* If the Ace of Cups (reversed) appears in the same spread as the Two of Swords (upright), a once happy marriage ends in divorce.
* If the Ace of Cups appears next to the Empress (upright), a much-wanted baby will be born.
* If the Ace of Cups (reversed) is around two Queens, the end of a female friendship is near.

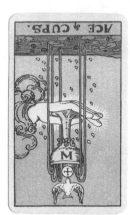

rather than allowing emotional baggage to reappear later.

One World Interpretation

Take care with your love so fine, in case you put it on the line.

KEYWORD: *challenges*

Rider-Waite Interpretation

A time to take stock of what the divine has given; nothing should be taken for granted. The client should cherish those around them and put in more effort. They are inclined to be obsessed about themselves, caring little how someone else is doing; therefore, more effort is required for relationships, both romantic and platonic. A partner's love could be distracted; maybe they are feeling unloved or jaded. Will it return to how it was? Everything needs attention, or all could be lost.

The client could be suppressing their emotions and not dealing with issues from the past. The pain from these problems could resurface, so it's best to seek help now

The Ace is upside down, signifying that something has been wasted or lost, and the waters are spilling out of the cup. Bad news is on the way, or it could be the end of a relationship or friendship for the querent. Things may have been difficult over the last year, but with a positive attitude, the outcomes should be positive if time and effort are put in.

> **MEMORIZE**
>
> ⌐•••⌐
>
> Things being lost or wasted ✳ Bad news, end of relationships and friendships ✳ Make more of an effort ✳ These are difficult times, but things will get better

Rider-Waite Tarot   One World Tarot

Two of Cups

Two hearts blend to be in love; blessings bestowed from those above.

CARD NUMBER: 38 **KEYWORDS:** soul mate

Rider-Waite Interpretation

A woman and man stand gazing into each other's eyes, about to pledge a commitment; unlike the Lovers, they are fully attired, showing the synthesis of the material world. Suspended over them is the caduceus of Hermes, a Greek messenger. The winged baton is entwined with two serpents depicting the ancient symbol of commerce and trade. However, it is now strongly connected as the symbol of medicine in the modern world. At the top of the caduceus is a lion's head, representing strength and passion in the relationship. This union signifies a bonding of the minds, encouraging the querent to venture into partnerships instead of remaining alone.

The Two of Cups is a happy, romantic card, and this water sign suit speaks of deep emotions and promises of forever love. The couple gazes adoringly into each other's eyes, oblivious of anyone around them; all they want is each other and their plans for the future. They are unaware of the other's faults, and there is a strong sexual attraction between them.

One World Interpretation

The card of true love, and some might even interpret it as the soul mate card. This is a relationship of the mind, body, and spirit, meaning that the couple is on the same vibration and has a unity based on love, good communication, and honesty. The Two of Cups can also represent the birth of a child or upcoming marriage. If this card comes out in a reading, the querent should either be in a happy relationship or they are about to embark on one. Some decks can even depict a reconciliation with a partner after a time apart.

Associated Cards with Upright Two of Cups

✳ If the Two of Cups appears around the Lovers (upright), a sexy, passionate, new relationship is starred.

✳ With the Two of Swords (upright) in the same spread, the likelihood of a new, positive relationship will follow a divorce or breakup.

✳ With other twos (upright or reversed), choices and decisions must be made.

✳ If the Two of Cups appears with the Ten of Pentacles, the client can enjoy a loving marriage with financial security.

✳ If the Two of Cups appears next to the Empress (upright), a pregnancy will be announced.

✳ If the Two of Cups (reversed) is situated next to the Fool (upright), the client will have lost the love of their life and must walk down another path.

MEMORIZE

Soul mate card: true love ✳ Love and passion ✳ Commitment and good communication ✳ Love and stars in their eyes

Rider-Waite Interpretation

The balance of unity is broken; rather than connecting, the couple will repulse each other and won't be able to communicate. Arguments will upset the client, and before they can go on to love again, they need to love themselves. A once-happy relationship or friendship will end, leaving the querent wary or mistrusting of any future partner. A time of reflection and healing is required before things can change.

One World Interpretation

Tears, trouble, and a broken trust; all could now turn to dust.

KEYWORD: *finalize*

The couple's relationship could face some obstacles that must be ironed out. They must come together to help each other; it won't be a time for them to pursue their individual problems. For harmony to be restored, the couple must be prepared to give and take. A work decision will suddenly appear out of the blue; whatever it is, it could impact both of them.

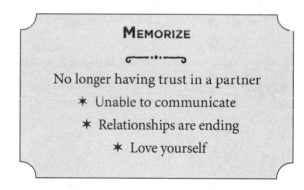

MEMORIZE

No longer having trust in a partner
* Unable to communicate
* Relationships are ending
* Love yourself

Rider-Waite Tarot *One World Tarot*

Three of Cups

A marriage and children surrounded with joy. Celebration to welcome a baby boy.

CARD NUMBER: 39 **KEYWORD:** joyfulness

Rider-Waite Interpretation

This celebratory card has three maidens dancing happily together. They are surrounded by blessings and abundance and do not have a care in the world. Life is good as they raise their goblets in the air. Above, the azure sky is cloudless, and in the grass are exotic fruits and flowers, depicting abundance. News of a wedding or the birth of a baby is ahead, so celebration is on the agenda. For the present, life is carefree, without obstacles or pain. Let the party begin! This is a time for the client to explore their creative side, attend classes, start a new course, or work on group projects.

One World Interpretation

The Three of Cups is a happy card, predicting parties and celebrations for the querent in the coming year. If the client is a female, she will be a social butterfly, surrounded by girlfriends. Families are also tightly bonded, and the client will spend quality time with loved ones. An unexpected new love may appear in the querent's life, leaving them happy and cheery. News of a pregnancy is ahead, and a healthy baby boy will be born. Weddings and engagements are also starred. If the person has been having a hard time of late, everything will come good in the end, as the Three of Cups promises stability. If the client is married, their relationship will deepen over the coming months.

Associated Cards with Upright Three of Cups

✳ Often this card will appear when many negative cards (upright or reversed) are in a spread. There is a message from the spirit world to hang in there as things will come good in the end. It promises hope when times are hard.

✳ If Pages are present (upright or reversed), the birth of a child is imminent, and the client will have a lot to do with the baby.

✳ If the Three of Cups appears around the Five of Pentacles (upright), a pregnancy could result in a caesarean section.

✳ When the Three of Cups (reversed) is directly next to the Tower (upright), a pregnancy might result in a miscarriage.

MEMORIZE

Celebrations and parties ✳ Harmony in families ✳ New love ✳ Weddings and the birth of a baby boy ✳ All will be well in the end

Rider-Waite Interpretation

A client's friend or family member could instigate an argument and sever their relationship for good. As the tension rises, the rift becomes deeper and deeper. Will it ever be the same again? Although someone looks forward to a new start or a hobby, others will show they are jealous and spend time dissuading them. The end of a romance will break a heart, but the person is strong, so they can move on.

One World Interpretation

Friends will be cruel, to your dismay, but do not let them have their way.

KEYWORD: *gossiping*

The querent will need some alone time or will find themselves excluded from social events. Friendships could turn sour, or groups of people might gossip and be cruel. Romantic relationships could be problematic, or the person may be in a relationship for all the wrong reasons. In some cases, overindulging in drugs and alcohol could be an issue, so suggest to the querent they take a hard look at their life.

MEMORIZE

Being or feeling alone ✳ Friendships broken ✳ In a relationship for all the wrong reasons ✳ Overindulging in drugs or alcohol

---

Rider-Waite Tarot   One World Tarot

Four of Cups

What do you want when you have it all? Give thanks for your blessings, lest you fall.

CARD NUMBER: 40 **KEYWORDS:** dissatisfied petulance

Rider-Waite Interpretation

A man stares moodily into the distance, his back resting on a stout tree that supports him. He is petulant with his lot in life but does little to change it. His thoughts are stubborn, and he refuses to change his attitude. He doesn't see the outstretched arm extending toward him, offering the cup filled to the brim. Three other goblets are on the grass in front of him, showing the opportunities that could be his. His lack of gratitude will be his undoing; this can also signify that he is self-obsessed, so much so that he ignores others' advice as he concentrates only on his own needs.

One World Interpretation

This will often indicate that the querent is dissatisfied with their lot in life or doesn't value the blessings around them. The grass always seems greener on the other side. General family issues will arise, or upsetting arguments can occur with close individuals. Disruptive issues emerge in their romantic relationships, leaving the querent lonely or isolated. The positive aspect of this card is that unexpected help will arrive, and things will become easier in the coming months. The outstretched hand indicates that the querent's spirit guide will give them everything they need to move into a more optimistic phase in their life.

Associated Cards with Upright Four of Cups

✳ If there are multiples of upright Wands, the querent is experiencing arguments or upsets at work, or they feel like they deserve a better job with a promotion or don't value the one they are in.

✳ If the Three of Swords (reversed) is nearby, the client might isolate themselves from friends and family.

✳ With the Three of Cups (upright) nearby, there is a good support network that will encourage them to have a more positive outlook on life.

✳ If this card is positioned in reverse and is around either the Nine or Ten of Swords (upright), depression could swamp the client, leaving them feeling suicidal.

MEMORIZE

⸺ •••• ⸺

Count your blessings ✳ Family issues and arguments with those around ✳ Feeling isolated and lonely in a relationship ✳ Spirit guides are close by and will offer help

Rider-Waite Interpretation

The man has a fit of the blues and is petulant, thinking others have everything while he has nothing. Karmic forces could take away the blessings bestowed upon him and force him to see the harsher lessons in life. Although he is an adult, his behavior is similar to a child; therefore, he's taking a long time to grow up.

One World Interpretation

A hidden gift is overdue; happiness now comes to you.

KEYWORDS: *being grateful*

In Tarot today, the reverse meaning of this card is quite positive. The client might have suffered extreme difficulties and felt disillusioned and depressed. Finally, they will turn a corner and enter a phase of happiness. However hard their life has become; they will eventually feel more optimistic. Encourage the querent to step outside of their shell and fully embrace life.

> **MEMORIZE**
>
> More positive and happier times ✳ Turning a corner ✳ A need to grow up ✳ Embrace life

Rider-Waite Tarot

One World Tarot

Five of Cups

Their love has faded far away and makes for long and lonely days.

CARD NUMBER: 41 **KEYWORD:** despondency

Rider-Waite Interpretation

A disgruntled man in a black cloak gazes down at the three toppled cups strewn on the ground, symbolizing his dissatisfactions and failures in life. Two upright cups represent new prospects for him, which he fails to see as he is selfishly entrenched in his misfortunes.

On the horizon, a fast-flowing river is spanned by a bridge, which leads to the sanctuary of a sturdy building. If he is brave enough to cross it, he will find a new and exciting way forward.

Feeling unloved, he finds that his days are repetitive and sad. The querent is desolate and without hope, as there is no one left to love him. He must accept part of the blame because of his bad behavior in the past.

One World Interpretation

A separation will occur in a romantic relationship, which could involve small children. The client will be full of regret and want to turn back the clock. The spilled cups could also symbolize that someone close to them is turning to booze and drinking far too much. Any memory issues around them could be linked to alcoholism. In some cases, this card can mean unrequited love; in others, the person or someone around them might feel desperate or suicidal. If you believe they are depressed, point out the two standing cups and assure them that everything will work for the best. Someone from the past, either male or female, will be in touch.

MEMORIZE

⊷ ⋯ ⊷

Feeling depressed ✳ Unloved and miserable ✳ Breakup of a relationship ✳ Drinking too much alcohol ✳ Unrequited love

---

Associated Cards with Upright Five of Cups

* When the Five of Cups appears with other fives, a difficult time will come in for the seeker, and they may suffer from depression or hopelessness.
* When the Five of Cups appears next to positive cards, such as the Sun (upright) or Ace of Cups (upright), any depression they face will be short-lived.
* With this card around Knights (upright or reversed), a young man will be off the rails and drinking far too much.
* With Queens (upright or reversed) in the spread, a female around the person could be demanding and needy.

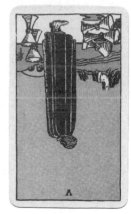

Rider-Waite Interpretation

The querent is feeling disappointed with their life. Things haven't gone according to plan, so they should scrutinize their misdemeanors. Because of these setbacks, they choose not to open up to those people who love them and are in danger of cutting themselves off. Over time, things will begin to change for the better, and they will feel much more optimistic and contented. New people come into their lives, and a different social circle opens up. A family feud or an argument from years gone by will suddenly be resolved, and happy reunions can be expected.

One World Interpretation

A time to be healthy; stop drinking wine, retune the body, and you will be fine.

KEYWORD: *abstain*

Someone close to them will need to care for their physical and mental health. Scrutinizing their diet and making a few changes could make them much healthier. This card in reverse can suggest some mental health issues, if not for the client, then someone close to them. If they try to improve their relationships, all will not be lost, and a positive reconciliation could occur. They must remain consistent afterward and show their partner the love and attention they need.

MEMORIZE

☞ ⋯ ☜

Feeling disappointed ✳ Take care of health ✳ Mental health issues ✳ Work at relationships ✳ Reconciliation

Rider-Waite Tarot

One World Tarot

Six of Cups

Touching hands with those from the past, reunions appear and friendships last.

CARD NUMBER: 42 **KEYWORD:** reunion

Rider-Waite Interpretation

Stepping forward, a young boy innocently hands a cup filled with flowers to a pretty girl. She gazes at him with adoration and respect as she accepts his gift. For a moment, they are lost in the joy and naivety of this act. This gentle interlude, unknown to them, will create their childhood memories.

In the background, an older man strolls away, leaving them to enjoy their childhood.

Both youngsters are standing, with solid walls around them, symbolizing financial security. They are encircled by five other cups filled with flowers, ensuring their happiness.

This Cup is a card of childhood and good or bad memories from days gone by. The client's past has formed their character, which could hold them back as the healing is incomplete. Soon this chapter will end, and happiness will be just around the corner for them. The family may have a celebration to look forward to, or news of a birth could be coming. The clan will meet for a much-needed get-together, barbeque, or catch-up.

One World Interpretation

Out of the blue, someone from the past comes along. Happy memories are recalled, and they enjoy the time together.

Another interpretation is that a past love will resurface and romantic feelings that were deeply buried will be rekindled. In today's readings, the client might find the reunion takes place over social media, or a chance meeting brings an old school friend back into their lives.

If your client is separated or divorced, arguments and disputes could arise over custody or alimony. If the querent has teenage children, an innocent relationship will bring their first crush. Do reassure the seeker that this should be a non-sexual union, unless the Lovers are in the same spread, and then they will need to make their child aware of contraception.

A new job offer could come unexpectedly, or the client might consider moving to a different location.

MEMORIZE

Innocent relationships ✳ Puppy love, non-sexual ✳ Healing nostalgia ✳ Celebrations, catch-ups

---

Associated Cards with Upright Six of Cups

* If the Lovers (upright) are in the same spread as the Six of Cups (upright), a teenage love affair could become sexual.
* With Strength (upright) in the spread, the client must put their plans into action before achieving their goals.
* When the card appears with the Two of Swords (upright), a custody battle could bring a negative outcome. The person would be wiser to settle things out of court.
* If the Six of Cups (reversed) is beside any Knights or young Queens, inappropriate behavior will cause a scandal

Rider-Waite Interpretation

The client is losing touch with everything around them, spending too much time dwelling on the past and thinking about previous relationships. Reminiscing over the past doesn't bring happiness, only sadness and regret; this is a time to learn from past mistakes and move forward. They may secretly rekindle an old relationship but keep it quiet as others may disapprove. These hidden agendas are likely to be exposed, so better to be upfront from the start. This card can also predict a financial windfall for the querent, either a small win or an inheritance.

One World Interpretation

Postponements cast you down. Have faith, for it will turn around.

KEYWORD: *waiting*

Relationships are about to collapse. The feuding of separating parents throws the reluctant children into the mix. Childhood security is no longer their future, while mother and father choose their new life. One of the children could go off the rails or even try to leave home. Rebellion adds to the overall mayhem. The client could find themselves around an immature adult, or someone they live with is refusing to take responsibility; this could be an entitled son or daughter in their twenties or a very needy parent. All blocks and obstacles will lift, so reassure them that things will turn around in the end. The client will come into a small inheritance within two years.

MEMORIZE

Puppy love ✳ New job ✳ Custody battles ✳ Someone is acting childishly ✳ Relationships end

Rider-Waite Tarot

One World Tarot

Seven of Cups

The cups are filled with many choices. Listen to those spiritual voices.

CARD NUMBER: 43 **KEYWORD:** decisions

Rider-Waite Interpretation

Here we see quite a mystical card. A man gazes at the seven cups before him and is confused. His arms are outstretched as if to say, which should I pick? Some vessels, like the dragon, hold fantastic items, but the snake vessel seems more sinister. The cups are surrounded by clouds representing the imagination and using one's inner voice to make the final choices.

When this card appears in the spread, the

client will have to make choices purely on their gut reaction. They will need to dig deeper to find the inner wisdom to get them back on track. As the soul transforms, it is essential to ensure everything is done correctly to improve one's karma.

One World Interpretation

Choices are ahead for the querent who may be confused, so care must be taken when making important decisions. Now is the time to examine their attitude and iron out any personality flaws. Each cup on this card represents unforeseen events, pleasant surprises, and invitations that will appear out of the blue. The querent will find themselves becoming more psychic, so tell them that it's essential to pay attention to their dreams and trust their instincts. Have a list of good books at hand so they can explore their spirituality, and encourage them to write down their dreams because they may come true.

Associated Cards with Upright Seven of Cups

✳ If this card is next to the World (upright), the querent must stop and evaluate their life and make sure they choose the right path.

✳ If it is next to the Two of Cups (upright), they must consider a loved one before making any life changes.

✳ If the Sun (upright) is in the spread, wonderful surprises are predicted, along with the chance to embark on a new, positive path.

✳ Should this card be reversed alongside the Hierophant (upright), a house move might fall through, and money could be lost.

MEMORIZE

Make decisions carefully ✳ Iron out personality flaws ✳ Surprises and unexpected events ✳ Listen to psychic intuition

The seeker or someone close to them might be experiencing strange and vivid dreams. Their guides could be trying to reach them in dream sleep. Practiced meditation can expand their psychic ability and even lead to experiencing astral projection. Don't abandon good ideas. Success is ahead, so keep pressing.

Rider-Waite Interpretation

The client could be faced with making lots of decisions at once and must choose what is best for their future rather than what is best for others. They could make bad decisions by rushing things too quickly, so they must clear their mind, go for a walk, or learn to meditate. It's time to connect with a higher power and ask a guide or deity for a more exacting answer.

> ### MEMORIZE
> ⟜ ·•·· ⟞
>
> Strange and vivid dreams ✳ Spirit guides trying to reach out ✳ Astral projection ✳ Success ahead, so stay on track ✳ Multiple choices

One World Interpretation

Dreams are strange but have great meaning.
Trust the guidance you are feeling.

KEYWORD: *dreaming*

Rider-Waite Tarot   One World Tarot

Eight of Cups

The past has gone and now you're free to embrace your life, and thus proceed.

CARD NUMBER: 44 **KEYWORD:** freedom

Rider-Waite Interpretation

A figure has his back to the eight cups on the ground; this represents someone turning their back on the past and choosing a different direction. The mountains symbolize that the journey might be challenging, and the water depicts the man's innermost emotions. The moon in the sky, lighting up the night, makes it easier for him to see the way.

All eights in Tarot mean good luck and good

fortune, and this card represents a pivotal point in changing one's life and making a new start. Time to drop regrets and nostalgia, as these only hold the client back. This card can characterize walking away from toxic relationships where many years have been wasted trying to change someone. The client must do what is best for them now.

One World Interpretation

This card is all about leaving the past behind and embracing the future. Although the client has focused too much on past events, they will soon start to live for today. Encourage them not to dwell on things they cannot change but to forge ahead and do something new with their life.

Being so disappointed with their past, the querent will have a strong desire for a change and is ready to try new things.

A blond person will enter their life, so look at the surrounding cards to decipher whether this is positive or negative. In general, the seeker will crave spiritual fulfillment.

Associated Cards with Upright Eight of Cups

✳ If cards such as the Two of Cups (upright) or the Lovers (upright) are in the spread, the client will have to choose whether they wish to remain or leave a current relationship. The mountains symbolize the potential for a difficult choice.

✳ If the Magician (upright) appears in the same spread, the client must try to ascend spiritually and work on their psychic abilities.

✳ If the Eight of Cups appears next to or around the Chariot (reverse), don't get involved in idle gossip; it could backfire.

✳ If the Eight of Wands (upright) is in the spread, the client could be thinking of living abroad and leaving their homeland for good.

MEMORIZE

Leaving the past behind ✳ Focusing too much on past events ✳ Seeking spiritual fulfillment ✳ A desire for change

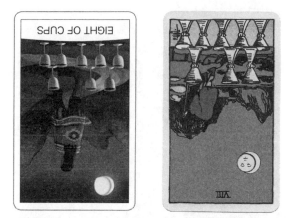

Rider-Waite Interpretation

The person is surrounded by indecision in their relationship and doesn't know whether to stay or go. If they remain, things must alter, so it's time to think seriously and be honest about whether those changes can be implemented. The past has sapped the querent's energy, but that will be replenished in time and bring happiness when it occurs. The soul has grown much wiser, building stronger foundations for the future. Onward and upward!

The client will desire to make more money and work hard to reap the rewards. A challenging new love interest is predicted, which could spell trouble for those already in a settled relationship. The querent could be self-centered, partying too much, and not having much thought for others.

Choices about where life is heading are at the forefront of their mind.

They could be around someone egotistical, and it would be best to move away from their disruptive lifestyle. Because of all the past drama, they might be feeling sorry for themselves.

MEMORIZE

Decisions about a relationship ✳ Feeling sorry for oneself ✳ Desire to make more money ✳ New love is on its way

---

One World Interpretation

A new love will brighten your day. Be sure they will not make you stray.

KEYWORD: *materialistic*

Rider-Waite Tarot

One World Tarot

Nine of Cups

This wishing card brings rewards to you, everything fine, pure, and true.

CARD NUMBER: 45 **KEYWORD:** wishing

Rider-Waite Interpretation

The man in this card sits on a wooden bench surrounded by cups. He is contented and satisfied with all his material and spiritual accomplishments. Merriment surrounds him as it is a time to celebrate. Traditionally, this is the "wish card" that promises all wishes will be granted.

The Nine of Cups is one of the loveliest cards in the Tarot deck, and it always brings optimism and upliftment to the client. Usually, there will be good news, a big celebration, or a visitor from abroad. It represents better times and no catastrophes; life should be tranquil for a while.

One World Interpretation

The Nine of Cups is the third best card in the Tarot deck after the Sun and the Ace of Cups. The nine radiates positivity and illustrates that the client's wishes will be granted eventually. The future is joyful, so whatever troubles they have encountered in recent months will be dispelled. They will experience good health in the next six to twelve months and delightful surprises. When this card appears in a spread, we ask the client to place their hand over it and make a silent wish. It's one of those positive cards that brings a happy ending to any unfortunate situation.

MEMORIZE

Third best card in Tarot ✳ Foretells of a happy outcome ✳ The wish card ✳ Joyful future ✳ Good luck

Associated Cards with Upright Nine of Cups

✳ When the Nine of Cups is with the Empress (upright), a much-wanted pregnancy is imminent.

✳ Around a selection of Wands (upright), the celebrations will likely be around work and employment.

✳ With this Nine placed near the Ten of Cups (upright), a wedding or engagement is predicted with a long and loving marriage.

✳ If this card appears next to difficult cards like the Tower (upright or reversed), the Ten of Swords (upright or reversed), or the Devil (upright or reversed), all troubles will disappear, making way for a brighter future.

✳ If the Nine of Cups is reversed with either the Two of Pentacles (upright) or the Three of Pentacles (upright), the client could lose a substantial amount of money.

Rider-Waite Interpretation

The seeker appears to have everything they want materially, but lacks in love and family time. Wishes and desires are delayed, and they will be tired of waiting for better times. Reassure them to be patient. Meanwhile, health issues will have to be addressed, and sensible eating could be on the agenda. Money problems can cause anxiety, so they might feel depressed.

One World Interpretation

Look after health, food, and drink. Your waistline has really got to shrink.

KEYWORD: *health*

People nearest the querent are taking advantage of their good nature. Someone around them is burying their head in the sand; it's time to "pop the bubble" and see the truth for what it is. Broken promises are soon to be discovered, and tears could be shed as someone's life is shattered. The client is either worried about their weight or that of someone close to them. Now is the time to start eating healthier.

MEMORIZE

Delayed wishes ✳ Overeating and drinking ✳ Taking better care of health ✳ Money problems ✳ Facing reality

Rider-Waite Tarot

One World Tarot

Ten of Cups

Romance and love are now complete. A painful past you'll not repeat.

CARD NUMBER: 46 **KEYWORD:** contentment

Rider-Waite Interpretation

A loving couple is standing together, their eyes raised in wonderment to the sky where ten cups are suspended in a rainbow. They lift their outstretched hands in thanks for all the blessings the creator has given them. Their son and daughter play happily nearby, where a secure home can be seen waiting for them on the hill. A river meanders in the distance, representing the flow of sentiment; everything is verdant, and the couple's everlasting happiness is complete; they have everything they have ever wanted and more besides.

When this card appears in the Tarot, it is classed as the second "wish card." This is true love, devotion, and a long-lasting relationship. It can sometimes be linked to the soul mate or twin flame. There will be a wedding for the client or someone close to them. The marriage should be blessed with children and loving relations.

One World Interpretation

One of the most outstanding romantic cards. Whenever this appears in a reading, the client will experience a loving and long-lasting relationship. If they are single, they may have had a problematic love life in the past but will have a happy marriage later. Although it will be a tender, stable union, they will still have to work at it from time to time to keep it thriving. If you make these predictions for a single person, their future partner will already own a property and have children.

Associated Cards with Upright Ten of Cups

✳ Dramatic changes are afoot if this card comes into a spread with any ten card (upright). If the surrounding cards are negative, the changes promise to be better.

✳ If the Ten of Cups is next to the Empress (upright) or the Two of Cups (upright), the couple will be planning a family. This should be successful.

✳ If this card appears next to three or more Swords (upright or reverse), the client needs to change direction and move away from negative people.

✳ A wedding will be canceled if the Ten of Cups is positioned in reverse and is next to the Five of Cups (upright).

MEMORIZE

❮ ━ ••• ━ ❯

Best relationship card in Tarot ✳ Finding a soul mate at last ✳ Children and families ✳ Nuptials to be exchanged

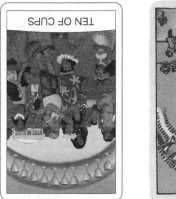 

Rider-Waite Interpretation

There will be a time of sadness for the client. Things seem hopeless, and the client could be feeling depressed and bewildered. Arguments with family members weigh heavy on their hearts as they keep trying to smooth the way with no success. Quarrels can arise from almost any direction; the client and their partner, who don't usually have a cross word, could go head to head in a screaming match. Family members will fall out, and sibling rivalry may upset the group.

Sometimes, the Ten of Cups in reverse can mean a painful past for the seeker, which makes them wary of a new commitment. It will take a great deal of time to recover from a previous relationship, and they may still lack trust, even years later. The client has learned many things from this old relationship and will be rewarded with a much better partner later. If a child is present in the cards, they may be disruptive or even try to run away.

> **MEMORIZE**
>
> ┌ ··· ┐
>
> Feeling let down ✳ Tears ✳ Family arguments and squabbles ✳ Bad past relationship ✳ Better relationship later ✳ A child is disruptive

One World Interpretation

Family rifts split people apart. Don't let this storm break your heart.

KEYWORD: *squabbles*

The Court Mentors: Cups

King of Cups, Queen of Cups,
Knight of Cups, Page of Cups

BIRTH SIGNS: Cancer, Scorpio, and Pisces

CAREERS FOR CANCER WATER SIGN: nursing, caregiver, horticulturist, schoolteacher, antiques, discovering ancestry, archology, realtor, chef, catering, social work, interior design

CAREERS FOR SCORPIO WATER SIGN: self-employment, financial advisor, engineering, psychologist, therapist, medical role, marketing, cleaner, laborer, psychic, Tarot reader, and medium

CAREERS FOR PISCES WATER SIGN: travel rep, sales rep, artist, creative drawing, crafts and pottery, writing, architecture, entertainment, caregiver, counselor, photographer, musician

Rider-Waite Tarot　　　　*One World Tarot*

Page of Cups

A crystal child is on its way. You are blessed is what they say.

CARD NUMBER: 47 **KEYWORD:** creativity
A child, boy or girl, aged birth–16

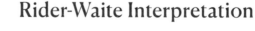

PAGE OF CUPS

Rider-Waite Interpretation

The card of inspiration. The image is of a water sign youth with a cup containing a fish that looks like it's about to leap out. In this card, the fish represents emotion, twinned with creativity. In many decks, the color theme is blue, which signifies communication and messages. This charming Page is open to new ideas and should be encouraged in all things creative.

One World Interpretation

A creative and psychic individual who possesses a sweet demeanor. If you establish that the Page is female, she is a kind and loving girl. If this represents a boy child, he will be extremely sensitive. In a reading, they will be connected somehow to the client; depending on their age, it could be a child they already have or a predicted baby for the future. For older clients, this could signify a grandchild, niece, or nephew.

The Page of Cups will love the family and be a social butterfly with many friends. They may not necessarily be academic and will sometimes struggle with schoolwork; their talents will lie in other directions, such as music, arts, singing, and dancing. From a young age, they will be spiritual and show signs of a psychic nature, talking to a deity or resonating with spirit helpers and angels. Some consider this type of youngster a "crystal child."

Other Meanings

New beginnings are highly starred for the client following a time of anxiety or depression. Changes will soon happen, so stick to long-term goals. Urge them to forget the past and forge on with inspiring new plans.

> **MEMORIZE**
>
> ⟜•••⟞
>
> The crystal child ✳ Psychic and creative, speaks to higher forces ✳ Connected to the client in some way ✳ Not academic, but more creative and artistic ✳ New beginnings ✳ Forget the past; look to the future

Associated Cards with Upright Page of Cups

✳ If this Page is around the Seven of Swords (upright or reversed), the child will suffer bullying at school. If the Page of Swords (upright or reversed) and Five of Swords (upright or reversed) are also present, a dysfunctional bully could be stealing their lunch money, or the child could be bribed or blackmailed into taking goods into school.

✳ With the Five of Wands (upright), the Page will find schoolwork too hard.

✳ If the Nine of Cups (upright) is present in the same spread, the youngster will receive an accolade for something.

✳ With the Magician (upright) nearby, they may experience strange dreams or possibly a memory of a past life in another century.

✳ If the Nine of Swords (upright or reversed) or Ten of Swords (upright or reversed) is present in the same spread, this will represent an unwell child or one prone to accidents.

A child's personality is changing. They will be sluggish and uninspired and have feelings of low self-worth. The Page could experience illness, suffering minor ailments. Creativity could be blocked, and, in some cases, if the Page is a teenager, they could mix with the wrong crowd or dabble in drugs. Encouragement should be given to reflect on a happier time and focus on the positive, not the negative.

Reversed Meaning

A little one to feel unwell. Time to do a healing spell.

KEYWORD: *unwell*

MEMORIZE

⌐—··—⌐

Personality changes ✳ Feelings of low self-worth ✳ Minor illness and ailments ✳ Mixing with the wrong crowd; dabbling with drugs

Rider-Waite Tarot   One World Tarot

Knight of Cups

A karmic lover will steal your heart. His love's so fine, you will not part.

CARD NUMBER: 48 **KEYWORD:** charming
Young man, aged 16–29

Rider-Waite Interpretation

Like a fairy-tale hero, this attractive knight in shining armor sits proudly on his steed to rescue the damsel in distress. He is intelligent and dependable with an artistic nature. Any relationship he has is likely to include a karmic connection. When he loves, he loves unconditionally, investing everything he has in his chosen partner.

One World Interpretation

This young man has good looks and charm; he is a favorite with the opposite sex and never has any trouble getting the girl. His charisma, aptitude, and flair make him very interesting, but he will wear his heart on his sleeve and be easily influenced. When you are reading for a young woman, this Knight will have some past life connection with her, so she may link with someone from a previous time.

Other Meanings

People will be coming for a visit, or the querent will be planning on visiting friends and family. A loved one will have opposing views, so disagreements are likely. A sudden trip could be connected to family or work.

MEMORIZE

⌐—·•·—⌐

Between 16 and 29 ✳ Good-looking and charming ✳ He is intelligent but wears his heart on his sleeve ✳ Karmic, past life connection

Associated Cards with Upright Knight of Cups

* When other male court mentors are in the spread (upright or reversed), the Knight may lose his love to another.
* Next to the Tower (upright or reversed), the Knight is playing with fire and could be injured in an accident due to his own naivety.
* With the Four of Cups (upright), he could end up being addicted to drink or drugs.
* The Five of Cups (upright) next to the Knight indicates he could come to regret his actions and will make changes to improve his life.

Reversed Meaning

He's hurt you in another life and brings only trouble, toil, and strife.

KEYWORD: *shallow*

A young man who is a Jack the Lad. He will rarely be faithful to one woman and leave a string of broken hearts in his path. He is a shallow and self-centered individual, thinking only of his next conquest. In love, he'll fail to treat his partner respectfully and have a childish approach, being jealous and hot-headed. He may have a brush with the law or overindulge in drink and drugs, and he refuses to focus on his education; instead, he's only interested in gaming and playing the field, but he will turn himself around in the future and become a lovely man.

> **MEMORIZE**
>
> A Jack the Lad ✳ Breaking hearts ✳ Shallow and self-centered ✳ Overindulging in alcohol and drugs ✳ Childish and jealous ✳ He will grow up to be a decent man

Rider-Waite Tarot   One World Tarot

Queen of Cups

Steadfast and loyal; good mother and spouse.
She adores her family, her children, her house.

CARD NUMBER: 49 **KEYWORD:** loyal
Woman, aged 16 onward

Rider-Waite Interpretation

A woman who is sensitive and intuitive, with a kind disposition. She is steadfast and loyal, always trusting her instincts. Being a nurturing type, she will always put her family before herself, and because of her wisdom, others will seek her out in times of trouble. She has had her share of hardship in life but tries not to dwell on the past. Her optimistic attitude will make her popular.

One World Interpretation

As a water sign, she will represent Pisces, Cancer, or Scorpio. Being at the center of her family is pivotal, so she will be an excellent homemaker, wife, and mother, always putting others' needs ahead of hers. Not much gets past this Queen as she is highly perceptive and relies on her intuition, but she can sometimes allow others to take advantage of her sweet character. Before you get to know her, she can be somewhat aloof or hard to engage with, but she will be forever loyal once she trusts. She will love her home, always keeping it spick-and-span, and be fond of animals and nature.

Her faults include sometimes exaggerating the truth, and she enjoys embellishing a good story.

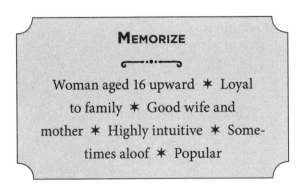

MEMORIZE

Woman aged 16 upward ✳ Loyal to family ✳ Good wife and mother ✳ Highly intuitive ✳ Sometimes aloof ✳ Popular

Other Meanings

The client's social life will improve, and they will accept invitations to parties or events. New friendships are also starred. Be careful what you believe; someone around the client will be telling untruths.

Associated Cards with Upright Queen of Cups

✳ If the Queen of Cups is around other Queens (upright or reversed) in a spread, she will delight in gossip.
✳ If a selection of upright Wands is present, she may follow a career path working with children, or have a job in the care sector.
✳ With the Three of Wands (upright), she might choose a career in counseling or helping others.
✳ With two or more Pages (upright or reversed), she may work with children as a nanny or childminder.

Reversed Meaning

She speaks sweet words—you'll be dismayed when all your secrets are betrayed.

KEYWORD: *manipulator*

This Queen tends to be two-faced and will gossip behind your back. She is clever with her words and can sometimes manipulate a situation to suit herself. Water sign Queens can often be anchored to the home, not engaging much with others, and they won't always make the right decisions. She may lack depth and sympathy for others. At work, this Queen is the type to steal other people's ideas and pass them off as her own. If she is a boss, her demands will be unreasonable and illogical, and her staff will dislike her.

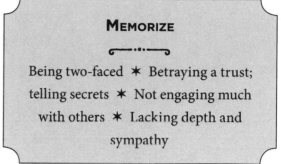

MEMORIZE

Being two-faced ✳ Betraying a trust; telling secrets ✳ Not engaging much with others ✳ Lacking depth and sympathy

Rider-Waite Tarot *One World Tarot*

King of Cups

A gentle man with a wise heart. Your secrets he will never impart.

CARD NUMBER: 50 **KEYWORD:** gentle
Male, aged 29 onward

Rider-Waite Interpretation

He sits upon his throne adorned in a blue tunic, which signifies his authority. This water sign King represents a man from the age of twenty-nine upward and is respected by all.

He holds his emotions together well, making him a great mentor to those who need guidance. He is reliable, gentle, and a good problem solver, yet he gives off an air of authority.

One World Interpretation

Being a water sign, this King can represent the signs of Pisces, Cancer, and Scorpio, and he is an excellent counselor. He is ambitious and determined in his career, emitting a solid and commanding influence. He will do well with anything he sets his mind to and will give 100 percent of himself to new business ventures. At home, he's a different character, keeping his thoughts very much to himself. He can sometimes be described as a little dull because of his lack of communication and is often inconsiderate as a husband or partner. This King will need to work hard at romantic relationships and show more love and intimacy to his spouse if he wants to remain married. He is a firm but gentle father figure who will lavish his children with everything they need.

MEMORIZE

Good counselor ✳ Good in business ✳ Noncommunicative and inconsiderate with love ✳ Firm yet gentle father type

---

Other Meanings

It is a time to put a lid on emotions and take control of a difficult situation. New friends and acquaintances will come in for the client, but they could leave as quickly as they arrived.

Associated Cards with Upright King of Cups

✳ If this card is around a group of Kings (upright or reversed), this usually pertains to business and work.
✳ If reversed and around the Three of Swords (upright), he will be looking to have an affair.
✳ If reversed and next to the Tower (upright or reversed), he could be involved in a brawl which leads to fighting.
✳ If reversed and around the Devil (upright) or Death (upright), he could have dark sexual desires.

Reversed Meaning

Find your own answers is the thing to do. He won't help, it's up to you.

KEYWORD: *controlling*

This King is not as he appears to be and cannot be trusted. He is a controlling character, always wanting his way, and could overpower a weaker partner or have a string of affairs. In business, he will entangle himself in double dealings or even gamble with the family money. He's the man who will spend each night drinking at the bar, leaving his wife to hold down the fort and raise the children single-handedly. He will never get involved in solving problems, but he will be very good at adding to them. As a father, he is noncommittal, and as the children get older, they won't have a very high opinion of him. If his marriage ends, he could be described as a deadbeat dad.

MEMORIZE

Not to be trusted ✳ He is a controlling man who wants his own way ✳ Strings of affairs ✳ Drinking and hanging out at the bar ✳ Deadbeat dad

The Suit of Swords

AIR SIGN: Aquarius, Gemini, Libra

SEASON: autumn

ALSO KNOWN AS: Spades, Pikes, Blades, and Daggers

REPRESENTS: difficulties, problems, illness, sorrow, bad luck, betrayal, trickery, arguments, and death

This is the most challenging suit to handle as it covers so much pain and torment. Emotionally, it represents heartache, illness, and litigation, not to mention death, surgery, and separation. To see a collection of Swords in someone's reading will indicate they have a rough time ahead of them. Sometimes if the reading is too dark and unhappy, it might be a good idea to ask the seeker to reshuffle and start again, but if the same cards are repeated, it will be your decision whether you wish to continue or not.

Rider-Waite Tarot   *One World Tarot*

Ace of Swords

Good news is coming, and victory is near. All of your worries will soon disappear.

CARD NUMBER: 51 **KEYWORD:** power

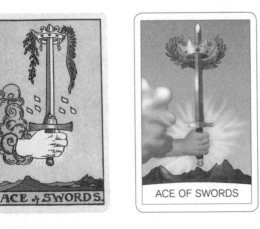

Rider-Waite Interpretation

The Ace of Swords portrays a masculine hand emerging from a white cloud, wielding a double-edged sword. The tip of the blade pierces a golden crown draped with cloth and encircled by a wreath of laurels, the sign of victory, triumph, and great attainment. All has been achieved through the energy of the divine. In the background, jagged mountains loom in a sinister way, meaning there are still more hardships ahead, and the complications will test the mental strength of the seeker.

The past had been tedious, with long days and nights filled with unhappiness and stress. Stay positive, because it will soon come to an end; a new beginning is on the horizon after the struggle.

One World Interpretation

The client will have a time of struggle, but victory will finally prevail. Even though the seeker may feel unhappy and depressed, there is a light at the end of the tunnel. Set goals for the future and forge ahead, as a more promising path is predicted. Through hardship, much has been learned, and wisdom has been acquired. It's also a time for karmic payback, so what has been sown must be reaped.

The person or someone close to them may have to seek medical attention, either blood tests or perhaps surgery. Legal matters could be on the agenda, including some documents to sign concerning court issues, income tax, or wills. Quarrels suddenly erupt out of the blue to create a bad atmosphere; this could take a few months to settle down, but eventually, harmony will resume.

Associated Cards with Upright Ace of Swords

✴ With the Ten of Swords (upright) in the spread, there will be news of an unexpected death. These two cards linked together are often referred to as the "funeral cards."

✴ If the Eight of Wands (upright) is present in the same spread, promising business opportunities will be on the horizon, but patience and lots of detailed planning are required.

✴ When the Tower (upright or reversed) is present, mental illness, dementia, and violence could disrupt the client's life.

✴ If other Aces (upright) are present in the same spread, dramatic changes bring about a happy outcome.

MEMORIZE

∾ ⋯ ∾

Struggle, but victory follows ✴ A better path ahead ✴ Unhappiness and depression ✴ Medical problems; blood work or surgery ✴ Karmic payback

Rider-Waite Interpretation

The client has great ideas but doesn't feel comfortable sharing them; they want to focus on the details first. As there will be legal issues on the agenda, they take no chances and double-check the small print. An operation for someone close by will relieve an ongoing health issue, but rest and recovery will be obligatory for the healing process to have a lasting effect.

One World Interpretation

Make sure to check that your body is fine. Better to enjoy a healthy time.

KEYWORD: *frustration*

Try not to overdo things, but go at a gentler pace; otherwise, there might be health complications. It will be a demanding time where the person may feel they are juggling balls and spinning plates simultaneously. They must not push too hard, or their nerves could suffer. Frustration will build, and delays may scupper the plans that seemed so safe and secure, leaving one wondering, "Will it happen, or won't it?" Documents might get lost in the post or be overlooked by others who are not doing their job correctly. News of a medical procedure comes out of the blue.

Rider-Waite Tarot   One World Tarot

Two of Swords

No solution can be found, and your head is spinning round and round.

CARD NUMBER: 52 **KEYWORD:** pressure

Rider-Waite Interpretation

A blindfolded woman wearing a white robe is seen holding two crossed swords. Her confusion is plain to see, as is her pain and indecision. The problems weigh her down, and there is nothing to ease the burden. She is stuck because no clear pathway is in sight, but her inner strength holds the two swords in perfect balance. Eventually, she will, with determination, find a resolution. The sea is behind her, and the islands offer no comfort, only hindrances. Water signifies emotions, and she must remain balanced to find a way out. To the right of her is a crescent moon, which means she must trust her intuition when making her final choices.

One World Interpretation

In modern Tarot, this is the divorce card. It may also appear when relationships or situations will end. A lack of communication in partnerships can leave the key players in limbo. The client may think they know their better half, but sadly, they will discover a hidden agenda and realize they've been kept in the dark. Everything is gridlocked, and the seeker will feel claustrophobic when a legal letter or news puts their life in turmoil. What to do and where to go? Emotional hardships are all around, with desolate feelings of being lost and alone. The seeker could make better choices if they were fully informed. A business partnership might end if the spread shows more than two Wands nearby.

MEMORIZE

Divorce card ✳ Relationships and situations are ending ✳ Legal letters ✳ Feeling lost and alone ✳ Everything blocked

---

Associated Cards with Upright Two of Swords

* When the Two of Swords (upright) is next to the Moon (upright), it can represent despondency and mental health issues.

* If the card is next to the Hermit (upright), spiritual help will be given to show an improved way. Keeping one's faith and asking for inspiration will bring hope and a clearer vision.

* If the Three of Swords (upright) is in the same spread, an adulterous situation is looming. The client has a choice whether to turn their back on the temptation or go ahead with it.

* If the Two of Swords (reversed) is present with several Pentacles in the spread, the client chooses not to address any financial issues or debt.

* The Two of Swords (reversed) with the Three of Swords or the Lovers indicates an unfaithful spouse with someone the client knows.

Rider-Waite Interpretation

Biting frustration and impatience magnifies problems for the seeker. Hissy fits will do more damage than good, so maturity must be shown before they can move on. They have the audacity to lay blame for the mess they have created at others' feet; this will put their closest friends and family members to the test because they have always supported them in the past. There are difficult decisions to make in the future, but the client has strayed down the wrong path, even though others have advised against it; this will cause more disagreements with family members turning their backs and walking away.

One World Interpretation

Your heart is broken; you've let yourself down. Start again, try not to frown.

KEYWORD: *foolhardy*

The querent should not disclose personal information to others until they can be trusted. Making decisions will be complex, and the seeker will be confused about which path to take. Someone nearby could betray them and bring their world crashing down; this might be a close friend or someone they love. A miraculous turn of events will occur, which will bring new beginnings and a fresh approach to the future.

> **MEMORIZE**
>
> Confusion ✳ Difficult decisions ✳ Betrayal of someone close ✳ Hopelessness ✳ Where to turn to ✳ Inner strength

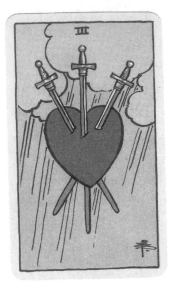

Rider-Waite Tarot

One World Tarot

Three of Swords

Separation, divorce, a tearful sigh. A time to be lost, a time to cry.

CARD NUMBER: 53 **KEYWORD:** infidelity

Rider-Waite Interpretation

To some, this is a worrying card as the three swords plunged into a human heart signify great heartache. To have one's heart broken, to be betrayed or abandoned, says it all. The ominous clouds in the background foretell more pain for the seeker, but once the tears have dried, a brighter future can be expected.

In most Tarot teachings, this card is classed as the eternal triangle—illicit affairs, usually with people who are already married and desire sexual thrills. Resentment and anger will mount in a family torn apart by broken love; this can suggest loneliness, separation, heartache, and upheaval. All trust is gone, with nowhere else to turn.

One World Interpretation

In today's Tarot, the Three of Swords only ever means adultery if it appears in the same spread as the Lovers. It is also one of the divorce cards and indicates acrimony and litigation. The client will feel weepy, so referring to the surrounding cards will help them see where the problem lies. A broken heart will take a long time to heal because a partner cares little for the chaos they have left behind. The separation will impact the family as love turns to anger and resentment. Small children will be unsettled, confused, and torn between their two warring parents.

Associated Cards with Upright Three of Swords

✳ The Lovers (upright) with the Three of Swords (upright) depicts an affair with someone who is married or in a committed relationship.

✳ If the Justice card (upright) is in situ with any of the Pages (upright and reversed), there will be court cases to finalize child support and custody.

✳ With the Seven of Swords (upright and reversed) in the spread, the perpetrator will dodge their financial responsibilities, and the abandoned partner will struggle to pay their bills.

✳ The Three of Swords (reversed) with the Lovers means one party in the marriage will cheat with someone known to the family.

MEMORIZE

Adultery with the Lovers ✳ Breakdowns in relationships ✳ Broken hearts ✳ Unhappy children stuck in the middle ✳ Divorce

Rider-Waite Interpretation

Life will never be the same; the good things will be thrown away for short-lived passion. There will be no way back now as a pathway of unhappiness is strewn with bitter debris. Someone is finding it hard to move on from a broken relationship and could spend months in emotional turmoil. They will never find happiness until they let go of the past and face the fact that it's over. In other teachings, this card reminds the client that saying sorry often smooths the way to a better future.

The client could hear news of a heart attack, miscarriage, or abortion. Someone might suddenly go missing, causing alarm and panic. Disorder and confusion will be rife with feelings of being unloved and abandoned. Self-esteem issues take away the last shreds of any confidence. Lies and deceit surround the client, and they will need to listen to their instincts for the truth.

There are similar meanings to the upright version, but hope and positivity come after the storm.

MEMORIZE

⌐•••⌐

Difficult decisions ✳ Acrimony ✳ End of a marriage ✳ Deceit ✳ Only means adultery with the Lovers

---

One World Interpretation

Acrimony, hurt, and a cheating lie; stand up straight and say goodbye.

KEYWORD: *lies*

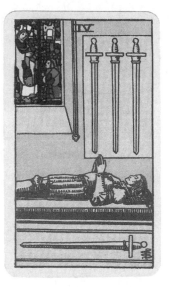

Rider-Waite Tarot

One World Tarot

Four of Swords

Meditation, contemplation, and rest. Soon you'll find this way is best.

CARD NUMBER: 54 **KEYWORD:** recuperation

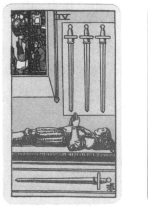

Rider-Waite Interpretation

The Four of Swords is a complex card depicting a knight in full armor lying horizontally on a tomb. Both hands are placed together in a position of prayer. He must get his energy back with meditation and inward thinking. A solitary sword lies beneath him, symbolizing his controlled point of concentration. The other three swords are suspended above him, pointing toward his head and chest. A woman and child observe him through a stained-glass window.

Reorganize one's thoughts, because deep thinking is required to start to heal the pain; the mind has been in turmoil, which has caused lethargy. Depression takes over as there seems to be no hope, especially in relationships or the workplace, where the seeker can feel stuck.

One World Interpretation

The Four of Swords can represent recovery after an operation or prolonged illness, and there will be a need to get one's strength back, but the healing time must not be rushed. The client may have to take time off from work to recover fully. Mindfulness is essential to balance the thoughts and realign the chakras for renewed energy. Those on a spiritual pathway might like to summon the angel of healing, Raphael, to assist with a speedy recovery. Also, using crystals to re-energize the body can aid in peaceful sleep. Soon things will pick up, and the person will be restored to their former strength and energy. There might be a short visit to the hospital or a much-needed break to a retreat to recharge one's batteries.

Associated Cards with Upright Four of Swords

✳ With the Judgement card (upright) close to the Four of Swords (upright), the person's karma is under intense spiritual scrutiny. Make sure things are done correctly to keep the energy flowing. Shortcuts will only undo all the hard work that has been achieved in the past.

✳ If the High Priestess (upright or reversed) is nearby, the querent could have dreams that come true, which will be helpful in making choices for their future.

✳ With the Five of Pentacles (reversed) in the spread, the client could have to undergo surgery that will take a while to recover from.

✳ With the Four of Swords next to the Five of Swords (upright), the client or someone close to them may be heading for a mental breakdown.

MEMORIZE

━ ·⋯· ━

Convalescing after an illness ✳ A healing time ✳ Meditate ✳ A troublesome time ✳ Take time to rejuvenate your energy ✳ A short stay in a hospital

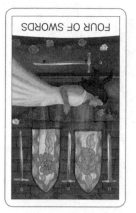 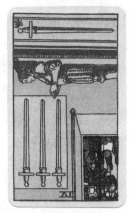

Rider-Waite Interpretation

The querent is advised to take time out and recharge their batteries, as their energy is at an all-time low. A short break to somewhere isolated would be a good idea; otherwise, they could burn themselves out. They must find a balance after the trials and tribulations that have dogged them in the past. The client is also discouraged with their life because nothing is happening the way they want.

Those who have always been trusted seem distant and indifferent. Friendships will come under the microscope, and a few will go on their way, but don't fret: soon inspiration will come, and optimism will brighten the days ahead. There will be no need to rush; take time to see what's around, and, as many people would say, stop and smell the flowers. At last new doors will open and allow exciting opportunities to come along. More options will be available to explore hidden talents, which should now be unleashed.

> **MEMORIZE**
>
> Recovery ✳ Meditation ✳ Don't rush ✳ Explore talents

One World Interpretation

Time to start something new. Take your time in all you do.

KEYWORD: *time*

Rider-Waite Tarot

One World Tarot

Five of Swords

News of death and an illegal will. Who owns what and tries to steal?

CARD NUMBER: 55 **KEYWORD:** failure

Rider-Waite Interpretation

A shady character holds three swords with two below his feet. Two men are walking away, implying that a battle has been fought and won. All the fives in Tarot are meddlesome and complex, with the Five of Swords being one of the worst. Friends could let the querent down, and no one is to be trusted. This is a time to choose associates carefully without divulging any secrets, as gossip could be rife. Health issues, which can be self-inflicted, will distress the person's life, and a hospital visit might be on the agenda.

One World Interpretation

This Sword is the card of theft and trickery, and it can also mean drug dealing, robbery, and criminal connections. It portends news of people going to prison, credit card theft, and embezzlement. It suggests an intrusive time when others will be out to get what they can, caring about no one but themselves. Someone's death could create a bitter outcome, and the querent may have an inheritance stolen from them. Don't ignore treasured items outside in the garden or yard, or leave a purse or wallet unattended; they might get stolen. If plans are thwarted and turn to failure, trust that this is not the pathway to go on, and wait for a better opportunity.

MEMORIZE

Theft ✳ Trickery ✳ Embezzlement
✳ Problems with wills ✳ Stolen
purse or wallet

Associated Cards with Upright Five of Swords

✳ Placed next to the Tower (upright and reversed), the Five of Swords suggests assault, murder, and accidents.

✳ If the card appears with the Three of Pentacles (upright and reversed), beware embezzlement or a ruined business. Also, watch out for internet scams.

✳ If the Five of Swords is placed near Knights (reversed), drug rings could bring violence when the debts are not paid. If the Sun (upright or reversed) appears nearby, there could be a good outcome, even though it might seem impossible at the time.

✳ If the card is next to the Nine of Wands (reversed), someone is stealing at work.

Rider-Waite Interpretation

A person in the client's family might be disgraced and shunned by the community or place of worship. Parents and siblings will wash their hands of the culprit, as the blame is unfairly heaped upon them. Old wounds from a past incident might resurface, and the querent will be worried that history could repeat itself. Asking for for-giveness is needed to clear the way ahead.

One World Interpretation

Explosive decisions cause distress. Everything will be a mess.

KEYWORD: *shame*

When the Five of Swords is reversed, the seeker could be in for a muddled and un-happy time. A can of worms is about to be opened, and deep secrets will be revealed. Others will have shame brought upon them, or they could hear news of someone they know going to prison. Life will be a mess, and the client will feel as if no one understands them. They could consider moving away or cutting ties with certain family members.

MEMORIZE

Muddled and unhappy ✳ Secrets revealed ✳ Disgrace and shame ✳ Cutting ties from a member of the family ✳ Feeling like no one understands them

Rider-Waite Tarot   *One World Tarot*

Six of Swords

Your lessons learned have paved the way. A new beginning and better days.

CARD NUMBER: 56 **KEYWORDS:** moving on

Rider-Waite Interpretation

A mother and a young child are rowed across the water toward a neighboring land. They are moving away from the sadness of the past. After the storm comes the light; it's been a long struggle, but they are nearly at the end of it now, so they must push on gently. A brand-new vista is in view.

One of the few Sword cards that offers

hope is the Six of Swords. The seeker's guide or guardian angel will assist; optimism will uplift the soul once more.

One World Interpretation

In Tarot today, we see this card as movement, which could mean changing jobs or leaving behind one relationship to pursue another. An accurate prediction is a change of home; the client will usually move out of the area and into a new district. Because of trial and tribulation in the past, the soul is wiser after the ordeals that have been experienced. You cannot teach what you have not learned. Travel plans could be made for a long journey on water or near the ocean or a lake. Peace is on its way, and the balance will soon be restored.

MEMORIZE

Changing jobs ✳ Leaving relationships ✳ Moving house ✳ A wiser soul ✳ Journeys near water

---

Associated Cards with Upright Six of Swords

* The Six of Swords next to the World (upright) brings great joy and adventure. Perhaps a long-haul flight to faraway lands.

* If the card appears with the Six of Pentacles (upright), extra cash will give security and allow time for some fun.

* When the Judgement card (upright or reversed) is in situ, it will showcase that important lessons of wisdom have been learned and will add to the client's positive karma.

* When the Six of Swords is placed near the Four of Cups (upright), it portends better health and mental concentration.

Rider-Waite Interpretation

Don't lose hope even though all seems at a loss. The client may be struggling with depression or perhaps is drinking too much. They know they need to do something about it but have to be in the right mindset. They should achieve it in the end. The seeker could have unfinished business with someone from their past, and they will need to address it before they can move on emotionally.

One World Interpretation

Stuck in a rut with no way out. It will end soon, without a doubt.

KEYWORD: *patience*

A house move may be delayed or fall through, or a vacation could be canceled— a time to take stock and get some equilibrium. The client will need to be patient; what is wanted will come, but not just yet.

MEMORIZE

House move to fall through ✳ Vacation canceled ✳ Wait and be patient ✳ Don't lose hope ✳ Struggling with weight ✳ Unfinished business with someone from the past

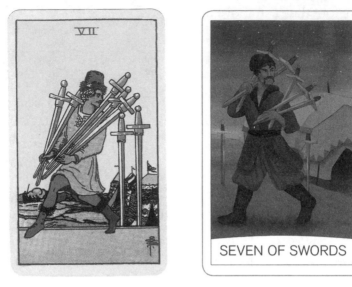

Rider-Waite Tarot   *One World Tarot*

Seven of Swords

Watch out, there's a thief about. Trust in no one, without a doubt.

CARD NUMBER: 57 **KEYWORD:** caution

Rider-Waite Interpretation

Traditional and modern-day interpretations show the Seven of Swords as the theft card. The man depicted on the card sneaks away without being seen. The smile on his face shows us that he is pleased with himself. He's obviously up to mischief and will have many fingers in the pie. It can also signify that a person could steal others' ideas or inventions.

One World Interpretation

Someone around the client must not be trusted. Mixing with people with criminal tendencies might cause them to have a brush with the law or even go to prison. The querent must trust their instincts. Any new ideas concerning business should be kept secret as others might profit from the seeker's talents.

Although they might wish to escape certain situations, such as relationships or work, it would be better for them to face their demons and honor their commitments.

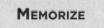

MEMORIZE

Someone not to be trusted ✷
Mixing with criminal types ✷
Trusting instincts ✷ Keeping ideas
secret ✷ Dodging commitments

Associated Cards with Upright Seven of Swords

* If this card appears in the same spread as a King (upright or reversed) and a Page (upright or reversed), a father won't show any interest in his children and will go on to be an absent parent.
* With the Knight of Swords (upright or reversed), Knight of Wands (upright or reversed), and Five of Wands (upright or reversed), this combination depicts a group of young men causing havoc. If the seeker mixes with the wrong sort, they could end up breaking the law. Gang warfare, knives, and guns could also be involved. There could also be illegal dealings linked to drugs and stolen goods.
* If the Seven of Swords is placed around the Eight of Pentacles (upright), someone could be cheating on exams.
* With the Five of Swords (reversed) in the spread, young people may be getting bullied over social media.

Rider-Waite Interpretation

Ideas could be stolen, so being discreet is a must. Someone around the seeker pulls the wool over their eyes; when the culprit is exposed, the client will change their opinion quickly. It's best not to believe all that is said.

Don't trust promises, and certainly don't loan any cash, as it will be a long time before it comes back, if it does at all. Someone will pressure the client and try to make them do something they don't want to do.

One World Interpretation

Delete your friends and let them be. Walk on by, and you'll be free.

KEYWORD: *manipulation*

Others will use every trick in the book to get what they want, so beware of manipulative people. The querent must display strong willpower and stay focused to keep on the correct path. Scammers are close, so if it looks too good to be true, it will be. The Seven of Swords reversed might also imply the seeker foolishly believes something to be true, even if it goes against everything they stand for. The message is to be careful and don't bow to someone else's influences.

MEMORIZE

Manipulative people ✳ Scammers; too good to be true ✳ Don't lend money ✳ Someone is putting on pressure

Rider-Waite Tarot

One World Tarot

Eight of Swords

Feeling abandoned, fearful, and lost. For mistakes you have made, you now pay the cost.

CARD NUMBER: 58 **KEYWORD:** restriction

Rider-Waite Interpretation

A blindfolded woman is bound with eight swords surrounding her. She is trapped and unable to see things clearly. The dark ocean is behind her, and she feels as if she is lost at sea.

When this card appears in the spread, there is a lot of sadness and hurt, and the person frequently feels betrayed and let down. Existing in a continual cycle of worry can create poor health. Restrictions are all around them, and there seems to be no way out. Because of the stress surrounding them, this can often depict signs that they might feel suicidal.

One World Interpretation

This Sword is the card of betrayal and separation, sometimes called the "divorce card." Because of anxiety, the individual doesn't have the strength to move on, so they are stuck without any hope. If the client is spiritual, a meditation with healing crystals could be beneficial, or a visit to a healer to align the chakras could unlock new healing energy throughout the body. The client will be confused about their future and have no clue as to how situations will play out. Today in Tarot, all eights signify good luck and hope; although this is a somewhat dismal card, things will improve in time.

MEMORIZE

⌒•••⌒

Betrayal and separation ✳ Divorce card ✳ Use meditation and healing ✳ Confusion over the future ✳ All will be well in the end

---

Associated Cards with Upright Eight of Swords

✳ The Eight of Cups and the Star (upright or reversed) can mean wonderful new beginnings that are totally unexpected with protection from one's guide. There's no gain without the pain.

✳ If the Eight of Swords is placed next to the Justice card (upright), a divorce is to be expected.

✳ If any Queen (upright or reversed) is present, the client has someone around them who wants to exact revenge.

✳ If the Eight of Swords appears around travel cards (upright and reversed), the client will have a fear of flying.

✳ If this card is in the reversed position beside the Tower (upright), the client or someone close by could be enduring domestic violence.

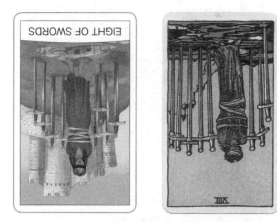

Rider-Waite Interpretation

The querent is deeply despondent with their back against the wall. All their efforts have been in vain. Because they didn't stop and see the red flags, they are dealing with the repercussions. The client needs to reform their behavior and aim to be kinder and less selfish toward others. The person has no self-confidence and believes they are not worthy of having the better things in life. Even if they do something good, they are constantly criticizing themselves. Many deep secrets from the past will continue to plague the person's mind, so it's time to clear away the skeletons in the closet.

One World Interpretation

Your lowest hour seems to have come; no hope now, nowhere to run.

KEYWORD: *dominance*

A dominant partner who shows signs of coercive control could even be physically abusive. There will be no reasoning, no battle to win, and much energy will be wasted, resulting in explosive quarrels. The client will eventually leave the partner, and after the separation, a new day will dawn, bringing hope and optimism.

With this bold step forward, they will start ironing out other problems in their lives, perhaps eating healthier and losing weight. Their confidence will soar, and they will finally be contented with their lot. Some good news and unexpected help are on the way to brighten the seeker's life.

MEMORIZE

Dominant partner ✳ Coercive control ✳ Explosive quarrels ✳ New and better times are ahead ✳ Change in behavior is needed

Rider-Waite Tarot   One World Tarot

Nine of Swords

Illness and death weigh on your shoulders. Too much to bear, too many boulders.

CARD NUMBER: 59 **KEYWORD:** fear

Rider-Waite Interpretation

A woman is seated in her bed, having awakened from a nightmare. The surrounding swords show the despair and sorrow of negative thinking. The soul is troubled, and without hope, worry will keep the client awake at night. There is no love or support, just loneliness, heartache, and feelings of being detached from the outside world. The fear she manifests will only bring more anxiety and stress. She must climb out of this depression to bring positivity in her life.

One World Interpretation

This card can depict death or a severe illness, and many Tarot readers consider it one of the most negative cards in the deck. Feelings of suicide, mental torment, and inability to live with oneself will become too much to bear. This sword can also depict a serious illness that cannot be treated, so look at surrounding cards to see the outcome. Either the client or someone close to them will have hospital visits or repeated clinic visits dominating their life for a long time. They will feel like there is little time left, but who would care anyway? This card can also suggest that they might have just lost the most precious person in their life, and to be without them will seem unbearable.

Associated Cards with Upright Nine of Swords

✶ When the Nine of Swords appears with the Tower (reversed), someone is feeling suicidal.

✶ When Strength (upright) or the Magician (upright) is in the same spread, the spirit world will intervene to change the mindset of the person suffering.

✶ If the Temperance (upright) card is nearby, miracles from the spirit world will bring in a wonderful new start.

✶ If the card appears around Knights (upright or reversed), a young man's mental health is dire. Seek medical attention quickly.

MEMORIZE

Death ✶ A serious illness that cannot be treated ✶ Mental torment ✶ Losing someone precious

 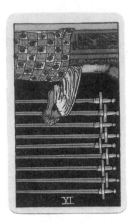

The Nine of Swords, in reverse, holds optimism and new blessings. The person's karma will be brilliant as the soul has become wiser and more empathetic. Their long journey of hardship will bring self-awareness and calm. A massive wall has been surmounted, and profound knowledge is waiting to be released to them. The client will now feel happy and contented.

Rider-Waite Interpretation

The client could be suffering from depression and may have entered self-destruct mode. They are frightened at what the future might bring and will lock themselves away for safety. If they have been struggling with personal problems, they must seek help from those closest to them. On a brighter note, a karmic lesson has been fulfilled, so the seeker can now turn a new page. The soul will be uplifted as fresh concepts are embraced for their future—a time to relax and heal.

One World Interpretation

You've passed the test of karmic law. Reap your rewards; your soul will soar.

KEYWORD: *blessings*

> **MEMORIZE**
> ⚬ ⋯ ⚬
> Fear of the future ✳ A time of depression ✳ Optimism and blessings ✳ Good karma ✳ Feeling happy and contented

Rider-Waite Tarot

One World Tarot

Ten of Swords

Deep distress and a broken heart. Life is unjust; you wish to depart.

CARD NUMBER: 60 **KEYWORD:** advancement

TEN OF SWORDS

Rider-Waite Interpretation

Representing death, a man lies face down with ten swords piercing his back. This sword card is full of doom and gloom and disrupts life. Plans could be scuppered, a business ruined, and the person's hopes and dreams could crash around them. Public shame and humiliation send them into a deep depression with a loss of face. Perhaps their life will never be the same again. Great strength is needed to survive in this difficult time.

One World Interpretation

Being one of the death cards, the Ten of Swords signifies bereavement. Slander and deliberate ruination will be plotted for someone else's gain, and the loser will come tumbling down. All that has taken years to build up will be smashed apart in seconds. Before signing documents, one must read the small print carefully. Unfair gossip will spread like wildfire to cause ruination. The person under fire will wish to flee and go into hiding to avoid any sudden media speculation. The end of something is inevitable; this could be a relationship, a job, or something important in the client's life. One of the worst cards in Tarot; study the surrounding cards to find any ray of hope.

MEMORIZE

╶─ ·ᐧ· ─╴

Death and bereavement ✳ Slander and ruination ✳ Read the fine print on documents

---

Associated Cards with Upright Ten of Swords

* When the Ten of Swords (upright or reversed) sits in the same spread as the Death card (upright), the client could be attending a funeral. Study surrounding cards to see if there are any applicable signs for the seeker. If not, it is likely that they may hear of death and perhaps attend the funeral to support someone else.

* If the Devil (upright) and the Ten of Pentacles (upright) are in situ, someone will maliciously interfere with another's life, especially their business world, and bring it to ruination.

* If the Ten of Swords (reversed) is next to any Pentacle, finances will improve, and a new venture is up ahead.

* If the Ten of Swords appears with the Nine of Cups (upright) or the Sun (upright), a brilliant resolution at the last moment will save the day.

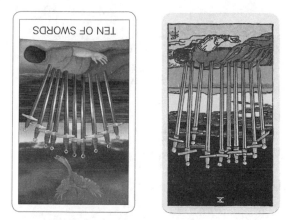

Rider-Waite Interpretation

When life is at its lowest point, the seeker is often given spiritual help. The soul becomes wiser and more empathetic, seeking more profound knowledge, so the trials, tribulations, and setbacks bring a deeper maturity. Something unfortunate may have happened in the past, but now it's time to close the door on it all. Emotional wounds are still open from an event that occurred previously, but the client will eventually address these issues and be able to make peace with it all.

This card has a positive outcome in reverse, saying that all the heartache and struggles are now behind them. Things will never be as bad as they were.

One World Interpretation

All is past, blessings to come. Lift your face to greet the sun.

KEYWORD: *movement*

A karmic debt has been paid, and a fresh start awaits after the storm with plans for expansion, movement, and success. The client has spent a few years being spiritually tested, but now they have passed their tests and can step out of the dark and into the light. They are surrounded by spiritual protection so that nothing can hurt them. A complete stranger will offer a new opportunity, and out of the blue, something amazing will happen. Search the house for lost objects as they will be found.

> **MEMORIZE**
>
> Karmic debts paid ✳ Spiritual protection ✳ A stranger brings an opportunity ✳ Lost objects will be found

The Court Mentors: Swords

King of Swords, Queen of Swords,
Knight of Swords, Page of Swords

AIR SIGNS: Gemini, Libra, and Aquarius

CAREERS FOR GEMINI AIR SIGN: writer, publisher, musician, linguist, hairdresser, beautician, makeup artist, tattooist, manager, supervisor, accountant, journalist

CAREERS FOR LIBRA AIR SIGN: graphic designer, dentist, fashion designer, wedding planner, florist, chef, pub owner, mediator, judge, police officer, probation officer

CAREERS FOR AQUARIUS AIR SIGN: homeopathist, counselor, therapist, reflexologist, humanitarian worker, vet, veterinary assistant, scientist, teacher, social worker, environmentalist

Rider-Waite Tarot

One World Tarot

Page of Swords

A child who wants to be the boss. Gain back the power, or all will be lost.

CARD NUMBER: 61 **KEYWORD:** feisty

Child, boy or girl, aged birth–16

Rider-Waite Interpretation

A young child stands with his sword pointing to the sky while looking in anticipation of what is coming. This Page is full of energy and determination and can be challenging. He will have a curious nature, asking endless questions and gathering information so he can decide the best course of action. His enthusiasm will help him do well in life, but he must be careful not to tread on the heads of others while he ascends to the top.

One World Interpretation

The client will try hard to psychoanalyze a male or female child who is stubborn, secretive, and introverted. A gentle approach is required to get them to open up about their worries and frustrations. If there is more than one youngster in the family, this Page might intimidate and bully another. A period should be set aside to help solve their anxieties.

This youngster can sometimes be disruptive, so the parents must find a balance of love and discipline. If left to their own devices, the youngster will rule the roost and show signs of precociousness. Modern readers can sometimes predict this child that's full of energy as having ADHD or a disorder that falls on the autism spectrum.

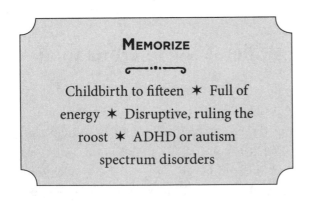

MEMORIZE

Childbirth to fifteen ✳ Full of energy ✳ Disruptive, ruling the roost ✳ ADHD or autism spectrum disorders

Other Meanings

Bad news is on the way, which will cause delays, and plans need to be rearranged. The client will be signing contracts or reading through important documents. This is a time of poor communication, so work on how best to approach introverted or sullen people.

Associated Cards with Upright Page of Swords

* If the Four of Cups (upright) is with the Page of Swords (upright or reversed), more love and attention are needed to give the child confidence.
* When the Five of Wands (upright) or the Seven of Swords (upright or reversed) is in situ, there will be a necessity to make sure the youngster has better friendships and isn't being influenced to behave badly or secretly.
* If the Page of Swords is next to the Devil (upright or reversed), a child might be violent and show signs of aggression, and could even bully other children or animals.
* When the Page of Swords is with any positive Cup card (upright), the child will be going through a phase and should grow up to be a respectable person.

Reversed Meaning

Unhappy children cause distress. Calm emotions are the best.

KEYWORD: *illness*

This young person can be full of self-importance and likes to stretch the truth, so it's best not to believe everything that is said. As they mature, they will show signs of being an interesting character with an upbeat personality. Clever, psychic, and a good judge of others—they might even be able to read your mind!

Swords are often linked to illness, so perhaps a child in the family is tired or unwell and might benefit from a visit to the doctor. There could be a minor or silly accident around them, but nothing too serious. Parents may feel the misery of dealing with a naughty child. No form of discipline seems to work. This card in reverse can often symbolize children with disabilities, either mental or physical.

MEMORIZE

Sick child ✳ Silly accidents ✳ Naughty and disruptive ✳ Not responding to discipline ✳ Mental or physical disability

Rider-Waite Tarot   One World Tarot

Knight of Swords

Gallant and sexy, a dream to behold. But if she's boring, he will grow cold.

CARD NUMBER: 62 **KEYWORD:** action
Young man, aged 16–29

Rider-Waite Interpretation

A young man spurs his white horse forward, prepared for battle. He is fearless and independent, not seeking approval from anyone.

This Knight can be fiercely competitive and never gives up. Although polite, he usually prefers his own way and will go to any lengths to achieve his goals. His personality is split into two. He is often a deep thinker with a vivid imagination, which causes him to frequently daydream, but he can also make rash decisions and then suffer the consequences later. He is opinionated from a young age and will enjoy debates.

One World Interpretation

This Knight is good-looking and sexy, loves flirting, and will probably flit from one partner to another. He will explore sex early on in his life and will always want to know what his partner is thinking. If his other half is dull or lacks personality, he'll get bored and be off like a shot to the next challenge. With careers, he is determined to get to the top, not caring much about who he steps on along the way. He can be outspoken, finding it hard to adhere to the rules. He's the type that might challenge his boss or complain about how things are run in the workplace. He could be hard to handle until he approaches the age of thirty, and then once he has sown his wild oats, he will usually settle down to be a good husband and father.

MEMORIZE

◈━━···━━◈

Good-looking and sexy ✴ Has sex early on in his life ✴ Likes an interesting mate ✴ Determined to get to the top

---

Other Meanings

Knights are cards of movement and will also represent journeys, so travel is highly starred. The client will make last-minute decisions and will not have much time to think about something before it happens; they could be inclined to rush things and cut corners. A journey might have to be canceled, and care must be taken for motorway travel as drivers might not be concentrating.

Associated Cards with Upright Knight of Swords

✴ When the Ten of Pentacles (upright) is in place, a raise or promotion will be around him very soon.

✴ If two Knights (upright or reversed) are present with the Lovers, this indicates gay men or a man exploring his sexuality.

✴ If this Knight (upright or reversed) has the Lovers next to him or is present with two or more Queens, there will be more than one woman in his life.

✴ If the World card (upright) is nearby, he will have a love of travel and will plan a trip in the coming months.

✴ With the Devil (upright or reversed), this Knight will be obsessive and perhaps a stalker type.

Reversed Meaning

This young Knight can be a pest. Step away; that is best.

KEYWORD: *pest*

This Knight could be a real heartbreaker, so the client might need to walk away if they feel they can't handle him. He will never stick to his plans, failing to do what he promised. Sometimes, he won't take no for an answer and will prove to be a pest. The querent would do well to stay away from him, or he'll go on to be a controlling type. Always short of money, he will tap his parents for funds. In his youth, he'll be irresponsible and an erratic driver, the sort of person to accrue a pile of unpaid parking tickets. Although he is young, he will like his own company; unlike most young men, he will be interested in classical music, history, and aliens from other worlds. A complex person but never dull! Certainly, a soul that has reincarnated before.

MEMORIZE

⌐–··–⌐

A heartbreaker ✳ Not sticking to plans ✳ Not taking no for an answer ✳ Controlling ✳ Erratic driver ✳ Unpaid parking tickets ✳ Interested in aliens and UFOs

Rider-Waite Tarot   One World Tarot

Queen of Swords

This air sign lady is very strong. Her wit is quick, and her friendship long.

CARD NUMBER: 63 **KEYWORD:** shrewd
Woman, aged 16 onward

Rider-Waite Interpretation

In her right hand, this Queen carries a sword that is lifted high, signifying her desire to discover the truth. Her left hand is raised in the air as if to accept all that will come to her. She is mature, shrewd, and often widowed or divorced. This Queen will be the family matriarch, and her words will be held in great esteem. She has a captivating knack for manipulating others; this charm extends to the opposite sex, from whom she will usually get what she wants. She is a wise counselor because she sees the situation for what it really is and, therefore, will come up with the correct solution.

One World Interpretation

She is the trickiest of the four Queens, as she can hide her thoughts. She will often be psychic and able to read others' minds, which puts them at a great disadvantage. Charming, witty, and erudite, her personality will change to fit the situation. She's a better friend than an enemy because, if you cross her, she will show a spiteful side to her nature and never forgive; this behavior comes from her wisdom and the past hardships and betrayals she has experienced. Sometimes this will leave her jaded. She has an edge to her and is nobody's fool. Men will love her physical beauty and find her intriguing. She is a wonderful mother, giving her children time, attention, and independence. Her positive attributes are that she is generous and kind; although she will help anyone, she will choose her closest friends carefully.

MEMORIZE

⌐ · ·· · ⌐

Divorced or widowed ✶ Wise counselor ✶ A better friend than an enemy ✶ No one's fool ✶ Wonderful mother

---

Other Meanings

The client's life is shrouded in mystery, so they strive to seek the truth. It is a time to assess life, and after a time of putting up with endless niggles, finally, changes will be made.

The person must attain higher standards, and it would be better not to put up with things as they are. And they must always consider the consequences of their actions. The client might have to stick up for themselves when difficult people challenge them.

Associated Cards with Upright Queen of Swords

* If the Queen of Swords has the Empress (upright) nearby with Pages (upright or reversed) around, we know she is the matriarch of the family. Her word will be law.
* When she's next to the Ace of Pentacles (upright), she might use her money to favor certain individuals to keep them close by.
* When she's next to the Two of Swords (upright), a broken relationship or marriage will still affect her, making her distrust other men.

✴ If she appears in the reverse position next to the Four of Wands (upright), she will be gossiping about a friend or neighbor.

Reversed Meaning

This Queen loves to gossip and put others down. Best to smile; don't make her frown.

KEYWORD: *formidable*

This Queen will love nothing more than to gossip about others. Because of this, she is formidable and can be deceiving. She has a strong presence and personality but can change her mood instantly, making her fickle and unpredictable.

She is bossy and sometimes rude, and she will be unpopular in the workplace. If she upsets a person, she feels no remorse and will immediately forget what she has said. This woman is a cunning manipulator and might even tell bald-faced lies to get her own way. Some of her redeeming factors are generosity, wit, and a love of the animal kingdom. She will also be very kind to anyone who is unwell or might need advice.

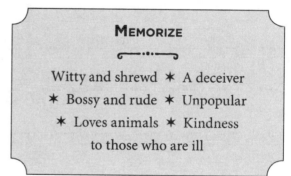

MEMORIZE

Witty and shrewd ✴ A deceiver ✴ Bossy and rude ✴ Unpopular ✴ Loves animals ✴ Kindness to those who are ill

Rider-Waite Tarot

One World Tarot

King of Swords

This air sign man gains deep respect. As your friend, he'll be perfect.

CARD NUMBER: 64 **KEYWORD:** responsible
Male, aged 29 onward

Rider-Waite Interpretation

The King of Swords is seated on his throne, looking forward as though prepared to face any challenges life may present him. He is a mature man who takes his responsibilities very seriously. He is often at the top of his tree, holding a job of accountability. This King has a great sense of fairness and is old-fashioned and reliable. For most of his life, he will try to lessen the burdens of those more unfortunate than himself, so his heart is kind.

One World Interpretation

This shrewd King misses nothing and watches how others negotiate to get to the top. His temper will rise when orders are ignored, as he hates a slapdash attitude or things left unfinished. As a professional, he can be the head of a company or an officer in the forces. In some Tarot cards, he can also be a doctor, a lawyer, or a leader in his field. At work, he will plot and plan to bring order and stability to those he oversees.

His nature is steadfast and romantic. When he is in love, he will treat his partner very well. He is not a spiritual type but is intelligent and will keep an open mind; because of this, he will be popular and well-liked by all.

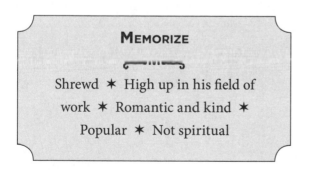

MEMORIZE

Shrewd ✳ High up in his field of work ✳ Romantic and kind ✳ Popular ✳ Not spiritual

Other Meanings

The client might have to consult a lawyer to deal with legal documentation. A visit to the doctor is a must to get a health checkup and ensure everything is okay. The seeker will be around builders or people who are experts in their field; this might involve having things fixed around the home.

Associated Cards with Upright King of Swords

* If the King of Swords has the Ace of Wands (upright) next to him, there will be a brilliant career opening up for him.
* When the Chariot (upright) is placed nearby, the opportunity to live and work abroad could bring wonderful new beginnings to change his life.
* The King of Swords (reversed) next to any upright Wands signifies a bully boss who will make everyone miserable at work.
* If he appears in a spread with the Five of Swords (upright) or the Seven of Swords (upright), he may have done a spell in prison.

Reversed Meaning

Strict and unbending, cruel and unkind. Compassion lacking is what you'll find.

KEYWORD: *bully*

The King of Swords, in reverse, can be un-kind and unfeeling, and his coldness can drive people away from him. Within his marriage, he will rule the roost and be a stern and autocratic father. He will often be a persistent bully by domineering his wife, partner, or colleagues. One day the con-sequences of his behavior will have to be addressed, much to his chagrin. He never turns his back on confrontation and enjoys the drama of a quarrel. He likes his own way and will stop at nothing to get it. He considers the home his domain, as he rules everything and everyone around him. He will be disliked by his children, resulting in them leaving home at a young age to escape his demands.

> **MEMORIZE**
>
> Unkind and unfeeling ✳ Rules the roost ✳ A bully at work and at home ✳ Disliked by his children

The Suit of Pentacles

EARTH SIGNS: Taurus, Virgo, Capricorn

SEASON: Winter

ALSO KNOWN AS: Pentacles, Coins, or Disks

REPRESENTS: wealth, business transactions, property, investments, and commerce

The Pentacle cards represent wealth, prosperity, property, and business. The success of these hard-working birth signs will manifest in the establishment of firm foundations of cash and security. When this suit appears in a reading, it can give you lots of information about the client's finances. As you will come to see, not all cards in this suit symbolize positive cash flow, as some can also point to the difficulties one might face. As Pentacles represent the earth signs, we see solid, dependable characters in the court mentors. They are the foundation of civilization, the workers producing structure and nurturing. These people are generous and will lend money to help their loved ones in a financial crisis. They have integrity, wisdom, and sound common sense, so their place in society is very important.

Rider-Waite Tarot   One World Tarot

The Ace of Pentacles

"Life is good" is what you'll say. A brand-new job, a better way.

CARD NUMBER: 65 **KEYWORD:** wealth

Rider-Waite Interpretation

The Ace of Pentacles is shown with a hand reaching out from the clouds. The palm holds a huge coin that is given as a gift from the gods. New-money energy is materializing; a brand-new opportunity is connected to financial success. The beautiful landscape beyond signifies a time of renewed growth. This is a very favorable card that represents riches and victory. It can also portend a fabulous new job, a pay raise, or a promotion. When this Ace makes an appearance in a spread, financial improvements are on the way, and perhaps a new house as well. Fate can smile on the seeker with a windfall, inheritance, or gift of some substance. It represents a more unrestrained monetary phase, and healthy investments will be implemented to bring security.

One World Interpretation

This Ace is the best financial card in the deck and promises a steady cash flow. An important document or letter with some good news for the family could be on its way. This is a time to invest in property or buy land to build a house; perhaps the client is making investments abroad or purchasing a holiday home. The seeker could be considering renovating a run-down house and then renting it out to bring in more income; this is undoubtedly a time when one must speculate to accumulate.

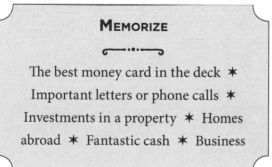

MEMORIZE

The best money card in the deck ✳
Important letters or phone calls ✳
Investments in a property ✳ Homes
abroad ✳ Fantastic cash ✳ Business

Associated Cards with Upright Ace of Pentacles

✳ If the World (upright) is present, the client may look at properties abroad and decide whether to purchase them.

✳ With the Magician (upright) placed nearby, trusting one's intuition and taking a gamble should pay off.

✳ If the Five of Swords (upright or reversed) and Seven of Swords (upright or reversed) is together with this card, then shady deals are on the table, and all that is being said is deceitful and not to be trusted.

✳ If this card appears with the Nine of Pentacles (upright), an inheritance or a lump sum of money will be flooding the bank account.

✳ When the Ace is positioned in reverse with the Two of Pentacles (upright), the client could let money slip through their fingers.

The querent or someone close to them is greedy for money; rather than share, they keep it all for themselves. A new job offer, a career change, or an innovative business venture may fall through at the last minute.

If the client is purchasing property, the buyers could suddenly drop out. Care must be taken not to overspend, or they will lose everything and end up in debt.

Rider-Waite Interpretation

All that has been gained could be lost, so caution is warranted for new business deals. The person could be feeling hesitant about spending money or making investments. Others will be out to make a fast buck, which could be with the client's cash, so they must guard it well. Embezzlement and corrupt procedures could cause ruination, and any internet business will have to be scrutinized; it's not a time to take chances.

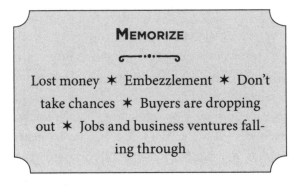

MEMORIZE

Lost money ✳ Embezzlement ✳ Don't take chances ✳ Buyers are dropping out ✳ Jobs and business ventures falling through

One World Interpretation

Try not to splash that cash around, or to the debtors you'll be bound.

KEYWORD: *losses*

Rider-Waite Tarot   One World Tarot

Two of Pentacles

Spinning plates and juggling balls. Gain control, lest they should fall.

CARD NUMBER: 66 **KEYWORDS:** monetary balance

Rider-Waite Interpretation

A man balances two coins in his hands. These symbols represent the need for careful management of his cash. On the horizon, two boats are dipping up and down in the sea; this indicates that the person must take control, however rough the ocean is. All twos in the Tarot symbolize choices and decisions, so the seeker might have two jobs or be juggling a failing business and must ponder whether to

continue or admit defeat. It's not a good time, so security measures must be put in place not to overspend. A second chance of cash could be offered to help, but caution is necessary to avoid misspending the money.

One World Interpretation

The client is juggling cash and robbing Peter to pay Paul. Bad management has come to knock on the door, and the credit cards could be in full use, but in the end, more significant bills will be looming, and loans might have to be taken out to compensate. It's the beginning of a slippery slope. Married couples have to decide whether to take on extra jobs to pull back the dwindling cash flow, but, in the end, it will prove hopeless, and hard lessons will be learned. The client might decide to get some financial advice and face up to their dwindling cash flow. This monetary crisis is short-lived, so do give them hope that all will be well in the end.

Associated Cards with Upright Two of Pentacles

✳ If there are Pages (upright or reverse) in the spread alongside the Fool, the children might be demanding expensive items to keep up with their peer group, or what money is remaining could be whittled away on trivial purchases.

✳ If the Two of Pentacles appears with Justice (upright), a warning of bailiffs and lawsuits is on the horizon.

✳ If this card appears in the same spread as the Tower (upright or reverse), the client might consider filing for bankruptcy.

✳ If the Sun (upright) appears in the same group of cards, all financial problems will soon be resolved.

MEMORIZE

❮—·•··—❯

Robbing Peter to pay Paul ✳ Credit cards maxed out ✳ Large bills and loans ✳ Take financial advice ✳ Make decisions over money ✳ Things okay in the end

Rider-Waite Interpretation

The seeker or someone close could be living beyond their means and refusing to see the consequences. Who is going to bail this person out? Maybe they will go, cap in hand, to a parent or benefactor to ask for financial aid. They will finally have to admit that their foolish and immature spending has made a real mess. The client will be swimming in debt, and their misfortune could implode into their workplace, too, resulting in the sack.

The client is overcommitted and juggling too many issues in their life. This could mean holding down a significant job while trying to raise a family and take care of others. Because there is too much going on in the person's life, it will be difficult for them to focus on one of their tasks properly. They must take stock and only attend to what is vital. This card can often mean that the seeker is neglecting their family life because they are so hell-bent on making ends meet. They have nothing left in reserve after paying the bills, and their health could decline through exhaustion.

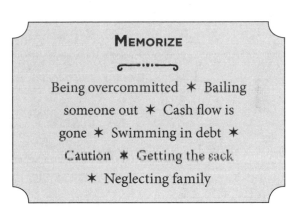

MEMORIZE

Being overcommitted * Bailing someone out * Cash flow is gone * Swimming in debt * Caution * Getting the sack * Neglecting family

One World Interpretation

Money's gone down the drain. Now in poverty you'll remain.

KEYWORD: *debt*

Rider-Waite Tarot

One World Tarot

Three of Pentacles

Use your talents to succeed, and to get the money you will need.

CARD NUMBER: 67 **KEYWORDS:** work success

Rider-Waite Interpretation

People are working on a project, and with hard work, the client has reaped the rewards and established more financial security. Praise can be given, and recognition from others will boost the person's ego. At last, things are improving, and cash will be saved in the bank for further investments. For those who work for a company, a salary increase or a promotion might be offered. Because of a job change, the client might have to train their successor to make the wheels run smoothly.

One World Interpretation

Today's Tarot readers will often refer to the Three of Pentacles as the "apprenticeship card"; however, if the client is mature, it can mean striving to be one's own boss through self-employment. They might, for a while, have to run their new business alongside their current job. Because this card is so positive, the extra effort will benefit the client in the long term.

The Three of Pentacles heralds a new time to forge ahead with a real career that might be in place for life. There will be much to learn, but the client will achieve greatness with hard work and dedication. If someone is striving for a degree or a higher qualification, this card represents the level of commitment that will be required, and it can depict a three-year time scale.

MEMORIZE

Apprenticeships and training ✳ Business owners and self-employment ✳ Degrees take three years ✳ Financially sound after hard work

---

Associated Cards with Upright Three of Pentacles

* If the card sits beside the Seven of Wands (upright), this could indicate the client is taking on more staff. If this doesn't relate to a self-employed person, they will be embarking on DIY projects around the home.
* When it is placed with the Six of Cups (upright), a new project will be about to start for a family member that will change their life.
* If the Three of Pentacles (upright) is next to the Devil (upright or reverse), look out for someone trying to ruin all that has been achieved.
* If it is next to the Ace of Wands (upright), the client will start their own business from nothing and could end up with a sizable income.
* Someone will fail their driving test with the Chariot (upright) and the Three of Pentacles (reversed).

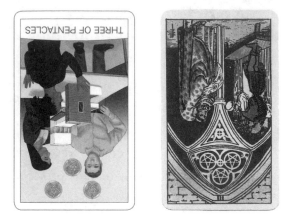

Rider-Waite Interpretation

The Three of Pentacles in reverse can mean a tricky situation is ahead for the person. An up-and-coming new business might be the querent's focus, but with a lack of foresight or bad management, it could be run into the ground very quickly. By thinking they can do it better, the client will leave everything extremely muddled and on a downward slope with their stick-in-the-mud attitude. A new business will be hard to get off the ground, and money and success will be on pause with no dividends to look forward to.

Arguments over money will occur in the client's life, and they will find themselves in a stalemate situation. One partner spends more than the other, leaving the bank account teetering. It's time to get some financial advice and perhaps restructure and consolidate. If they or someone close to them is studying, the work will be too hard, and the person could fail any exams they are taking. Any self-employed ventures will come to a grinding halt, and business could be slow or even flop.

> **MEMORIZE**
>
> ⌐•••⌐
>
> Business not getting off the ground ✳ Lack of foresight ✳ Bad management ✳ Quarrels over money ✳ Self-employed ventures flop

One World Interpretation

Keep your eye on the ball. Tread carefully, or you will fall.

KEYWORDS: *business loss*

Rider-Waite Tarot   One World Tarot

Four of Pentacles

Material things can be provided. Relationships become divided.

CARD NUMBER: 68 **KEYWORDS:** the miser card

Rider-Waite Interpretation

A man sits clutching a coin, with his feet placed on two others. One coin balances on his head, signifying his connection to the spirit world. He is so fixated on protecting his cash that he cannot move and is stuck in one spot. This card can relate to investing money or opening a savings plan. The person has no financial worries, but rather than enjoying the steady flow of wealth, they will stash it away for fear of losing it. The Four of Pentacles is, by and large, a positive card for money growth, showing there is plenty of cash to pay the bills and a little extra left over for small investments.

One World Interpretation

Cash is obtained by hard work and dedication, and with this comes better dividends in the future. This Pentacle is also classed as a social-climbing card, where new social groups can introduce the seeker to influential people, but they must be careful with money and take no chances. Instead, they would be best served by going steadily and building a security network around business and finance. The client must refrain from becoming a workaholic and get a balance of work and play. All work and no play makes Jack a dull boy. The urge to build things bigger and better will be apparent, but not at the family's expense. Cash isn't the be-all and end-all; everything must be done in moderation.

Associated Cards with Upright Four of Pentacles

* If the Four of Pentacles (upright) is mixed in with others from its suit and sits alongside the Justice card (upright), new financial growth spurts will herald a beneficial period. This can indicate business mergers and new innovations; an exciting and fertile time will be ahead.

* When the Hanged Man (upright) is present, financial situations will be at a stalemate for at least a year. This doesn't represent failure, though, just a time of slowing down, during which patience will be required.

* If this card shows itself in the reverse position next to a court mentor, someone is being miserly with money.

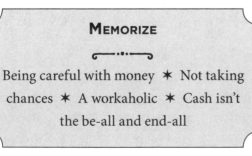

MEMORIZE

Being careful with money ✳ Not taking chances ✳ A workaholic ✳ Cash isn't the be-all and end-all

Rider-Waite Interpretation

Money is slipping through the querent's fingers, and they no longer have control over their finances. It's time to reevaluate their cash flow. Someone around them isn't paying their way, and they could be holding on to their own money while spending someone else's.

The client is feeling unprotected and may detach from those closest to them. The world seems manic and out of control, so they feel safer retreating and being on their own.

More modern interpretations sometimes refer to this as the "miser" card.

Money will be the person's god, and the need to make extra will consume their every thought. It doesn't matter how much is in the kitty, it won't suffice—the brain will want more!

Selfishness, jealousy, and envy play their part, too, because the querent might want what others have got. Sharing their riches with friends or family will be out of the question.

> **MEMORIZE**
>
> ⌐—·••·—⌐
>
> The miser card ✳ Not sharing money with others ✳ Being mean and selfish ✳ Always wanting more ✳ Feeling unprotected

One World Interpretation

I am rich, but you are poor. Don't come knocking on my door.

KEYWORD: *miser*

Rider-Waite Tarot   *One World Tarot*

Five of Pentacles

Care and concern for the sick. Look at your cash and fix it quick.

CARD NUMBER: 69 **KEYWORD:** poverty

Rider-Waite Interpretation

The image shows a lame man next to an impoverished woman. They are out in the cold and appear to have hit rock bottom. All fives in Tarot are troublesome, and this one is no different. Poverty could suddenly be forced onto an unsuspecting person or family member, causing their fortunes to take a tumble. The financial situation around them has not been handled well, heads have been buried in the sand, and there is no magic wand to put it right. Will the house be lost, or the business fall into ruination? There seems to be little optimism for the future.

One World Interpretation

There is a real need to watch someone's health, and elderly family members might require assistance and hospital care. There may be a discussion about admitting an older person into a nursing home or palliative care. This Pentacle can also represent death and funerals. You will need to look at surrounding cards to establish whether the situation has some hope.

During a time of poverty, no amount of penny-pinching or balancing the books seems to work. All is lost, with no bright horizon ahead. The ego will be at rock bottom, and blame could be placed on others' shoulders because of the mess, which is like a tangled ball of string. The client could also have a terrible fear of being homeless.

Associated Cards with Upright Five of Pentacles

* If the Five of Pentacles (upright) has the Star (upright) and the Wheel of Fortune (upright) nearby, miracles can happen and quickly. In the eleventh hour, the hand of fate comes in like a guardian angel to save the day.
* When the Strength card (upright) appears, karma has tested the person to see how strong they can be.
* The Five of Pentacles (reversed) around the Tower (upright) means that someone in the family might be diagnosed with dementia, or someone might feel so low that they contemplate suicide.
* If the card appears next to the Ace of Pentacles (upright), eventually, their finances will come good again.

MEMORIZE

The elderly falling sick * Nursing homes * Poverty and financial hardship * Funerals

Rider-Waite Interpretation

After a time of great difficulty, the storm dies down, and the sun begins to shine. At last, things are starting to look up. Cash could be given to the client to pay the bills, and a new business or job will be on the horizon. Faith will gradually return, and optimism will flicker into the soul. A new day is dawning, and there can be happiness once more. It's a time to trust others, so let the sadness of the past fade away, and look ahead to a bright future.

Life is finally getting better, and there's a light at the end of the tunnel. After a time of hardship, fresh ways to make money suddenly materialize; perhaps a new job or a gift of cash. Debts and credit cards will be paid off, health matters will improve, and any medical results will shine out positively. The client will start to cheer up and find themselves able to laugh again. The lessons they have endured over the recent months have been necessary for their spiritual development and their karma.

> **MEMORIZE**
>
> ┍━━•··•━━┑
>
> Karma ✳ Things are starting to look up ✳ Cash is given to the client ✳ Happiness for the future ✳ Health matters improving

One World Interpretation

Lift your chin and you will see just how happy you can be.

KEYWORD: *optimism*

Rider-Waite Tarot　　　*One World Tarot*

Six of Pentacles

Someone soon will make a gift. This will give your heart a lift.

CARD NUMBER: 70　**KEYWORD:** gifts

Rider-Waite Interpretation

A man stands with a set of scales in one hand and is seen giving cash to the unfortunate people at his feet. He is weighing his finances and balancing the books. This is a beneficial card showing that the client will easily pay their bills. The man is being generous with his money, lavishing gifts to bring joy to others' lives. Unexpected presents can be given either by friends or by a legacy. These offerings will come at precisely the right time, and it will seem like the universe is sending them a blessing.

One World Interpretation

Hard work pays off, and the fruits of one's labor will start to pay dividends. At last, a move forward, where new doors will open. Within business, it might be a good idea to expand or move to a bigger venue. A new phase has begun and should be around for a year or so. Make hay while the sun shines. Karma might expect the client to share some of their money with close family members or someone in need. A helping hand or recommendation will boost profits and bring in new clients if the querent is in business.

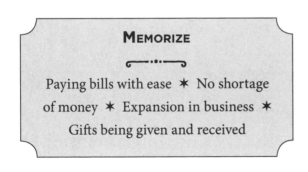

MEMORIZE

◚ · ∙∙ · ◚

Paying bills with ease ✳ No shortage of money ✳ Expansion in business ✳ Gifts being given and received

Associated Cards with Upright Six of Pentacles

* If this card is in the vicinity of the Sun (upright), a fantastic stroke of luck is on its way.
* If the Six of Pentacles is placed next to

the Empress (upright), business matters will blossom, and there will be thoughts of opening a different branch.

* If the Ten of Cups (upright) appears, a wedding will be on the agenda, and a special gift will be given to the bride and groom to help them with their home or honeymoon.
* When the Six of Pentacles (reversed) is next to the Two of Pentacles (upright), the person could have money stolen from them.

Rider-Waite Interpretation

The client is generous with their money, but others are not reciprocating, and the client is in danger of being used or taken for granted. While it's generous and kind to give, the person must not be mistreated, and the client will need a change of approach. This is not a time to take on extra debt; it would be wiser to protect the money they have and squirrel it away for a rainy day. For those in relationships, a partner might be spending money unwisely or even frittering it away; this results in the couple quarreling over finances.

One World Interpretation

Deceit and robbery are around. What is taken can't be found.

KEYWORDS: *change passwords*

Someone will ask the client to lend them some money, knowing full well they cannot pay it back. Warn them against being overly generous.

Caution is needed as a financial loss could arise through human error or ex-travagance. Take note of bill receipts and credit card fraud, and change all internet passwords, as scammers might empty the bank account. Check bank statements and don't leave any property unattended; even a coat could be stolen from a bar or café. If the person has filed for divorce, the chattels will be split down the middle. This could apply when a home is for sale or the client downsizes their house.

MEMORIZE

Internet scammers—change passwords ✳ Financial loss through human error ✳ Don't lend money, you won't get it back ✳ Theft ✳ Others taking advantage ✳ Partners frittering money away

Rider-Waite Tarot

One World Tarot

Seven of Pentacles

So much work, but little gain. Your back will hurt; feel the pain.

CARD NUMBER: 71 **KEYWORD:** development

Rider-Waite Interpretation

A farmer waits in his field to gather his crops. He has toiled wearily and is now ready to reap the rewards. The Seven of Pentacles is a card of hard work, but with no immediate payment in sight. Although the graft has been put in, a waiting period will now be set in place. Have the seeds sown, germinated, or failed? Only time will tell. It is essential to have hope and not allow oneself to be negative. The client must try hard not to take loans from others; these will end up as additional millstones around their neck. Instead, encourage them to keep striving because the fruits of their labors will eventually come to fruition.

One World Interpretation

Money worries cause a lot of pressure in the household. The client endlessly slogs to make ends meet, but still there is never enough. Much time will be spent trying to work things out within the family unit. Increased responsibility and unpaid work will be necessary all the same. Despite the financial troubles, they will have enough to manage; they just can't see it yet. Warn the querent against taking out loans or credit cards; this will leave them short of funds later. Children suddenly become disrespectful or difficult to handle, so a firm approach is needed to nip things in the bud.

MEMORIZE

⌐ — ••• — ⌐

Money worries ✳ Finances will be okay in time ✳ Naughty children need a firm hand ✳ Don't take out loans

---

Associated Cards with Upright Seven of Pentacles

✳ If the Seven of Pentacles is next to a Page (upright or reverse), there could be disagreements about children, but a way must be found to bring harmony to the home.

✳ When the Two of Pentacles (upright) is nearby, it indicates juggling money to make ends meet. Time to consolidate loans and get on top of the finances.

✳ If the Hermit appears (upright), all will be well; just be patient and keep the faith because a new phase is about to start.

✳ When the Seven of Pentacles appears next to the Three of Pentacles (upright), a self-employed venture is taking time to get off the ground.

✳ If the Six of Pentacles (reversed) is next to the Tower (upright), the client will become extremely depressed and will worry about money.

Rider-Waite Interpretation

The querent will spend a great deal of time and money on something that just isn't producing rewards. They must reevaluate this project and decide whether it's worth it. They will also be wasting much time at work, doing mundane chores instead of dealing with what matters. For those in relationships, much time and dedication have been spent on their partner, but they could have an inner fear of losing them. The relationship isn't turning out as they thought it would, and no progress has been made.

The reverse is very similar to the upright meanings, but despondency becomes overwhelming when there seems to be no end in sight. The client is pressed with financial obligations coming from all directions. Any monies due are delayed so that they will be chasing payments. Money will improve over the coming months, so all will be well in the end. Taking care of any health problems that stress may have caused is essential. Ensure the diet is balanced, and don't skip meals because of a loss of appetite.

MEMORIZE
⌐—·••·—⌐

Depressed over money worries ✳ Chasing payments ✳ Finances will improve ✳ Stress-related health issues ✳ Eat properly, and don't skip meals ✳ Relationships are not turning out as they hoped

One World Interpretation

Don't give in, keep plodding on. Soon your worries will be gone.

KEYWORD: *improvement*

Rider-Waite Tarot　　　　*One World Tarot*

Eight of Pentacles

Learn your trade and gain your skills. This in time will pay the bills.

CARD NUMBER: 72 **KEYWORD:** training

Rider-Waite Interpretation

A young man sits patiently, carving out the Pentacle shape on a coin; this represents making one's own money. In the distance is a town, but he prefers to be on his own, away from the hustle and bustle, so that he can focus intently on his project. This card of opportunity and new beginnings is also known as an apprenticeship card. New projects will need careful consideration. Get ready for a brand-new start, as it could be a life changer and a way to make lots of money in the future. An offer of work or study might come out of the blue, and it will seem as if fate has arranged it. Grab it with both hands, as it will be a gift. The number eight is a destiny card linked with one's karma.

One World Interpretation

As the Eight of Pentacles is an industrious card, expect some action. The client or someone close to them might embark on a training course, from mechanics to doctoring. It might also represent a training course for work, which will enhance their résumé. Perhaps thoughts of self-employment need to be put under scrutiny to begin a brand-new way of life. Out with the old and in with the new! Things are about to change positively for the client. There could even be a small grant given to help solve a financial hiccup.

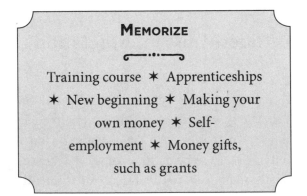

MEMORIZE

Training course ✳ Apprenticeships ✳ New beginning ✳ Making your own money ✳ Self-employment ✳ Money gifts, such as grants

Associated Cards with Upright Eight of Pentacles

✳ A young man will think of his new career if this card is near a Knight (upright or reverse).

✳ With this card around the World (upright), the client may be considering working abroad.

✳ If the Justice card (upright) is with the Six of Pentacles (upright), a legacy will come to help a new enterprise or business.

✳ When the Lovers (upright) are in the spread, choices will have to be made when one of them has a work opportunity in a different district.

✳ If the Eight of Pentacles appears around any Page (upright or reverse), the youngster will be taking exams or seeking qualifications.

✳ If this card appears next to the Chariot (upright), someone will be taking their driving test.

Rider-Waite Interpretation

The client will be focused entirely on themselves, and with hard work and dedication, they hope to improve their life. They are grateful for all they have, even if things are not always positive around them, and remain thankful for their blessings. The person must be careful not to be obsessed with making everything perfect. If they are too nit-picky, they might miss what is really important. Any projects or new ventures will take time before they come to fruition, which might frustrate the client, but things will work out well later on.

One World Interpretation

Money comes in later life, after trouble, toil, and strife.

KEYWORDS: *failed exams*

Anyone around the client who is taking exams might sadly fail and have to re-sit them. They need to study harder and not leave anything to chance.

The client is working hard but is frustrated in their job and could feel like throwing in the towel. A stubborn boss who refuses to have a fresh approach annoys them, so they feel at a loss to perform their tasks properly. Because of this, the querent will seek something else, which in the end could work out very well; it's just taking that leap of faith and having the courage to change one's life. It will all be worth it in the end.

> **MEMORIZE**
> ⌐—··—⌐
> Failing exams ✳ More study needed ✳ In the wrong job ✳ Change your life ✳ A draconian boss

Rider-Waite Tarot   One World Tarot

Nine of Pentacles

You have it all, safe and sound. What is good you have found.

CARD NUMBER: 73 **KEYWORDS:** good times

Rider-Waite Interpretation

A striking female stands in all her glory, surrounded by coins, revealing her wealth. Her world is one of exotic travel and exhilaration. At last, a new time has come to enjoy the pleasures of life. Money will be stable, and extra cash can provide for some luxury. Appreciating Mother Earth and nature, the seeker is beckoned to explore new countries and widen their knowledge. They might also take a new interest in gardening or desire to grow their own vegetables and fruit.

One World Interpretation

Unexpected cash is on the way, and it may allow the client to pay off existing loans or perhaps even the mortgage. This card represents a time of abundance and freedom without any money worries. Look back and be pleased with the progress that has been achieved. The client will focus on their home, buying new furniture or changing the décor. There will still be time and money left for travel, and a trip overseas will take place within a year. Don't feel guilty about splashing the cash; it's been hard-earned, and, after all, money is just an energy.

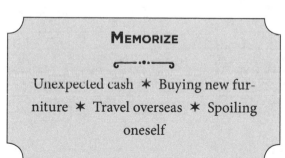

MEMORIZE

Unexpected cash ✳ Buying new furniture ✳ Travel overseas ✳ Spoiling oneself

Associated Cards with Upright Nine of Pentacles

✳ If the Ace of Pentacles (upright) sits directly next to the Nine of Pentacles (upright), a huge lump sum will arrive

and flood the bank account. If the Ace of Cups (upright) is also in the same spread, this could indicate a lottery win.

✳ The Nine of Pentacles (upright) can represent foreign travel; if it is next to the World (upright), a different continent will be visited; water or beautiful scenery will lift the soul to make it a memorable time.

✳ If the Ace of Wands (upright) is nearby, a lucrative deal could be on the agenda to bring in even more money.

✳ When this card is shadowed by the Five or Seven of Swords (reversed), take care with shady investments or potential fraudsters.

Rider-Waite Interpretation

Those who run their own business may not charge enough for their products or services. This card is about self-worth, so perhaps the client must implement some changes to feel better about themselves. They could be so preoccupied with working and making money that they fail to have time to enjoy or spend their wealth. A balance of work and play must be in harmony if the client is to be happy.

One World Interpretation

It all looked good, but now it's a mess. Stop and think about what's for the best.

KEYWORD: *collapse*

When the Nine of Pentacles is in reverse, this could be a cause for concern. All that has been built up could suddenly collapse, perhaps because of unwise investments. If there were to be a sudden stock market crash or canceled orders, the client's business might be liquidated.

Alternatively, the client may have all they need financially but have no love or tenderness in their life.

MEMORIZE

Unwise investments ✳ Businesses going into liquidation ✳ Money is good, but no love ✳ Not making time for pleasure

Rider-Waite Tarot

TEN OF PENTACLES

One World Tarot

Ten of Pentacles

Prosperity is on its way, bringing travel, luck, and better pay.

CARD NUMBER: 74 **KEYWORD:** security

Rider-Waite Interpretation

TEN OF PENTACLES

An affluent couple is displayed on this card, along with a gray-haired man; he is the patriarch of his family and has toiled most of his life to bring financial security to his kinfolk. Pentacles surround the group of people; this idyllic setting symbolizes their wealth and financial security.

Generally, the Ten of Pentacles is a prosperous card. It will be closely connected to the family in a caring and supportive way and will also provide security for the children.

A loving couple could be in a marriage or living together, and although they are financially secure now, they have both independently struggled over the years to get where they are today. Their relationship is so strong that nothing should affect them. This card will often represent a successful family business without any interference from outside influences that otherwise could put a wrench in the works. With this card will come sound investments, good insurance plans, and private schooling for the children and grandchildren.

One World Interpretation

The Ten of Pentacles can be associated with unearned money, so property, inheritance, and businesses might have been handed down through each generation. Stocks and shares will bring in additional benefits, along with property and land investments. This card has a solid religious theme, so everything will have to be done fairly to ensure one's karma is on track. The Ten of Pentacles brings security because everything has been thought out carefully, and so financial abundance and family harmony will be enjoyed for many years.

Associated Cards with Upright Ten of Pentacles

✷ If this card comes in with the Two of Swords (upright), the couple is unlikely to split as they have a firm foundation to their relationship.

✷ The Ten of Pentacles (upright) has tight-knit family values, and if you see Pages, Knights, Kings, or Queens around (all upright or reversed), it will represent a gathering.

✷ If the Nine of Swords (upright or reversed) makes an appearance, a funeral could take place, and if the Justice card (upright) is present as well, an inheritance or gift will be given. If the Five of Swords (upright or reversed) is nearby, someone could question the will and cause a delay.

✷ With a young Knight (upright) in the spread, an apprenticeship will be offered with a cash dividend to help him on his way.

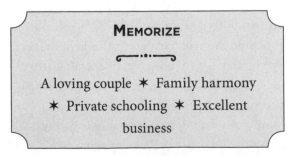

MEMORIZE

A loving couple ✷ Family harmony ✷ Private schooling ✷ Excellent business

Rider-Waite Interpretation

The client may feel trapped with their wealth and want to try to live their life another way. Money and security will be in question, and what was once taken for granted now needs attention because of lack of foresight in the past. A relationship or marriage could struggle, and one party might feel like walking away. The person discovers their job is on the line and will be worried as a result. With money not flowing freely, they must take every care to tighten the purse strings.

The client might have problems with their pension or insurance.

Traditions come under the microscope, and the younger family members will want a more modern approach; friction could rip through the household, splitting it in two. Religious values will also be under pressure as others question their beliefs and ideas. Taxes may be too high and leave the kitty very low, but the family still tries to keep up with the Joneses. Foolishly, the spending continues as they refuse to see the red flags that are up ahead.

> **MEMORIZE**
>
> ⌐—··—⌐
>
> Problems with pensions or insurance ✳ Young family members causing friction ✳ Taxes are too high ✳ Keeping up with the Joneses ✳ Foolish spending

One World Interpretation

The cash has gone to who knows where. Take stock now, the cupboards are bare.

KEYWORD: *friction*

The Court Mentors: Pentacles

King of Pentacles, Queen of Pentacles,
Knight of Pentacles, Page of Pentacles

EARTH SIGNS: Capricorn, Taurus, and Virgo

CAREERS FOR CAPRICORN EARTH SIGN: building structures, architecture, antiques, security, banking, nursing, childcare, law, finance, medicine, factory work, forklift driving, truck driving, investments

CAREERS FOR TAURUS EARTH SIGN: singing, music, gardening and agriculture, interior design, house renovating, self-employment, herbalism, working with animals, sales, entertainment, retail, catering, baking

CAREERS FOR VIRGO EARTH SIGN: office work, banking, hospital or healthcare work, clothes styling, accounting, agenting, publicity, event planning, managing, data analysis

Rider-Waite Tarot   One World Tarot

Page of Pentacles

This Page will study to reach their goal. Kind-hearted child, a gentle soul.

CARD NUMBER: 74 **KEYWORD:** intelligent
Child, boy or girl, aged birth–16

Rider-Waite Interpretation

Traditionally, this card can represent a male or female earth sign child up to sixteen years of age. The image in this deck shows a young person standing in a field of flowers, gazing at a coin in their hand. The mountain behind depicts that later on in life, obstacles could be ahead. The child is sweet-natured and studious, and they will be thinking of their future and exploring which avenue will be the best for them. This Page will apply themselves in school and will usually be a straight-A student.

One World Interpretation

The earth signs are known to love food and for being creative in the kitchen, but large appetites can mean a bigger waistline. The Page of Pentacles might have to be careful with their diet and portion control.

This youngster will like to study or research topics and be easygoing and helpful. They often exhibit musical skill or love drama, acting, singing, and dancing. As they are measured, they will grow up to be entrepreneurs and might even have their own businesses. If they work for others, they will earn a position of responsibility. At school they will do well with their studies, but they are inclined to daydream and have trouble concentrating. Later, this child will have no problem getting into the university of their choice and will go on to have a dazzling career.

Other Meanings

The Page of Pentacles represents good news, usually within the family unit. This stretch of luck may affect people's lives, particularly if they had previously faced insurmountable difficulties. Someone will offer sound advice that could help solve an ongoing problem, bringing a fresh new start. Friends or family might be considering moving house; this should bring about a good outcome.

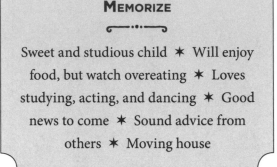

MEMORIZE

Sweet and studious child ✳ Will enjoy food, but watch overeating ✳ Loves studying, acting, and dancing ✳ Good news to come ✳ Sound advice from others ✳ Moving house

Associated Cards with Upright Page of Pentacles

✳ If the Empress (upright) is in front of the Page of Pentacles (upright or reverse), this will often signify the birth of an earth sign child (Taurus, Virgo, or Capricorn). As the Pentacle child represents good news, this might be a long-awaited pregnancy that will bring joy to the family.

✳ If the Page is reversed with the Five of Swords (upright) or Three of Swords (upright), an abortion or miscarriage could bring sadness.

✳ When this Pentacle child has the Chariot (upright) or the World (upright) in place, a wonderful journey will soon be on the horizon.

✳ If the card appears around the Eight or Nine of Pentacles (upright), the youngster is destined for university, and the parents will have to support the youth financially for up to five years.

Reversed Meaning

Dreamy child, out of place. Once all grown, they'll win the race.

KEYWORD: *gawky*

When the Page of Pentacles is reversed, this can show an unhappy and muddled child. They will find it difficult to make friends, especially at school, where they might be tongue-tied or gawky. If the youngster has siblings, they will often feel different or left out in the family, so creative parenting skills must be implemented to help the situation along. A bigger problem for this Page can be laziness or a daydreamy nature, so when trying to focus or study, they will face tremendous obstacles. Signets transform into swans when they get older and will flourish in later years to become very successful.

> ### MEMORIZE
> ⌐─··─⌐
>
> Daydreamy or lazy ✳ Feels gawky or different ✳ Needs careful parenting ✳ Will flourish later

Rider-Waite Tarot   One World Tarot

Knight of Pentacles

Striving ahead, a knight so fine. Caring and loyal, patient and kind.

CARD NUMBER: 76 **KEYWORDS:** gentle and kind
Young man, aged 16–29

Rider-Waite Interpretation

The Knight of Pentacles sits astride his horse, inspecting the gold coin in his hand. He is taking time to assess his future and choose the right path. This earth sign Knight has a lot going for him as he intends to strive ahead and achieve his goals. His focus is especially on money, work, and property. He has great patience, so he'll wait for suitable openings and plod on until his goals are met. As he doesn't give in, he must be careful not to neglect his relationships in pursuit of financial gain. He will be loyal to his friends, family, and wife later, and he will accrue property, status, and respect as he matures, but sometimes he will be a little dull as he thinks only of work and business.

One World Interpretation

When this Knight is young, he is shy around women. Once he catches up, he will enjoy flirtations and sex. He's destined for university and will choose a challenging career that might take many years to train for. He will love food and show off his culinary skills to impress others. As he becomes immersed in the business world, he will leave behind his hobbies and other such things because he aims to climb the ladder of success. Yes, he will be competitive, but not at the price of someone else's demise, as integrity and genuine kindness are in his heart. As he has a love of animals, he would make a great vet and, in the process, build up a thriving business.

> ### MEMORIZE
> ⸺ •••⸺
>
> University type ✳ Enjoys sex and flirting ✳ Love of food and animals ✳ Climbing the ladder to success ✳ Patient and loyal

Other Meanings

The client's financial situation will improve, but they still need to be cautious not to overspend. "Spend a little, save a little" is a fitting motto. A vacation will be planned, and the person will find themselves flying to an exotic country.

Associated Cards with Upright Knight of Pentacles

✳ When the Emperor (upright) is next to the Knight of Pentacles (upright), there could be a big business deal up ahead. He might be asked to spearhead or manage a large corporation.

✳ If the Seven of Wands (upright) is nearby, caution will be needed as fierce competition from other companies could bring acrimony.

✳ If other Knights (upright or reversed) are placed around him, he will be working in a male environment in an elevated position. His management skills will have to be slick and controlled.

Reversed Meaning

Careless with cash and not too bright, his future is ruined with a lack of foresight.

KEYWORD: *entitled*

If the Knight of Pentacles is reversed, he will find it difficult to hold down a job. He is arrogant and entitled, thinking only of himself, so his parents will be at their wit's end. This Knight will go through his twenties not wanting to work; instead, he'll be content feeding off his family and not contributing financially. Any career he has will come crashing down around him because of laziness and apathy.

If left to his own devices, his funds will be depleted as he faces the road to ruin. Debts will start to stack up, and banks could confiscate credit cards. Romantically, he's too selfish to be in any deep or meaningful relationship and will probably not treat his partner very well. He isn't abusive, more neglectful, only concentrating on matters that involve himself.

MEMORIZE

Arrogant, lazy, and entitled ✳ Won't hold down a job ✳ Parents at their wit's end ✳ Stacking up debts

Rider-Waite Tarot

One World Tarot

Queen of Pentacles

This earth sign Queen is good as gold. She makes her money till she's old.

CARD NUMBER: 77 **KEYWORD:** sophistication
Woman, aged 16 onward

Rider-Waite Interpretation

The Queen of Pentacles sits upon her throne, surrounded by symbols of success. Her striking clothes symbolize her beauty, inside and out. She has very refined tastes, and as luxury is on her list, she will undoubtedly love her creature comforts. She will adorn her home with opulent furniture, perhaps antiques, and serve fine cuisine and wines while entertaining.

Being a history lover, she will collect artifacts and enjoy learning every detail of her past. When in society, she will be eloquent, erudite, and up to date with what's happening in the world.

One World Interpretation

This Queen is not frightened of hard work and will be pretty comfortable wheeling and dealing in the business world. She'll enjoy making her own money and won't be beholden to any man. Her heart is kind, and she'll have many friends, always making time for them. This Queen hates poverty, so perhaps she has experienced hardship in her past. As a mother, she will be strict but fair and will encourage her children to study and be proactive in their hobbies. As a wife, she can be loving but occasionally bossy. Being an avid animal lover, she will have a keen interest in green issues and will strive to protect her environment.

MEMORIZE

Works hard and makes her own money ✳ Hates poverty ✳ Enjoys business deals ✳ A good wife and friend ✳ Interested in green issues

---

Other Meanings

The client will strive to balance their home life with their work schedule. Security is essential, and so they may feel torn between the two. It's a time for the seeker to look inward and concentrate on their nurturing side.

Associated Cards with Upright Queen of Pentacles

* If the Queen of Pentacles is next to the Hermit (upright), it shows she is spiritually protected and could be given information about her life in dream sleep.
* She is intuitive and a lover of animals, so she often gives money to charities. This is the case if the Strength (upright) card is nearby.
* If the Lovers (upright) card appears, she will have to make a choice of either her love life or her career; usually, she will choose well because she is wise.
* When the Queen of Pentacles (reversed) is next to the Tower (upright), she will cause a tremendous rift in the family.

Reversed Meaning

Do not cross her, that's the truth. She won't forget, she has no ruth.

KEYWORD: *unpredictable*

The Queen of Pentacles is a very different character when she is positioned in reverse, acting selfishly and falling into unpredictable moods. If her finances are at rock bottom, she will be looking for a rich husband to ensure that money and luxury will always be in place. As she is a social climber, she will carefully select friends that can introduce her to affluent people; once their help is given, this Queen will drop them to move on to the next. In modern-day terms, you would describe her as a gold digger, marrying for money and not for love.

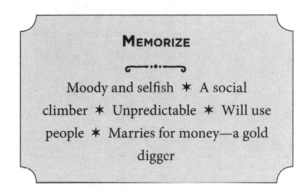

MEMORIZE

Moody and selfish ✳ A social climber ✳ Unpredictable ✳ Will use people ✳ Marries for money—a gold digger

Rider-Waite Tarot

KING OF PENTACLES

One World Tarot

King of Pentacles

This earth sign man has stacks of money. Treat him well, feed him honey.

CARD NUMBER: 78 **KEYWORD:** responsibility

Man, aged 29 onward

KING OF PENTACLES

Rider-Waite Interpretation

He sits upon his throne, surrounded by wealth that represents his authority. Around him, carved into the throne, are images of bulls that might signify the King's birth sign as Taurus. He is usually a wealthy man with cash squirreled away in different bank accounts; he'll have investments abroad and will love to wheel and deal. He will stand by his decisions and double-check everything. As this King is shrewd, nothing will get past him; he's learned from his mistakes in the past.

One World Interpretation

The King of Pentacles is good-looking and not short of money. He might have worked hard to earn his wealth, or he may have inherited it from his family. He is high up in his field of employment; he may be a banker, vet, stockbroker, doctor, or high-ranking manager. In his life, he will have multiple irons in the fire, so he may accrue several small successful businesses and larger ones possibly spread around the globe. He is very traditional and likes houses with character and history. Perhaps he might renovate an old rectory or manor house where he will wine and dine those who are of the same social standing. This King is passionate about love, and once he has the right partner, he's usually loyal and will be a good friend and lover.

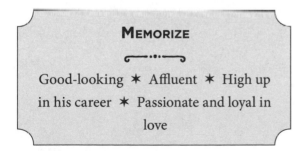

MEMORIZE

Good-looking ✳ Affluent ✳ High up in his career ✳ Passionate and loyal in love

Other Meanings

The client will go through a time when they are organizing their finances. Everything in the bank is in order, and some monies are left over for luxuries. Any projects the client has been working on will soon come to an end. They have achieved a lot in a short space of time.

Associated Cards with Upright King of Pentacles

✳ If the King of Pentacles (upright) is next to the Wheel of Fortune (upright), a legacy or a windfall could be on its way.

✳ When placed next to the Tower (reverse), a huge amount of money could be lost through others' bankruptcy or illegal dealings.

✳ If the Hierophant (upright) is in the same spread, alongside the Ten of Cups (upright), family values and religion will be present, perhaps with a marriage or a christening to attend. If the World card (upright) is there as well, the celebration could be taken abroad.

Reversed Meaning

He loves his money and way of life. And wants a carer to be his wife.

KEYWORD: *nitpicky*

When this King is in reverse, we have a grumpy character who can be moody or morose. Others will find him tiresome and irritating as he will nitpick about everything. His wife will run around after him, acting as his chattel. He will have money but will tend to keep it to himself and secretly hide some of his fortunes to ensure his nest is always feathered. Ultimately, he will end up a lonely old man whom no one likes or wants to spend time with.

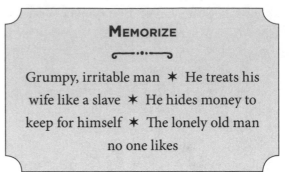

MEMORIZE

Grumpy, irritable man ✳ He treats his wife like a slave ✳ He hides money to keep for himself ✳ The lonely old man no one likes

5

Card Groupings & Techniques

This is probably the most essential part of the Tarot journey, so give it special attention. After studying and memorizing all seventy-eight cards, you will, in time, become familiar with their upright and reverse meanings. Don't worry if it seems a mammoth task; you'll get there in the end, as everyone must go at their own pace.

Some people who are new to Tarot will read each card individually without merging them with other cards close by. When the Tarot is read this way, the forecast will likely be disjointed, and the client might not be able to relate to the reading. Also, one reading will be very much like another. A preferred way to get clarity for a better-detailed prediction would be to group the cards together and then blend them into one another; this should go on to demonstrate a unique situation for each client.

CASE STUDY: BELETA
How It Can All Go Badly Wrong

Many years ago, when I was teaching Tarot to a group of students, one particular woman, albeit psychically gifted, always appeared to be over-confident. Later, after completing our Tarot and palmistry courses, she decided to pursue a career as a professional reader. All was well for a year or two, and then one day, I opened our weekend newspaper and there, splashed all over the front page, was a story about charlatan Tarot readers ripping off the public. I was shocked to see the woman involved was my ex-student! She had visited a party of six female clients in their home and gave them all exactly the same reading. Later, they got together and played their recordings back to each other. They were all furious and felt duped out of their money, so they contacted the tabloid press. The woman had obviously ignored the part of the lesson where she was taught to blend the cards and instead read each one individually. She was mortified by the publicity and subsequently immigrated to another country.

Expect to put in a lot of effort if you want to become an expert at card groupings; it won't happen overnight. Seeing all ten cards in front of you at once can be daunting, but your readings will have more perception when you get the hang of it. Here, we can find all kinds of details that will hopefully amaze your client. No two people's lives are the same, so no two readings should be the same. Of course, we humans tend to have similar problems in our day-to-day lives, and your predictions will likely be centered around work, love, family, health, etc. Delivering the fine details in a reading will not only elevate your psychic skills but also impress your client.

So How Do We Go About Grouping the Cards?

One of the reasons we added the "Memorize" sections shown in every card description in this book is because these short reminders help connect one card to another immediately. It's handy to learn these for accuracy.

Let's start with a simple example. We know that one of the meanings of the Empress card can signify a pregnancy, but if you look at the surrounding cards, you might be able to see who the pregnancy is for and whether everything will go according to plan.

EXAMPLE : *Empress (upright), Ace of Cups (upright), Queen of Pentacles (upright)*

Here, you can see that the Queen of Pentacles is likely to be pregnant, and the Ace of Cups depicts a joyful occasion where everything goes according to plan. By twinning these cards together, we can see there is nothing scary here and all is well.

EXAMPLE: *Empress (upright), Nine of Swords (upright), Queen of Pentacles (upright)*

Here, we see the Queen of Pentacles is to become pregnant, but because the Nine of Swords points toward health concerns, there could be some complications. Blurting out a prediction like this will worry the client, so by examining nearby cards, you can ascertain whether the pregnancy will be okay; if not, it's wise to err on the side of caution and move the reading on by dealing some more cards.

EXAMPLE: *Empress (upright), Nine of Swords (upright), Queen of Pentacles (upright), Ace of Cups (upright)*

We know that when the Ace of Cups is in a spread, it trumps a negative card, so you can relay to the client that the pregnancy could be a little challenging—perhaps she might suffer with a few symptoms or have a period of morning sickness—but all in all, everything will be okay.

EXAMPLE: *Empress (upright), Nine of Swords (upright), Queen of Pentacles (upright), Ace of Cups (upright), Page of Cups (upright), King of Wands (upright)*

We've established that the Queen of Pentacles could suffer health concerns in her pregnancy, and with the Ace of Cups in the spread, we are sure that all will be well. With the Page in attendance, we know the pregnancy will go full-term and result in the birth of a beautiful baby. This child is gentle and won't be difficult to raise, they will love their family, and they will be popular and have lots of friends. Although they are not very academic and might sometimes struggle with school-work, their talents will lie in other directions, such as music, art, singing, and dancing. (By bringing in the personality of the child, we can see how the prediction is lengthened and how it provides a much more detailed account of the scenario.) The King of Wands (we know him as the nicest King of all) is likely to be the father. He will adore his child and play an active role in their life.

The client has much more information, and by adding a few extra cards, the reading can take on a completely different slant.

EXAMPLE: *Empress (upright), Nine of Swords (upright), Queen of Pentacles (upright), Ace of Cups (upright), Page of Cups (upright), King of Wands (reversed)*

Here we have the exact same set of cards, but instead of the King of Wands being in the upright position, we now see him in reverse.

Reverse Meaning for the King of Wands: *arrogant and unpopular; usually divorced; a disinterested, unloving father; lazy and verbally aggressive*

Here we can ascertain that the father of this child will more than likely be separated from the mother, so perhaps they've divorced, and he's a deadbeat dad because he's arrogant and unpopular and disinterested in his child.

EXAMPLE: *King of Pentacles (upright), Three of Pentacles (upright), Two of Wands (reversed)*

Let's say you are reading for a married woman. The King of Pentacles would likely be her husband. He could be self-employed or in business (Three of Pentacles), and has made firm plans for the future but seems blocked at every angle (Two of Wands, reversed).

These few cards only give us a snippet of information, so then we would deal some more cards from the top of the deck to see the outcome.

EXAMPLE: *King of Pentacles (upright), Three of Pentacles (upright), Two of Wands (reversed), Three of Wands (upright)*

The King of Pentacles is surrounded by obstacles at work and might benefit from receiving some more advice (Three of Wands). You can then bring in other meanings connected to the Two of Wands (reversed) and inform the client that situations could be tedious, but things will change for the better in time.

There are occasions when you have a selection of cards in front of you, and no court mentor will be present. When this happens, you might be at a loss to know who the predictions are directed toward. Before placing the other cards in their vicinity, a reader might choose a court mentor card to serve as the client's representative (we call this the "significator"). The majority of the time, any cards displayed in the spread will be directly related to the client or someone close to them, like a son, daughter, parent, or partner. Whether the court mentor card is present or not, you'll still have to use your psychic ability to determine who the prediction is for.

EXAMPLE: *Three of Swords (upright), Five of Pentacles (upright), Five of Cups (upright)*

We see an issue with a marriage, potentially resulting in a divorce. There could be arguments and upsets with the rejected spouse, and any children in the family could be left feeling confused (Three of Swords). This disturbance could impact the client's health, and as a result, illness might follow. The client's finances could be dire, and they'll be concerned about their financial security (Five of Pentacles and Five of Cups). One person in the marriage will be full of regret and want desperately to turn back the clock. They might use alcohol to blur the edges and end up in a very dark place.

EXAMPLE: *Three of Swords (upright), Five of Pentacles (upright), Five of Cups (upright), the Hermit (upright), the Moon (upright)*

The client is probably not receiving the whole picture as lies and deceit are present in the spread; perhaps their partner may be keeping something from them. They might have an inclination that something is suspicious, but they won't address it for fear of finding out the truth (the Moon). Even though the client is going through a tough time in their life, a male guide protects them spiritually and provides them with love and support. Clearly, this is a time for spiritual growth, and the person in this situation needs to learn something. Their actions are being spiritually monitored, so however hard it is to be civil, they must approach their issues in the correct way (the Hermit).

Grouping the Suits

The Tarot doesn't always spell things out as clearly as we have stated above, and you will often find the cards are jumbled and don't correlate. In this instance, you will need to separate those cards that make sense and then perhaps combine the remaining cards, which hopefully focus on a different topic. One good way of doing this is to start by grouping the suits together. We know that Wands represent work, so if there are two or more Wands in a spread, look at them and the surrounding cards to see if they fit.

EXAMPLE: *Three of Swords (upright), Five of Pentacles (upright), Five of Cups (upright), the Hermit (upright), the Moon (upright)*

GROUP 1: KING OF CUPS, FIVE OF WANDS, NINE OF WANDS, TWO OF PENTACLES

The King of Cups is having a bad time at work, and colleagues could be temperamental or up in arms about how things are being run (Five of Wands). The company may be under reconstruction, leaving everyone feeling confused about their future (Five of Wands). He could be overcome with anxiety or may not be feeling well, struggling with a stress-related illness (Nine of Wands). Perhaps a devious person at work is making things worse (Nine of Wands). The King is juggling his finances, robbing Peter to pay Paul, so maybe his wages are not enough to keep him afloat (Two of Pentacles).

GROUP 2: TWO OF CUPS, TEN OF PENTACLES, THE LOVERS

If he hasn't met her yet, the King will meet a wonderful partner with whom he shares much in common (Two of Cups). He does, however, need to make a choice about this new love. Does he take a chance or not? One thing is for sure; the relationship will be passionate (the Lovers). In the future, the King will be in a loving and committed relationship that is financially sound (Ten of Pentacles).

SPARE CARD: THE HERMIT

This King has a male guide in spirit who will oversee everything in his life. If he needs help from above, encourage him to connect with his protector. You might prefer using this card as a means of timing, foretelling the above to happen in or around Virgo time, August or September.

Other Interpretations

When you memorize the key points to each card, it's straightforward to jump to the first thing you remember, but learning additional facts about each one will make your readings much more interesting. Below is an example of one of the spreads we have just looked at, but this time, we use a different slant with the cards' other meanings.

EXAMPLE: *Three of Swords (upright), Five of Pentacles (upright), Five of Cups (upright)*

The client is worried about money and debt (Five of Pentacles); they often feel unhappy and tearful (Three of Swords). Because they see no end to their troubles, they drink too much and may have suicidal tendencies (Five of Cups).

EXAMPLE: *Three of Swords (upright), Five of Pentacles (upright), Five of Cups (upright)*

The client is unwell and may have to visit his doctor or perhaps have tests (Five of Pentacles). Because their health is getting them down, they feel hopeless (Three of Swords). This could be related to a drinking problem; maybe they're an alcoholic? Although there seems to be no way out of the predicament, all will be fine in the end (Five of Cups).

You may be confused about which interpretation you use, so just follow your instincts, and you should settle on the right one.

Test Yourself

In this section of the book, we will give you some random groupings to try out for yourself. The answers are below, so when you have finished, compare yours to ours. They don't have to be exactly right, but there should be some similarities.

EXERCISE 1: Page of Wands (upright), Four of Swords (upright), Nine of Cups (upright)

EXERCISE 2: The Lovers (upright), Three of Swords (upright), Two of Swords (upright)

EXERCISE 3: Queen of Cups (reversed), Seven of Swords (upright), Two of Swords (upright)

EXERCISE 4: King of Wands (reversed), the Devil (upright), the Tower (upright), Five of Cups (reversed)

EXERCISE 5: The Star (upright), Five of Pentacles (upright), Four of Swords (upright), Ace of Cups (upright)

EXERCISE 6: Death (upright), Ten of Swords (upright), Queen of Wands (upright), Sun (upright)

༆ ⸺ ••• ⸺ ༘

CARD GROUPINGS ANSWER SHEET

EXERCISE 1: Page of Wands (upright), Four of Swords (upright), Nine of Cups (upright)

ANSWER 1: *A child in the client's life (Page of Wands) will become unwell and must undergo a period of recovery (Four of Swords).*

All will be well in the end, and worries will disappear (Nine of Cups).

ANSWER 2: *A sweet-natured child around the client (Page of Wands) might need a spell in the hospital followed by lots of rest (Four of Swords). The client must not fret because all worries will soon disappear.*

EXERCISE 2: The Lovers (upright), Three of Swords (upright), Two of Swords (upright)

ANSWER 1: *The client or someone close to them will be embroiled in an affair (the Lovers and the Three of Swords together). They are already in a relationship so they will be committing adultery. The marriage may not withstand this affair and could end in divorce (Two of Swords).*

ANSWER 2: *The client is already in a relationship or married, but their life will turn upside down when their soul mate makes an appearance. There will be confused,* unhappy children who feel stuck in the middle of the mayhem. The karmic pull of the soul mate is so strong that the client may be unable to resist (the Lovers and the Three of Swords). The relationship or marriage is unlikely to last, and they will deal with legal matters (Two of Swords), perhaps resulting in a divorce.

EXERCISE 3: Queen of Cups (reversed), Seven of Swords (upright), Two of Swords (upright)

ANSWER 1: *An unfavorable woman is around the client. Beware of telling her any secrets as she is untrustworthy and will betray the seeker's trust (Queen of Cups, reversed). This female could also have criminal tendencies (Seven of Swords, upright), and so the client is advised to end this friendship immediately (Two of Swords, upright).*

ANSWER 2: *At work or in business, the client has a female boss who is disliked by all. She will ask the impossible and probably plagiarize her colleague's ideas and pass them off as her own (Queen of Cups, reversed). The client will feel like running away from the job (Seven of Swords, upright) and will finally leave (Two of Swords, upright).*

EXERCISE 4: King of Wands (reversed), the Devil (upright), the Tower (upright), Five of Cups (reversed)

ANSWER 1: *The client is around an arrogant and abusive man who is generally unpopular (King of Wands, reversed). He may* become physically violent and have bizarre sexual fetishes, or he may be addicted to pornography (the Devil, upright). Things will come to a sinister head, and the client could be in a dangerous position; they will need to exit as soon as possible (the Tower, upright). The client might be drowning their sorrows due to the drama and be under great stress (Five of Cups, upright).

ANSWER 2: *The client is around a man who could be suffering from mental health issues or depression (the Devil, upright); perhaps he has been made redundant from a long-standing job (the Tower, upright). He is lazy around the house, unloving toward his family (King of Wands, reversed), and may even have a problem with alcohol or drugs (Five of Cups, reversed).*

EXERCISE 5: The Star (upright), Five of Pentacles (upright), Four of Swords (upright), Ace of Cups (upright)

ANSWER 1: *The client, or someone who is elderly and close to them, will go through a period of ill health (Five of Pentacles, upright) and need to take some time to heal (Four of Swords, upright). This situation might impact their finances (Five of Pentacles, upright). The client mustn't worry because spiritual protection is around the patient (the Star, upright), and a healing time will begin (Four of Swords, upright, again). The outcome is positive, and everything will be alright in the end (Ace of Cups, upright).*

ANSWER 2: *The client's finances are at rock bottom, and they will be penny-pinching and trying to balance the books (Five of Pentacles, upright). The worry over money could make them ill (Four of Swords, upright). Although this is challenging, help from the client's female guide will bring a more positive future (the Star). In the end, the cards foretell a happy outcome, and the client might even get an invitation to a wedding or engagement (Ace of Cups, upright).*

EXERCISE 6: Death (upright), Ten of Swords (upright), Queen of Wands (upright), the Sun (upright)

ANSWER 1: *In a set of cards like this, there is only one answer, and that is because the Death card has appeared with the Ten of Swords. The client will hear news of a death and have to arrange a funeral or attend one (Death, upright, Ten of Swords, upright). The deceased is likely to be a female (Queen of Wands, upright). There are no cards of sadness in the spread, only the Sun, which cancels out all negativity and suggests that the client will not be grieving but supporting others.*

6

Spreads

Dealing the Cards and Spreads

There are many ways to shuffle and lay out the cards into spreads, and over time, you will find one that you feel comfortable with and will probably use all the time. However, you might prefer to learn a few different ways and mix them up.

Below, we have included a few of the most popular spreads for you to try, but before you set about learning these, there are a few basics to follow.

Shuffling and Choosing

When you begin the reading, ask the client to take the pack of Tarot and shuffle the cards for around four to five minutes. Most decks are larger than the average playing cards, so it may take them a little while to get used

to handling them. Don't be surprised if the client struggles a bit, as stray cards will most definitely slip out of the pack, and some will even land on the floor. It is always an excellent way to break the ice.

Place the stack face down on the table in front of the client and ask them to cut the cards into three piles with their left hand. We favor the left hand because it is nearest to the heart. The client must now concentrate on the three stacks and choose two piles they feel most drawn to. If the client can't decide, ask them to hover their left hand over each pile and concentrate on any sensations the cards might give off. Sometimes, if it's the correct pile, the energy emanating from the cards can feel cold or warm, or their hand might tingle slightly. Once the client has chosen two stacks, place the first on top of the second and set aside the discarded pile. These are the cards you will use throughout the reading.

Recent past   *Present*   *Future*

The three-card spread above can be used in one of two ways.

* Card 1: the recent past
* Card 2: the present
* Card 3: the imminent future

Of course, it's highly unlikely that you will get all the information you need with only one card to represent each period in the client's life, so you would have to deal on to each card to see a clearer picture emerging.

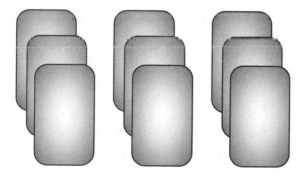

You may decide not to use the past, present, and future time frame at all, instead just focusing on the future. In this instance, you can group the cards as a whole or read them horizontally or vertically.

THREE, THREE, THREE, ONE SPREAD

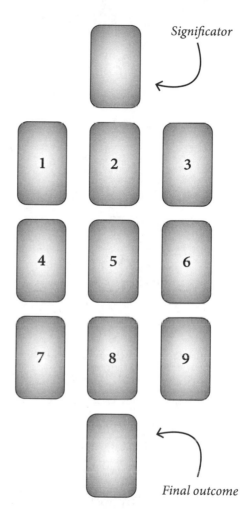

Significator

Final outcome

With this spread, you would begin reading the cards in order, interpreting cards 1, 2, and 3 as a group. Repeat with the second row and see if any relevant information pertains to the first row. If not, the second row would be read separately as a new group. Next, read cards 7, 8, and 9 in the same way. The last card, number 10, will foretell the outcome.

THE FIVE-CARD CROSS

THE HORSESHOE SPREAD

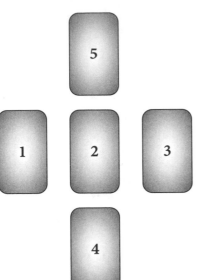

This spread works for any future forecasts you might like to make. You will note there is no significator here. If you like to use a significating card, you can place it in the center under card number 2. Just group the cards together as best as you can.

✶ Card 1: the recent past. This card will probably give you some idea about events that have taken place over the past few months and how they affect the client today.

✶ Card 2: present day. Here you will have an inclination of what is happening around the client now, how they are dealing with situations, and what their state of mind is.

✶ Card 3: imminent future. This card shows the reader what is to come for the client very soon, and it also shows anything that may be hidden from them or what they might need to know in order to go forward.

* Card 4: the significator's feelings; how the client is thinking and feeling toward the situations in their life. If this portrays a negative card, then you will know they are struggling with something; if it is positive, then they will probably have an optimistic approach.

* Card 5: influences. Here we can see if there are others around the client that might influence their life in some way. Again, positive cards might mean they have a good supportive network; negative cards would show that someone is hindering them.

* Card 6: what the client should do. The card that appears in this position determines what kind of advice you give to the client. If a spiritual card pops up, you might advise them to try connecting with their guide. If a more practical card is positioned, then they might move ahead with a plan of action.

* Card 7: This card represents the final outcome, so you would hope it's a positive card. If not, you can always deal on top of the card to see if you can give hope.

THE CELTIC CROSS

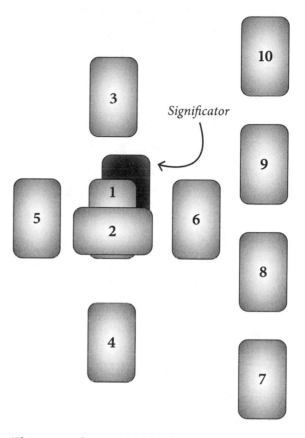

Significator

This spread is probably the most common of all and can be read in one of two ways.

THE TRADITIONAL INTERPRETATION

* Card 1: the present time. This card will give you a look at what is taking place for the client right now.

* Card 2: what is challenging them. This card shows the reader any issues the client might have been dealing with over the past month.

* Card 3: what to focus on. Here you will be able to give advice and pass on to the client what they need to do.
* Card 4: past events. This card can foretell the recent past, usually within the last twelve months.
* Card 5: the client's strengths. You can give information regarding their strengths and how to better use them.
* Card 6: the imminent future. Here, you can get a good look at what will be happening in the coming months.
* Card 7: the cards' advice. This can be instructions from the spirit world to help the client overcome any problems.
* Card 8: those people around the client. This would display either the types of individuals in the client's life right now or those to come soon.
* Card 9: the client's hopes and fears. Cards placed here will guide the client on how best to act on fears and/or their desires.
* Card 10: the final outcome.

Because timing in Tarot is very difficult to predict, we find that reading the cards (as above) can sometimes get muddled. You may find that the card that was supposed to represent the future has actually taken place over the recent past, or the client's hopes and fears are positioned where the final outcome should be. Over the years we found a better way of reading the Celtic Cross.

THE ALTERNATIVE INTERPRETATION

Cards 1, 2, 3, 4, 5, and 6 represent everything that has taken place in the recent past and present. These cards will deal with the issues relating to how the client has felt, how they feel now, and how they plan to go forward. You can group these six cards together to get a more in-depth look at the client's life. Cards 7, 8, 9, and 10, going up the right-hand side of the spread, are cards that predict the future. You can still use card number 10 as the final outcome.

EXAMPLE SPREAD: *Reading for a thirty-year-old woman.*

Let's start with the Moon. The client has been around someone who is lying to her; she must trust her instincts at this time. As this is also the psychic card, perhaps she had an inkling that someone was telling her untruths. The Nine of Wands also suggests that the client is around a deceitful person, so these two cards group together nicely. The Moon can also represent gynecological issues, and the Nine of Wands minor health problems, so you would predict a period of ill health around her. The High Priestess is crossing the Moon, showing us she has a female guide. Because of this, we know that she is spiritually protected, so nothing will affect her too much.

The Ace of Wands. Here we see a new job

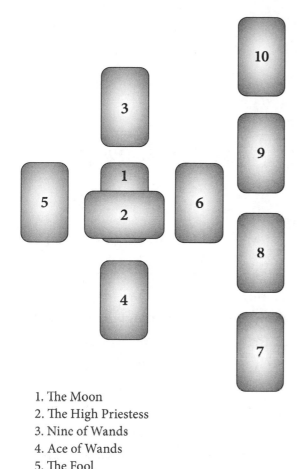

1. The Moon
2. The High Priestess
3. Nine of Wands
4. Ace of Wands
5. The Fool
6. Six of Pentacles
7. Ten of Cups
8. Two of Cups
9. Nine of Cups
10. King of Swords

cles sitting to the right, we know straight-away that this new job will pay well, as this is the card of not having any financial worries.

Now we focus on the right-hand side of the reading and study cards 7 through 10.

You can see that these cards are foretelling a relationship. With the Ten of Cups, we can see that the client has had at least one difficult relationship in her past, but now an excellent new companion is on the horizon for her. The predicted partner has probably been married or had a long-term relationship before and could possibly have children. The Two of Cups signifies that her new relationship will truly be wonderful, and she might feel like she has met her soul mate.

Because both the Ten of Cups and the Two of Cups represent a wedding or engagement, you can easily predict that she will have a long and lasting marriage. The client may have secretly wished for someone like this to come into her life because the Nine of Cups is positioned above. The King of Swords (her new partner) rests in the position of the final outcome, so here you could give the client some information on his personality type.

This is just a brief example of how you would go about grouping the cards together in a spread like this. Of course, once you thoroughly study the cards, you could potentially find at least two scenarios that might apply to the client.

for the seeker, but because the Fool is positioned nearby and we know that this card represents a time before something has happened, it's unlikely the client has started her new job yet. The fool also tells us of a new path ahead, so the client must be patient and wait for the job offer. With the Six of Penta-

7

Situations You Might Face

In your career as a Tarot reader, your clients will be sure to arrive with an array of different problems. Some will be run-of-the-mill, and others will leave you open-mouthed. Still, most people go to psychics either out of curiosity or because they are totally lost about what to do next. As a result, readings are usually in-depth and packed with surprises. The hardest part for any reader is that they only have about an hour to identify the issue and then provide guidance, support, and a solution. There will always be one person who enters the room with an odd situation that leaves you scratching your head or wishing you could have done more to help. At other times, with some of the difficulties you see, you'll have no trouble finding the correct answers.

Providing the person with spiritual direction is helpful when dealing with challenging issues. You may also explain to them why certain things happen in life, so they can understand why they are being tested with different lessons. The more life experiences they go through, the wiser their soul will become. This section lists some of the common problems you might encounter. We will also include a section on spiritual lessons, which you can digest and pass on.

Romantic Relationships

The subject of relationships will come up with most people you read for. Four out of five readings will be geared toward partnerships and marriage, and these can become repetitious. Even if the seeker has the perfect marriage, there will undoubtedly be information you can give them about their partner. Suppose the client is in a problematic relationship. In that case, the Tarot will indicate this, and you will more than likely find the suit of Cups or Swords present in the spread. Extramarital affairs are also common, with either the questioner secretly seeing another person or a close friend or family member deciding to start a passionate love affair. Unfortunately, it's extremely rare to see a perfect union in the cards; there is usually a glitch, if not now, then in the future.

Squabbles in a Marriage

Arguments and upsets in relationships happen all the time; sometimes, the couple can work through them, and other times, it leads to separation and divorce. If your client has reached the end of their tether, they may ask you if they should remain in the partnership or leave it. Psychically, you may feel the relationship won't stand the test of time, but you must never influence them to leave unless they're unsafe. Because each of us is born with free will, persuading someone to follow a specific route could potentially interfere with their karma. We can only see a glimpse of the actual situation; therefore, if the client decides to leave, it must be their choice. There's a strong prob-

ability that children will also be involved in the mix.

Often, the relationship can be strained because of outside influences; this could be the case with difficult in-laws or other members of the family. In many instances, if the person is able to focus on one problem at a time, it may help them untangle the ball of string, and things might look clearer for the couple. Before the questioner decides to walk away from their partner, ask them to think back to when they were happiest. Maybe this could be achieved again, especially if they enlist the help of a therapist or family counselor.

Suppose the female is unsure about her future. If she left her partner, she might be worried about how to raise the children independently. Or her concerns may revolve around limited finances; this is when the cards are good at giving guidance and shedding light on the different scenarios she will have to go through. Ask her to shuffle a fresh pack of cards for at least three minutes, then tell her to cut the pack into three with her left hand (the hand nearest the heart) and choose one of the three piles. Take ten cards from the top of this stack and lay them facedown in two vertical lines, five cards in each. The first set of cards is the path she is on right now, so try to group the cards together and interpret them as a whole. The second line is the alternative path, so you will see what might occur should she leave him. This way, you can give the seeker two sets of circumstances which might guide them into making the correct decision. If they choose path A, this will happen, or if they decide on path B, the other will happen. In most struggling marriages, the couple is so bogged down with day-to-day life that they might have lost their emotional connection. The answer could simply be to spend more time together and, for once, put the relationship first.

Spiritual Lessons

Every single person we meet in life is pre-planned before they reincarnate. Nothing is left to chance, so in effect, our lives are spiritually orchestrated. For our soul to evolve, we have to experience things first-hand and work hard on relationships, romantic or otherwise. In the afterlife, we constantly gravitate toward our own soul family, meeting up and spending time with them. There can be twenty or more individuals in this group, each on a similar vibration and all learning similar lessons. Before we embark on a new life, sometimes a soul agrees to reincarnate with others from a different soul family. One group might be on a higher frequency than another, so by spending time with them on Earth, the younger soul can ascend at a faster rate.

There will also be a lesson somewhere for the more evolved soul; they might need to learn patience or muster strength in a specific area of their personality. When reincarnating into a new family group, one can often feel different from other family members or like an outsider; this is one of the key signs that the person has reincarnated outside of their soul family.

We agree on our itinerary before each new life. The people we meet will be pre-arranged, and the challenges we face will be designed to test us; this explains why we sometimes feel as though we have known someone for a long time when we first meet them. In truth, we most likely belong to the same soul group and have had many previous incarnations together.

In our lives, we may encounter a driving force that pushes us to start relationships with particular people, even when we know in our hearts that they are not the right fit. When we look back on these relationships, we might wonder why we married or set up a home with someone who is clearly not on the same page. In situations like these, before we reincarnated, we probably agreed to spend time on Earth with that person for learning purposes. Putting two people together from different soul groups can cause clashes of personality as one partner may not be as thoughtful or kind as the other. It's common for one person in the marriage to have enough and walk away, seeking someone on a higher vibration with whom they can connect better. Spiritually speaking, it's not wrong to leave a relationship, even if you've agreed to be in it, because we ultimately have free will and must move through our lifetimes at our own pace. Any unfinished relationships will occur again in a different life until the lessons are completed.

In most cases, these spiritual trials are for the couple. One partner might be snappy or bossy, while the other will show signs of submission. It's not unusual for the spirit world to pair couples like this so that the passive partner can gather strength and stand up to their opposition. When the roles are reversed, the more dominant person may have to learn what it's like to lose a partner because of their actions. Although their personality may not change significantly in this lifetime, the soul remembers everything after death, allowing them to improve their character in subsequent lives.

Difficulties with Exes

When a relationship ends, many people who have been in love with their partner or spouse find themselves dealing with a challenging stranger. The first flushes of love subside, and the cracks begin to show; this decline often happens subtly over many years, and the once love of their life is now their bitter enemy.

This scenario is a common problem in Tarot readings. If your client is female, you might see a King in the spread next to the Tower or the Devil, and the Two of Swords could be present, signifying the breakup. If it's a man, a Queen will take center stage with lots of Wands or Pentacles, showing battles perhaps with property and finances. Most of the time, there are children involved, and the situation may be quite upsetting and stressful for them. When conducting the reading, it's possible to perceive that one side is more at fault than the other. If this is the case, it's best to be careful with the advice you offer. No one likes to be told they're in the wrong, but sometimes, it can be the person you are reading for that is the perpetrator; you may have to gently point them in the right direction.

Another possibility is that one spouse in the marriage cannot let go and refuses to move on, but before jumping to any conclusions, remember you'll only hear one side of the story. She might be complaining that she can't shake off her ex, but she fails to mention she still hooks up with him for sex twice a week. If you see something like this in the cards, you'll need to press the client to see if she is sending out mixed messages to him. Of course, it could be much worse, and an ex-partner might be stalking her. In situations like this, you might encourage her to get the police involved. Sadly, very rarely do exes get along or co-parent happily together.

SPIRITUAL LESSONS

Our spirit guides will put us in challenging situations and in the presence of difficult people to see how we deal with the matter. For example, if a woman is around a strong male who likes his own way too much, her lesson might be to find inner strength and stand up for what she wants. Suppose she allows others to dominate her. In that case, she will have to continually reincarnate with these kinds of individuals until she has learned to stand her ground.

If we show signs of cruelty and resentment or retaliate badly to an ex's actions, we have failed. Putting ourselves in the other's position and trying to understand why they are acting in a certain way is a more favorable approach. You've all heard the saying "rise above it"; this is what we hope to achieve. People usually behave badly when they are unhappy or hurt. Showing kindness instead of anger will often smooth the way for better relations. It's very difficult to be vile toward someone who is being nice to you; therefore, from a growth perspective, self-control is expected and will demonstrate your spiritual elevation.

Unsafe Relationships

If you've established that the questioner is in a dangerous relationship, you should step in and do your best to convince them to leave. Believe it or not, coercive control and domestic abuse are prevalent in society today, albeit hidden away and conducted in secret. Controlling partners can put the client in fear, leaving them isolated from friends and family. If they have been cut off from those they love, you could be a lifeline for them; so during the reading, give them the strength and encouragement they need to stand up for themselves. If you are recording the reading, for your own safety, it's always best to turn the recording device off. In these situations, the person will rarely be able to maintain their privacy, and the reading could end up in the wrong hands. When you are faced with this issue, the session can take longer than the usual hour, so expect to go overtime. Ensure that you have phone numbers for shelters or refuges to pass on.

CASE STUDY: BELETA
Toby

When I run a Tarot course, I usually ask each student to bring a practice reading they've done for someone to class. The rest of the students then try to decipher the cards. Megan's mixture of cards was extremely bizarre and frightening. The Devil, the Tower, the Ten and Five of Swords, and lastly, the Death card. The man that had selected them was a friend of hers.

A few weeks later, my husband and I were invited to Megan's house where a demonstrator taught us the benefits of essential oils for health, beauty, and massage. There was a lovely group of about ten or twelve friendly folks present that I would class as new-age types. The house was small, and most of them had already taken a seat when we arrived. One place was empty beside a dark-haired man, whom I guessed to be in his late thirties. The little sofa was snug, to say the least. I smiled politely as I sat down next to him. Immediately the hairs on the back of my neck stood up. His brown eyes flicked over me curiously and were as cold as ice. All I wanted to do was flee the house and get back to the safety of my own home. Later in the eve-ning there was a coffee break, and I approached Megan. "Who's that man, Megan? He gives me the creeps!"

"Oh, he's okay . . . he pops over a couple of times a week for coffee; his father's a minister in our church, that's how I met him." Something was terribly wrong; my guides were urging me to speak to her. I knew she was going to move in a month or so. Holding both her hands, I looked deep into her eyes. "Megan . . . promise me you won't give him your new address?"

"Beleta, stop it . . . you're really frightening me. Why are you talking like this? He's a nice guy; you've got it all wrong."

"Promise me?"

She shrugged her shoulders irritably. "Okay, okay . . . now, can we just drop this?"

Six weeks later, Toby strolled into a local hospital, and a young nurse was in another room attending to a patient. He grabbed the nurse from behind, plunged a large bread knife into her neck, and stabbed her five more times. Her young life was over. The selection of Megan's Tarot cards had said it all.

SPIRITUAL LESSONS

There's nothing wrong with being a gentle, nonconfrontational person so long as you respect yourself. The spirit world will introduce controlling characters to people's lives to give them the strength to walk away. We often reincarnate with strong-minded people if we have a weakness in our character. A gentle soul who wouldn't hurt a fly or a submissive person will often fall foul of abusive partners. In readings, you will see henpecked husbands, monstrous mothers, nagging wives, and difficult in-laws, to name a few. It's how we deal with these people that really matters. Suppose we allow ourselves to be a door-mat. In that case, we will probably have to keep reincarnating in similar circumstances with similar people until we complete the lesson and demand the respect we deserve. Encourage the client to stand firm and make changes to their life. Once a lesson has been learned, we won't have to reincarnate and do it all over again. Of course, some people are married to violent partners and cannot find the strength to leave for fear of getting physically hurt. Remember, it's no mistake that you have met this person, so do everything you can to get them help; the rest is up to them.

Extramarital Affairs

Because human beings are generally not monogamous creatures, it is not surprising that affairs are probably one of the most common situations you might face in a reading. There are two cards in the Tarot that will tell you an affair is imminent or happening, and this is when the Three of Swords (the adultery card) and the Lovers are in the same spread. The same meaning applies whether the cards are in the upright position or reversed. You can gauge from

this that the client or someone around them is having an affair. Of course, this situation will often end with someone getting hurt, so it's a scenario you will need to handle carefully. If you've established that the client is playing away from home, it's best to gently encourage them to make a decision. The reading can become complicated when you turn over the cards and discover that it's their partner having an affair, because now you'll have to determine whether or not the client knows! This is tricky because you don't want to be the bearer of bad news, so rather than coming straight out and asking, "Is your partner having an affair?" you'd be better to remark that the relationship will face some difficulties, and you'll have to decide later whether to stay together. If the affair hasn't occurred yet, you are providing the customer with a snippet of information they might relate to later.

Spiritual Lessons

Sometimes your guides will introduce a new person into your life to help you leave a current relationship. Not all marriages or partnerships are destined to last. Before you reincarnate on Earth, it may have been decided that you would spend ten years with a partner before changing direction. There are many reasons why the spirit world does this. For example, you can no longer learn anything new with your current companion, or you are meant to be supportive in the relationship to help your partner through a harsh lesson. Once the assignment is completed, you are fated to walk a different path.

Let's say you are reading for a man, and he wasn't a particularly good father in his previous life. The lesson is repeated, and following a failed marriage, he will be tested again to see if he can maintain a good relationship with his children.

Other scenarios occur when it's our destiny to have another marriage. It's time to learn new things with a different partner. Remember, you always end up where you are meant to be, and the spirit world orchestrates everything.

Family and Children

Families come in all shapes and sizes, and most people who have readings are always very interested to know what is in store for their loved ones. There are numerous blended families these days, with many men raising other men's children, and grandparents supporting their adult kids that work full-time. When there are court mentors in the spread, the Tarot can sometimes be confusing, and deciding which Queen or King represents which person in the family can often be a night-

mare. At times like these, it's best to use your psychic instinct to see if you have a feeling of who they might represent. This can take lots of practice, but once you tap into those psychic feelings, you'll come to recognize them again in any future readings.

Disruptive Children

> **CARDS THAT MIGHT BE PRESENT IN A SPREAD**
>
> Any *Pages* or *Knights* (upright or reversed), *the Chariot* (reversed), *Five of Wands* (upright of reversed), *Nine of Wands* (upright), *Seven of Swords* (upright), *Seven of Wands* (upright), *Two of Swords* (upright), *Three of Swords* (upright or reversed), *the Empress* (upright), *Seven of Pentacles (upright)*.

Usually, if there are three Pages in one reading, the client will have three children or three grandchildren if the querent is not of childbearing age. Because the four Pages traditionally portray either sex, again, you would have to psychically determine whether the child you are talking about is male or female. The seeker will often help you and might say, "It sounds like you are talking about my son," or "It's not my son that is being naughty; it's my daughter." You will immediately be forgiven for getting the children mixed up because you mentioned that she had a naughty child. Once you have found out she has a girl, you can take that card out of the spread, put it to the side, and then deal a few cards around it to see if it gives you more information.

Disruptive children often appear in a reading, and the client nearly always feels powerless and at a loss. Nine times out of ten, the child will turn themselves around and grow up to be a very decent person. However, there are still those cases where a teenager or young adult is out of control and perhaps dabbling in drink and drugs. When other options like doctors and therapists don't work, we encounter worried parents who are left with you as their only option. As we have mentioned earlier in the book, usually we don't read for clients under the age of eighteen. Still, on rare occasions, we will if the young person is suicidal or heading down a dangerous path.

CASE STUDY: LEANNA
Guiding Youngsters

Years ago, while reading for a troubled teen, I could see her hanging around with the wrong crowd and sneaking alcohol, cigarettes, and marijuana. I gently explained to her about the spirit world and angels. I told her that her guide wasn't happy and that her smoking would eventually leave her with severe chest and throat conditions. That young woman is now in her forties and still comes to see me from time to time; she told me she hasn't smoked a cigarette since that reading all those years ago and only drinks on special occasions. In this instance, with the help of the Tarot, I was able to put this young teen back on the right path.

With younger children, behavioral issues often give the client grief, so all it will take is some common sense and sound advice from you on how to proceed. Most readers are parents; therefore, you might have shared similar experiences and can offer alternative ways of dealing with the problem. There is always a reason why a child is acting up, and when the client has no idea what is wrong, you can deal extra cards that might reveal the cause.

ADHD and Autistic Spectrum Disorders

Over the last thirty years, these children have been popping up in readings all the time. Sometimes, the disruptive child you see in the cards has a medical condition, which explains why they act up. Because the Page of Swords is a strong-minded child, this card can sometimes represent a youngster with a mental health condition. Alternatively, you might see other Page cards around lots of Swords or those representing poor health. If the child is a teenager, one of the Knights might present themselves around a selection of Swords and, perhaps, the Justice card if they are getting into trouble with the law.

In most cases, the client is worn out and can't see a way forward. Still, you can give hope because, with these types of children, professional help is available. Sometimes, the client might not even be aware that their child is on the spectrum, so having a reading may be the very thing that prompts them to get some medical advice.

SPIRITUAL LESSONS

Because the world is like a giant school, before we reincarnate, we choose to undergo specific lessons to further our spiritual development. Often, a child on the autistic spectrum has opted to come into a body that is wired differently. They probably decided to help themselves fully understand what it is like to live with some limitations and to also help other souls ascend by reincarnating with them. It's not just the parents and family of these children who are learning these lessons but also the doctors, healers, teachers, and social workers that will have some involvement in the child's life.

These children are believed to come in with a great deal of spiritual protection, with a guide permanently close by. They may also show signs of being psychic, speaking to imaginary friends or predicting future events. When they finally pass away at the end of their lives, their souls will be completely pure and have gained incredible wisdom.

Child Abuse

CARDS THAT MIGHT BE PRESENT IN A SPREAD

Any Pages (upright or reversed), *Kings, Knights,* or *Queens* (upright or reversed), *the Devil* (upright), *Two of Swords* (upright), *Five of Swords* (upright), *Seven of Swords* (upright or reversed), *Ten of Swords* (upright or reversed), *the Tower* (Upright or Reversed), *Five of Wands* (upright), and *Nine of Wands* (upright).

Sadly, instances that depict a child being bullied at school or, even worse, being sexually abused or mistreated occur quite regularly. It can be disconcerting to see in a reading. Asking clients if they have a child who seems depressed or acts out of character is an excellent way to start the conversation. Depending on their response, you might advise the client to investigate more, perhaps speak with the youngster in private, and identify the root of the issue. Children who bully or terrorize others in school probably live in a home with many problems. A child might replicate an adult's actions, or their violent outbursts might be a way to get someone to pay attention to them.

You do have to be very careful how you word things if you feel a child is being abused. The Tarot doesn't always clearly spell things out; sometimes, the spread might mean something completely different. Try tuning in psychically, and if you still believe something doesn't look or feel right, sow a seed in the client's mind and perhaps suggest that the youngster receive some counseling. It would then be up to the parent to decide whether or not to take further action.

CASE STUDY: BELETA
Opening a Can of Worms

The beautiful cottage was set in a couple of acres of Yorkshire countryside. It even had roses around the door. It would be a long evening ahead for me as I was there to do seven readings. As I walked into the sumptuous lounge, everyone greeted me in a friendly way, and Eva, my host, showed me into a cozy dining room, which was perfect with a small round table ready for the Tarot cards. The first two readings were pleasant and successful, so I prepared myself for the next, a young girl called Lilly. As I began laying the cards out in front of me, I knew something was strange. Before me was the Seven of Swords, the King of Swords, and the Devil, followed by the Lovers and, finally, the Tower. I used a very pictorial deck, and the significator I selected was the Queen of Swords, who had tears streaming down her face.

I asked the girl if her childhood was troublesome, and she nodded. "This King of Swords looks sinister to me," I said. "Did he harm you or act inappropriately?"

Then it suddenly dawned on me; the cards all indicated that she'd been sexually abused from a young age. She gazed at me imploringly and tortured a tissue in her lap. I took a deep breath and asked her gently if she had ever been sexually abused. She started to sob. "I've never told anyone before," she whispered. My heart went out to her, and after she had dried her tears, I encouraged her to see a therapist who might be able to help her deal with her anguish.

After she left, my next client, Gemma, who was about twenty, smiled brightly and told me how much she was looking forward to her reading.

As my mind was still on Lilly, I decided to use a different deck of Tarot, and as I laid out her selection of cards, I couldn't believe my eyes. Gemma's cards were nearly identical to Lilly's. How could I see precisely the same thing? I felt my guide was nearby urging me to continue, so I gently asked if she had been sexually abused when she was younger.

She paled visibly. "How do you know that no one knows these things?" And then she, too, started to cry.

I gave her the same advice and told her she needed some counseling, and after she left, I leaned back in my chair wearily. What a night this had turned out to be!

Suddenly, Eva entered the room, and it was evident by the look on her face that she was furious. "Beleta, why have you made both my daughters cry? What on earth is going on?"

I had no idea these were Eva's daughters, not that it would have changed anything, and because I pride myself on confidentiality, I told her I couldn't discuss their readings and that she must speak to her girls for the answers. She flounced out angrily and summoned them to come into the reading room. After a few minutes had passed, Lilly and Gemma both admitted that their father had abused them from an early age and had even coerced them into having full intercourse as they grew older. It became apparent that neither girl knew it was happening to their sibling. Eva left the room, told everyone to go, and then broke down.

Some months later, Eva rang me and told me her husband had been due to appear in court, but a few days before the hearing, he hung himself on a rafter. She said she was relieved it had all come out, but now she faced the difficult job of supporting her daughters so that they might heal.

The ordeal was so traumatizing that for months I even contemplated giving up my career.

Tarot is indeed a potent tool that can unlock the secrets hidden within.

SPIRITUAL LESSONS

What a difficult lesson to undertake, yet so many people find themselves in this situation. In truth, there are predators in this world, and sometimes, they can't be avoided no matter how hard you try. The people who commit these diabolical acts on children are young souls that haven't reincarnated much. They manipulate and torment others for their own gratification, unable to control their selfish needs. Upon death, they will go to a place reflecting their soul's vibration, so it's likely to be a dismal afterlife. They are still loved by the spirit world, though, whose inhabitants spend much time trying to help them evolve and improve their souls.

A more profound lesson is learned for children who intimidate or torment others. Perhaps in a past life, the victim was a bully and now must understand what it's like when the shoe is on the other foot. It's a harsh lesson, but you cannot fully understand how the other person feels until you've experienced it.

Sibling Rivalry

> ### CARDS THAT MIGHT BE PRESENT IN A SPREAD
>
> Any *Pages, Knights,* or *Queens* in pairs or trios (upright or reversed), *the Chariot* (reversed), *Five of Wands* (upright), *Nine of Wands* (upright), *Seven of Swords* (upright), *Seven of Wands* (upright), *Two of Swords* (upright), *Three of Swords* (upright or reversed)

Conflict and tension can arise among any siblings, whether they are young children or have reached maturity; this can be the bane of a parent's life, but perhaps it's their inability to parent correctly. The likelihood of young children making friends and going on to have healthy relationships with their siblings is good, but when they reach adulthood their relationships can turn fractious. Your client will know which child is the offender, but they are in a difficult situation because they don't want to appear to be taking sides. When a parent chooses a side, it frequently comes at a cost to their relationship with the other child, so they must be very diplomatic and tread carefully.

> ## CASE STUDY: BELETA
> ## When the Cards Come to Life
>
> *Dr. Ross was a beautiful soul who, as a general practitioner, had helped so many of her patients through the years. I could sense she was distracted and not herself. Looking deeply into her card selection, I felt a little shiver run down my spine as the Page of Cups took my full attention. Suddenly in the picture, the eye of the child dropped down onto the cheek, and I blinked to clear my vision. What had I just seen?*
>
> *"Um . . . has there been an upset or a trauma with a child's eye?" I asked tentatively. "The Sun card is next to it, which means all should be well."*
>
> *She gasped, with tears in her eyes. "Beleta, as we speak, my grandson is having major surgery to his eye; he was playing with his brother, and they were throwing a pair of scissors at each other, which pierced his retina, ripping it. My daughter is inconsolable."*
>
> *"Tell her all will be well, and he won't lose his sight." She was ringing her daughter's cell phone as she left to give her the news. Needless to say, all was as the cards had predicted.*

SPIRITUAL LESSONS

Sometimes a pair of souls will have to repeatedly reincarnate together to settle their karmic differences. On the other hand, one soul, which might be more evolved than the other, has consented to reincarnate as a brother or sister to assist the other in moving up the spiritual ladder. When an evolved soul reaches adulthood on Earth, they can and often do opt out of communicating with their sibling, only seeing them on holidays such as Thanksgiving or birthdays. By skipping the lesson, they will probably have to go through a similar situation again in another life. Giving the client this information often helps them take a step back and view things differently. In circumstances like these, there is very little the parent can do other than respect their children's decisions.

Monsters-in-Law

> ### CARDS THAT MIGHT BE PRESENT IN A SPREAD
>
> Any *Knights, Kings,* or *Queens* (upright or reversed), *the Moon* (upright), any of the four *Fives,* (upright or reversed), *the Devil* (upright), *Strength* (upright), and *the Empress* (upright)

Even the happiest marriages might suffer when someone in the family strongly dislikes another. Circumstances can vary, such as when a pushy mom does not give her daughter any peace or a father or step-parent belittles a son.

Extended family issues are common, especially between in-laws. One parent-in-law might not like how the son- or daughter-in-law raises their children, or the mother-in-law doesn't think the wife is good enough for her son. Many in-laws feel compelled to intervene and go into parental mode, defending their offspring. No matter how old the child is, a parent's instinct is to protect them, but when a parent meddles in their offspring's marriage, the adult child is more inclined to stay in the relationship. Unless the client's child is in danger from an abusive partner or spouse, offer gentle support, but encourage them to take a step back so their child can learn their lessons. We mentioned before that every relationship, good or bad, is for a reason. It might be part of their child's karma to spend time with a particular person so they can grow and evolve. The client may have to bite their tongue.

Additionally, when a parent interferes with their child's relationship, the youngster may distance themselves from the parent or use lies to disguise what is happening to avoid a confrontation. If the parent keeps her ideas to herself and is simply available for the child when they want to vent, she will be much more in control and likely to obtain the truth. Again, it goes against every parent's nat-ural instinct, but in the end, one must remember every person must go through life at their own pace.

If you are reading for someone who has an obnoxious in-law, keep in mind that sometimes perfect marriages end because the in-law won't stop interfering. Always try to encourage the person to keep working on their marriage.

SPIRITUAL LESSONS

Lessons here are for all parties. Example: If a problematic mother-in-law disrupts your marriage, your response to her behavior will be spiritually monitored. Never stoop to her level; instead, try rising above it.

If you've attempted to resolve the issues between yourself and your in-law and found that nothing seems to help, it might be time to put some space between you. Agree to disagree and avoid socializing. From a spiritual standpoint, you have tried hard and shown self-restraint; the fault now sits with the in-law.

A second example arises when the lesson is for the husband. He has probably gone through his life already with a strong mother who might have been controlling or bossy. His assignment here is to stand up to his mother and put his wife and her happiness first. Until he accomplishes this, he will repeatedly reincarnate with a similar type of parent.

Example 3: The mother-in-law is having the reading, and she is constantly complaining about her daughter-in-law. She could be correct, and her son's wife might be difficult, but you should still offer the same advice. Gently tell her not to interfere with the marriage as it's her son's karma to undergo the lesson. Maybe her time would be better spent making sure she has a good relationship with her grandchildren.

The worst-case scenario is when a grandparent is denied visitation with her grandchildren. However you look at it, they have reincarnated into the same family for a reason. Unless the child is unsafe or in danger, no one should deny a child the right to get to know their grandparent, as it interferes with the karmic balance.

Absent Parents

> ### CARDS THAT MIGHT BE PRESENT IN A SPREAD
>
> Any *Kings, Queens,* or *Pages* (upright or reversed), *Five of Pentacles* (upright), *Six of Pentacles* (upright), *the Tower* (upright or reversed), *Two of Swords* (upright), *the Devil* (upright or reversed)

When marriages and relationships end, sometimes the tension between a couple is so bad that it's easier for one party to walk away than stay and fight for the right to see a child. The animosity between the partners can become so intense that visits start to wane or become so inconsistent that they cease altogether. When conducting a reading, you will more often see absent fathers than absent mothers, so in this section we will refer to the male gender—no offense meant.

Sometimes, it's not the father's fault. The mother will deny access because she is not receiving enough child support or doesn't like her ex's latest girlfriend. He might be unable to afford a lawyer to fight for the right to see his child, so he has no choice but to stay away. Other times, a father gets married again, and the new wife doesn't want anything to do with his children. Sadly, you will see a lot of this if you choose Tarot as a profession. Rather than stand up against his wife, he backs down for a quiet life. These situations can rile the mother, and the mama bear comes to the surface again. Whatever the case, whether it be a jilted mother or a father who has been browbeaten, it is best if both parents are constantly in the child's life. You will undoubtedly read for those children whose father has abandoned them when they are grown up, and this can leave them feeling isolated and rejected. Some are so affected by it that they need a lifetime of therapy. But remember, the child, in another life, might have been an absent parent themselves.

What goes around always comes around.

SPIRITUAL LESSONS

When the above situation arises, in whichever form, there is always a spiritual test in place. The natural balance will be upset, and their relationship will be hindered if one parent prevents the other from seeing their child. This is never good and is often frowned upon spiritually. A parent must only intervene and stop visitation if they believe the child to be in danger. For the child's welfare and mental health, the parent must also try to be cordial and understanding with the other parent, no matter how challenging this may be. This earns brownie points in the spirit world, and the parent or guardian will have passed their test.

The absent parent is not completing the spiritual lesson and will unavoidably accumulate negative karma because their behavior has affected the life of another. Above all, all parties' welfare and spiritual development come from reaching compromises and endeavoring to do the right thing.

Blended Families

> ### CARDS THAT MIGHT BE PRESENT IN A SPREAD
>
> Any *Pages, Kings, Knights,* or *Queens* (upright or reversed), *Four of Wands* (upright), *Ace of Swords* (upright), *Nine of Swords* (upright), *the Lovers* (upright or reversed), *Two of Cups* (upright or reversed), *Two of Swords* (upright), *Three of Swords (upright)*

We are seeing more and more men bringing up other men's children and instances of grandparents who are not related to their grandchildren by blood. It's not always easy to love another person's child. These relationships can work well, but sometimes it's a recipe for disaster, and you'll see chaos erupting with every turn of a card. The types of problems you will face can be widespread. Here are a few examples.

YOU'RE NOT MY DAD!

Your client falls in love with a new man and, after a while, introduces him to her children. One child acts out and throws repeated tantrums, disliking the stranger who has suddenly shown up in his life and refusing to stop until he's gotten rid of him. In cases like these, the new man has a challenge ahead of him because he's somehow going to have to win the youngster over. If you are reading for the stepparent and see that there is a light at the end of the tunnel, perhaps suggest some strategies they can use to smooth the waters.

DON'T TREAT MY CHILD LIKE THAT!

A woman meets and moves in with a new man, yet he raises her children very differently from how he raises his own. The man is then resented by the client because, in her opinion, he is treating her children too harshly. This frequently happens in readings, and more often than not, nobody is to blame. He may be a strict father figure who watches a mild-mannered mother allow her children to get away with bad behavior, or she might undermine him and instruct him not to discipline her children at all. Despite their differences, if you believe the couple can make a go of it, you could suggest they get some family counseling.

THE DIFFICULT EX

If the client has left her husband and moved herself and the kids in with her lover, the husband can cause no end of trouble for her and her new man. Once he's realized

his wife isn't coming back, anger can set in, and sadly, any children in the relationship will end up being used as pawns. The new man is embroiled in a bitter battle because now he has the difficult job of raising children that are not his, and he has to sit back and watch his new partner fighting and squabbling with her ex. Whether you're reading for the new man or the woman who has left her husband, sometimes it makes more sense for them to live separately until the tension has died down.

One of the worst things when couples separate is that one parent will likely criticize the other. Often, little children become very confused and can even go on to lose an excellent relationship with their parent because they believe everything the other parent tells them. Unfortunately, this is a common scenario, and if you come up against it, perhaps offer some spiritual advice.

SPIRITUAL LESSONS

As we have mentioned in previous sections of this book, everything we do and say is spiritually noted. So, it's essential to be aware of this and handle every situation with thought and care.

For those entering a new family environment, it's always best to put any children's needs above your own. Suppose the child is stressed out with the new person living among their family. In that case, moving out and working on the relationship gradually from afar might be best. The new couple's lesson is to help the child adjust to the circumstances; to do this, they must show patience and kindness.

Even if there is no blood link between a child and their step-grandparents, the child may well be a member of the same soul group. The spirits will always connect people who are destined to be together. If they are from separate soul groups, they are meant to have some sort of influence on one another's life.

Even if a mother detests her ex-husband, she must never bad-mouth him to her children. It's so hard to remain neutral, but it's imperative not to comment or manipulate the child's mind. After all, the mother's relationship is now over with her husband; however, the children still have to remain in their father's life because they are not finished with their lessons.

The youngsters will eventually arrive at their own conclusions about the other parent. They should do so without outside influence. If you fail this test, you are again meddling with your child's karma, which doesn't bode well. We all start learning life lessons the moment we are born; therefore, support a child and give them lots of time and attention, but avoid giving your opinion; just let the child know they are loved.

Unloving Parents

> ### CARDS THAT MIGHT BE PRESENT IN A SPREAD
>
> Any *Pages, Knights, Kings,* or *Queens* (upright or reversed), *Four of Cups* (upright), *Five of Cups* (upright), *the Empress* (upright or reversed), *the Emperor* (upright or reversed)

You might occasionally read for someone who, for whatever reason, believes they have nothing in common with their parents. There may be a hole in the client's life due to their distant mother or father not spending time with them. This can really leave scars, especially if they feel a sibling is more loved than they are. Many parents will favor one child over the other and make no secret of it. This frequently impacts how they raise their own kids, either by being overly involved or repeating history and becoming aloof themselves.

You will frequently encounter clients with firsthand knowledge of what it was like to grow up around alcoholics and drug users. These clients can be severely traumatized and may require additional support to deal with their upbringing, mainly if an alcoholic parent has been abusive.

The seeker may be able to accept the situation and value their interactions outside of the family environment if you provide them with a spiritual explanation of why it occurs.

Spiritual Lessons

In the afterlife, we are encouraged to re-incarnate into certain families for various reasons. As mentioned before, when an individual experiences rejection or feels like an outsider, it clearly indicates that the person is from a completely different soul group. The reincarnation process is long, and by the time we have finished, we must have experienced every single human emotion possible. It's not wrong to be angry or to walk away from a parent who is obnoxious or has never given you any love. Still, it's better not to cut a parent entirely out of your life because you may have agreed to reincarnate with them to help them evolve. However, there will be times when it will be impossible to remain in a relationship with a disruptive parent as their behavior might bring nothing but misery. At times like these, perhaps put some distance between you, and leave the door ajar in case you are needed.

It could, of course, be all centered around karma. In one life, the client might have been a mother who became an alcoholic; this time, she must reincarnate with a similar parent to learn what it's like. We cannot truly understand a situation until we learn the firsthand lesson.

Health Issues

CARDS THAT MIGHT BE PRESENT IN A SPREAD

Any court mentors (upright or reversed), *Five of Pentacles* (upright), *Nine of Swords* (upright), *Ten of Swords* (upright), *the Devil* (upright or reversed), *the Tower* (upright), *the Moon* (reversed), *Nine of Wands* (reversed), *Five of Cups* (reversed), *Nine of Cups* (reversed)

If you read cards regularly, the subject of health will often crop up. Sometimes, it won't be the client but someone close to them suffering from bad health, so getting the prediction right is imperative. You must also be very careful what expressions you use when predicting health matters. However psychic you feel that day, don't try to diagnose a health condition when reading the Tarot. Most of us are not licensed doctors or mental health professionals.

Doing this could leave them worrying for months, even years, that someone they love will become ill. Because timing is often flaky in Tarot, sometimes one prediction could take up to five years before it comes about. It's best to say something like, "I can see someone having to visit the doctor, or possibly having an outpatient appointment at the hospital, but it's nothing sinister, so don't worry." Suppose they go on to experience a loved one with a terminal illness. In that case, it's far better that your prediction was only partly correct, as you will have saved them months of unnecessary anxiety. We always say, "If in doubt, leave it out."

Sometimes the client will be faced with an ailing parent and might have to care for them at home. You will have to gauge in the reading whether the questioner is tired or overwhelmed. Many clients struggle to look after a dementia patient with little or no support.

The cards will often indicate that the sick person might need extra care, and you can guide the client to reach out to the authorities for help. This might involve them having to stand aside and put their mom or dad in a care facility. These are tough choices, so in these situations, we always advise the client to do what is best for the parent.

CASE STUDY: LEANNA
When Readings Save Lives

Many years ago, a regular client of mine arrived for her reading, and as the cards unfolded in front of me, I could see there was something sinister going on with her health. All the negative health cards were present, along with the Tower, Death, and the Nine and Ten of Swords. I psychically tuned in and sadly felt it might be cancer. Not wanting to frighten her, I told her she must get a checkup with her general practitioner straightaway, and then played it down by saying she might be lacking in some vitamin or another, or her blood pressure might need checking. The rest of the reading went along as usual, and as I was seeing her out, I reminded her again to book an appointment at the doctor's office. Thankfully, she listened to my advice and called me a few weeks later to say she had been diagnosed with breast cancer and was starting chemotherapy. I never told her I suspected cancer and how I had struggled with my conscience since our meeting. I didn't feel confident enough to give such a pessimistic prediction. If I'd been wrong, I could have affected her mental health as she might have constantly worried about contracting cancer throughout her life. She still visits me all these years later and always says how that reading really did save her life.

SPIRITUAL LESSONS

When a person is unwell, they are at their most vulnerable, so anyone caring for or nursing someone who is ill always scores highly in the spirit world. Our guides will watch us to see how we handle the situation and, if asked, will even help us by giving us the strength we need to keep plowing ahead. When we care for someone, we can often be pushed to our limits, possibly not feeling 100 percent ourselves. Our intention must be pure, and no resentment should be present. When faced with these circumstances, we must do our absolute best and show kindness and compassion. Some people are natural caregivers, and others have to work at it. Whatever the case is, we are in this predicament for a reason.

Death

╭─────────────────────────────╮
│ **CARDS THAT MIGHT BE**
│ **PRESENT IN A SPREAD**
│
│ *Death* (upright), *Nine of*
│ *Swords* (upright), *Ten of Swords*
│ (upright), *the Tower* (upright),
│ *Five of Swords* (upright)
╰─────────────────────────────╯

Predicting death is always tricky in Tarot, so it's important to exercise common sense and determine your client's personality type. Every time you bring up death in a reading, you must be very careful how you convey the message to avoid upsetting the client. Some people you meet will approach the topic with detachment, while others will be more sensitive.

If someone around the questioner is to die, more often than not the Death card will appear in the spread, next to or alongside the Nine or Ten of Swords. If these other cards are not present, the interpretation will steer away from death and indicate the end of an era. If Death appears with the two Sword cards above along with the Tower, then the meaning is far worse and suggests a death caused by trauma or accident. Because it's virtually impossible to guess how the client will respond to bad news, whichever scenario you are faced with, it's always best to play it down. Some people might argue and say the Tarot reader is wrong to withhold information, but you are not God, and more to the point, you could be mistaken. Anything can cause a false prediction, from the reader having an off day or the client not shuffling the cards correctly. Often, a psychic will foretell a death in the cards and leave a worried or anxious client concerned for their loved one's health and well-being. It's far better to tell the client there is a death in the cards but that it's no one close to them. You might also say they could be attending a funeral, but they will only be there to offer moral support. If someone close to them does pass away, they will remember you predicted the death but will forgive you for the lack of details.

SPIRITUAL LESSONS

I am incredibly fortunate to have a stepfather who practices clinical hypnosis, and over the years, I have undergone many hypnotic sessions where he regressed me not into a past life as such but to a time between each of my lives.

During my sessions, my stepfather instructed me to remember everything I learned, so you might find parts of the following helpful to pass on to your clients.

Birth and death are the cycles of life; when one life ends, the soul will enter the spirit world and usually wait until other members of their soul group return home. Once everyone is back and all have rested from their life on Earth, the cycle begins again. Since everyone has free will, we are not told to reincarnate; it's a choice. If you decide not to keep revisiting Earth, the soul family members who wish to progress might choose to reincarnate without you and eventually reach a point where they would leave you behind. This motivates us to continue with the reincarnation process.

One of the things that became apparent was that life and death are continuous, and that Earth is just one of many planets we visit during our reincarnations. The entire purpose of life is to learn through experiences and to elevate our consciousness. Depending on what kind of death we have, we spend time with our spirit guide when we leave our earthly body and adjust to our new ethereal form. If we had a painful or violent death or spent many years suffering from a particular illness, we are taken to a spiritual hospital as soon as we pass over. Here, the soul is healed, cleansed, and realigned. Many higher beings are present during this procedure, all working in unison to prepare us for the next phase. Once we have undergone this process, we can travel to where our loved ones wait. In the spirit world, our family is so excited to meet with us again, so although our death means sadness and grief for the people we leave behind back on Earth, our spiritual friends are delighted.

Everyone is different, so our final destination is attuned to our consciousness and will reflect the type of soul we are at that precise time of death. If you were a keen gardener in your earthly life, you might have a special garden where you can continue to enjoy the outdoors. If you love to sail, you might dwell near the ocean or spend your time on a magnificent boat. Everything in the spirit world is tailor-made to your needs and is even more beautiful than anything you can imagine on Earth; each flower, blade of grass, and drop of water contains its own consciousness, and the scenery is breathtaking. Those who have lived a decent life and who have put the needs of others first will end up in a place that reflects their inner beauty, so their spiritual home is likely to be fantastic. However, the final resting place might not be as picturesque if they were a destructive or shallow soul on Earth. There is no hell, so to speak, but for those people who murder or hinder the lives of others, their afterlife is much darker and dismal, just like their soul.

One interesting thing I learned was that we are not judged for our wrongdoings when we pass over. Each individual will judge themselves; this takes place during something called a "life review." Here we see a playback of our life, the good, the bad, and the ugly; this can be a very emotional time for the newly passed soul.

We must, however, feel the consequences of every wrongdoing we commit against others, and so we are made to ex-perience the same pain we inflicted for a short while. This helps us to truly understand where we went wrong. Once the life review is over, we can settle down into our afterlife and spend time with our loved ones and beloved pets that have passed.

I experienced so much in my regressions; the information warrants a book of its own, but for now, when you are faced with a client who is grieving for a loved one, reassure them they are in a beautiful place and will be there to meet them when their life is over.

Work, Business, and Money

CARDS THAT MIGHT BE PRESENT IN A SPREAD

Any Wands (upright or reversed), any Pentacles (upright or reversed), *the Chariot* (upright or reversed), *Three of Pentacles* (upright or reversed), *the Emperor* (upright or reversed), *Eight of Pentacles* (upright or reversed)

Because they occupy a large percentage of our daily lives, work and money are at the forefront of most readings. The Ace of Wands, which foretells a new job, and the

Three of Pentacles, which suggests your client may be self-employed, are two essential cards to look out for.

There's a wide variety of situations you'll be faced with when work-related cards are in a spread. Your client might have a problematic or stern boss whose demands are illogical, or the boss might even go so far as to bully or undermine them them in the office. The client could be bored out of their brains and secretly yearn for a change of career, or they might seek a different job because the pay is so bad. Over the years, we have found that many social workers, police officers, nurses, and industry workers are the most stressed of all and will leave their roles after many years of service because it adversely impacts their mental health. If you come across a client who is unhappy in their job but afraid to leave for fear of the unknown, it's always wise to encourage them to look for a more suitable position. The cards will also indicate if a new job is on the horizon, so you can look at the surrounding cards to see if it's a good move.

Younger people fresh out of college might do a fair bit of job hopping, so you might see more than one occupation spring up in the cards. These types are interesting because you can help them choose the best path.

The most challenging people to read for are those who own big or small businesses. They have more time and money invested and can fixate on the company's growth. You might look for positive Pentacle cards in the same spread for a favorable outcome.

SPIRITUAL LESSONS

Work is one area of our lives where fate and destiny prevail, and the spirit world will intervene and place us where we belong. Because we spend so many hours of our day in our employment, many of the lessons we must learn pertain to our jobs. Ordinarily, we wouldn't choose to be in the company of some of the people with whom we spend each day, but there is always some spiritual reason why we do. Before we reincarnate, with the help of our guides, we decide which field of work to pursue. This can sometimes explain why even from a young age, a person can have a calling to work in a particular role. Those souls who choose professions to help humanity, such as doctors, surgeons, nurses, midwives, social workers, caregivers, counselors, therapists, and others, are highly favored by the spirit world. Taking on such a huge responsibility and giving their life over to the needs of others will earn them a high score when they finally go home.

Psychic Encounters

> ### CARDS THAT MIGHT BE PRESENT IN A SPREAD
>
> *The Magician* (upright), *the Hierophant* (upright), *the High Priestess* (upright), *the Hermit* (upright), *Temperance* (upright), and *the Star* (upright)

This is not a common subject, but it is worth a mention. Occasionally, you will read for someone who has just discovered they are psychic. For many, it can be a frightening experience, so they come to you seeking clarification. Others are just as keen to learn how to hone their skills and best understand them. Deep down, the client might have always known they were different because psychics are often born with a gift. If someone never connects with their skill and pushes it to one side, it will surface at some point, and they will encounter something strange. The client might be able to experience predictions in dream sleep, or have a gut feeling something is about to happen—some lean more toward being mediumistic and will see a ghost or hear a spirit voice. When the Magician comes into a spread around other spiritual cards, this means that it's your job to persuade the client to explore this side of their personality. Often, the best way to sharpen your psychic skills is to use an outlet like Tarot, palmistry, runes, the pendulum, etc.

On rare occasions, a client will visit you because their young child is showing signs of a psychic nature and telling the parent all kinds of weird and unusual things. Sometimes you will have to reassure the client that there is nothing wrong and assist them in helping their youngster come to terms with it. Imaginary friends play an essential role in a child's life and can often be the child's guide.

> ### CASE STUDY: BELETA
> #### Out of the Mouths of Babes
>
> *Leanna was the most challenging child to raise, as, from the age of three, she would see spirit lights and ghosts and have imaginary friends she would talk to in the middle of the night. I come from a long line of psychics, so it didn't surprise me that she might have acquired the gift. From the age of five, she would predict all kinds of little things, and then one day, while I was doing laundry, she innocently remarked that I wouldn't stay married to her father. Leanna loved her dad, so this was quite alarming. When I asked her what she meant, she said she'd had a dream where I was standing on a rock, out at sea, with a man dressed in Roman clothing. She said I wore a blue*

306 THE MAGIC OF TAROT

chiffon gown with a long matching scarf that was blowing high into the air, and I was frightened of falling into the crashing waves below, but the Roman man kept me safe. She sent chills along my spine when she insisted we were together in another life; this was bizarre because I had never discussed reincarnation with her, as she was far too young to understand. Leanna never mentioned it again until she was ten years old and encountered my current husband, John, for the first time. He was entering my house for a reading, and she passed him in the hall. She pulled me to one side and whispered, "That's the Roman man in my dream," then skipped off happily to play with her friends. I was astonished! Although I hid it well, my marriage was in tatters, and once I had separated from her father, a relationship began to form with John. Years later, the three of us visited a place in Devon, England, called Hartland Point, and as we watched the waves crashing around us, John pulled me to stand on a nearby rock. I was scared to go any closer, but he reassured me I'd be safe. At the time, I was wearing a long blue scarf which was billowing behind me in the wind, and then suddenly I realized Leanna's dream had come true!

SPIRITUAL LESSONS

Little children have just crossed the border from the spirit world to Earth. They can come in with vivid memories from their time in spirit or recollections from another life. An excellent TV show that portrays this phenomenon is *The Ghost Inside My Child*, which features children who give extraordinary details about their former time on Earth. Before we reincarnate, our memories of previous lives are usually wiped away, but in certain instances, this fails to happen, and these children will continue to remember. However, as the child matures, the memories generally fade, usually when they reach the age of seven.

Unbelievably, each of us is born with a psychic ability. We can use our sixth sense in the same way we use our five senses daily.

Also, every person on Earth is born with a guide who watches over us, so when we get a hunch or a gut feeling about something, we are actually receiving information from our guide. They can adapt how we think and feel by speaking to our subconscious, so if you wake in the morning with a fear or dread, your guide will alert you that something unpleasant is about to happen. It's so important that we trust our instincts and listen to the warning bells.

Those who see or sense spirits and ghosts are referred to as "sensitives" or "mediums" and can communicate with supernatural beings. Never show panic or anxiety because dark forces thrive on fear and will feed off that energy. Instead, be bold and courageous, and tell it in no uncertain terms that they must leave. Often, that's all it takes. Cuss and swear if you have to!

Hauntings and Psychic Attack

We haven't included a list of cards you might come across with this topic, because a haunting is difficult to discover in a spread—there are no cards that represent it. The client might tell you they think there are spirits in the house and ask you how to get rid of them. Most of the time, ghosts and spirits are simply described as the lingering energy left behind by previous occupants of a building. There are, however, spirits who, for whatever reason, fail to cross over and attach themselves to a property; they can make things go bump in the night or observe the present occupants purely out of curiosity. Most ghosts are harmless, but some are highly aggressive and will crash, bang, or even touch someone.

Demonic energy is more worrying, and it can manifest as dark shadows, produce foul smells, and, in some cases, take a form that can assault a person physically. These kinds of entities are difficult but not impossible to get rid of. To rid the home of spirits or demons, tell the client to wear black obsidian for protection and to smudge the house with white sage. Sage acts as a spiritual disinfectant and can clear away negative energies.

SPIRITUAL LESSONS

For whatever reason, there are those spirits who don't realize they have died and will remain in the place most familiar to them. The spirit guide of one of these beings will try endlessly to get them to cross over into the light, but the soul can be so confused that they choose to stay. They may have unfinished business, or their death might have been dramatic and they are still traumatized. Eventually, they will succeed, even if it does take a few hundred years.

Other entities, like demons, arrive in this world through portals. The Earth is full of them, and these gateways can open and close at will. Demons are not human; they are manifestations of evil energy left behind by others' sinful acts, which attach themselves to unsuspecting people or dwellings. They feed on a person's fear and will enjoy the chaos they create. You will often see paranormal investigators or priests banishing them from properties. Although it's not an easy practice, it can work. Whoever is clearing a home or establishment of demonic energy needs to be fearless and show great strength. The perpetrators hate anything to do with godliness or religion and will retreat if the person shows relentless bravery. Unfortunately, one of the downsides is that these entities can be fascinated by a psychic's energy and can sometimes make themselves visible. You may be dropping off to sleep when you see a monstrous face or dream of demons holding you down. If this ever happens, a sure way to get rid of them is to recite the Lord's Prayer, or call upon the archangel Michael for protection. Also, for some bizarre reason, they respond to profanity, so show no fear and, in your mind, tell it in no uncertain terms to go away.

8

Tarot as a Profession

Studying Tarot as a profession is a satisfying career for those who wish to help others. Not everyone will be cut out for it, though, as it takes a certain amount of self-confidence to tell a stranger all about their life, past, present, and future. Before you decide if this is the occupation for you, it's always best to spend at least a year practicing the readings for family and friends to build up your psychic self esteem. Over the years, some might naively remark that it must be easy to lay a few cards on the table and then charge money. It is not at all! Essentially, a Tarot reader is a spiritual counselor and will deal with many underlying issues. You will frequently read for people facing challenging circumstances; the medical profession might be unable to help, and the client's previous therapies may have been ineffective. Hence, they visit a psychic as a last resort.

In contrast, a therapist's job is more straightforward because they can ask the right questions and get to the root of a person's problems. A Tarot reader must identify the issue in just sixty minutes, offer solutions, and provide spiritual counseling. It can be very stressful and, not to mention, tiring. With every person you see, a different story unfolds, and as the reader, you must try to give this person 100 percent of your time and focus. Some predicaments the clients might face will be pretty bizarre, and after a while, nothing will surprise you. Still, most of the time, you'll be dealing with everyday problems and will not have any trouble guiding and giving advice.

Many budding readers will feel the weight of their responsibilities when performing consultations and opt out of the job as quickly as they stepped into it. Those who continue will develop their own techniques while dealing with these differing situations. Another thing to remember is that you cannot treat every client in the same way, as there are many diverse personality types. What can be said to one person freely won't apply to another.

Five out of ten clients will have challenging problems, so be ready for everything and try to use good judgement when counseling them. Problems encountered could include domestic abuse, sexual assault, drug and alcohol addiction, terminal sickness, and grief.

If you are not a qualified counselor, you might feel overwhelmed; keep a few accredited therapists' phone numbers on hand to support the person after they leave you. Because of the responsibility and the seriousness of some situations, many experienced readers will go on and train to become a therapist or counselor; this is something you might want to consider doing in the future.

Working from Home

WHAT YOU MIGHT NEED

When you're ready to do readings for a living, you'll need to consider whether to work from home or rent a modest premise nearby. Running the business from one's house is usually the preferred choice. It's very common for most of your clients to arrive either in groups or early, so if possible, have a waiting area for them to sit in until it's their turn. Working from home also brings with it some risk. Not everyone is honest and trustworthy, and we have had items stolen on many occasions—books, DVDs, ornaments, and toiletries from the bathroom, such as hand creams, toilet rolls, medicines, and perfume. These are just a few things that can go missing, and although it doesn't happen every day, it still occurs about three or four times a year. If you are lucky enough to have a waiting area you can clear of valuables, then all the better. The bathroom should be emptied, too, with just the basics on show. You might prefer not to allow clients to wait at all and ask them to remain in their car until their appointment time. It's a tough decision.

CASE STUDY: LEANNA
Letting in Strangers

When I was starting out, I lived in a property with only one toilet upstairs, so I didn't have much choice but to let a group of clients use the bathroom. Later, after saying goodbye to them all, I found that my jewelry box in my adjoining bedroom was completely empty. As there were four people at the party, it was difficult to make accusations, and of course, when I did confront the woman who originally called to make the appointment, she was adamant it wasn't any of them.

CASE STUDY: BELETA
Wandering Clients

Two women were booked in for a reading, and as I read for one, the other sat waiting in an adjoining room. I live in a bungalow, so my bedroom was on the same floor. After reading for the first woman, I walked into the waiting room to invite the second one in, but she was nowhere in sight. As I opened my bedroom door, she was rifling through my underwear drawer. Needless to say, she was marched straight off the premises!

It's a mystery why this happens, but nearly every person you see will need to use the bathroom at least once when they visit, usually on the way in and again on the way out. After having so many incidents over the years, we chose to keep our expensive soaps, shampoos, and beauty products out of that bathroom. On the flip side, nine out of ten people you read for will be very respectful of your home, but you must always be aware that even the sweet ones might be a tad light-fingered.

For those that prefer to rent a room or space somewhere, this brings fewer problems. It's unlikely you will have a waiting area, so if you read in groups, the others might go away and do some shopping for an hour until it's their turn. However, you will need to factor in the expense of the premises and your daily commute time.

Setting the Scene

It's professional to give your consultation room a comfortable ambience. We keep ours neat and orderly and have a good-sized table for laying out the cards. We tend to avoid using bright reds or gaudy interiors when decorating and go instead for gentle, pastel, or neutral colors; this creates a calm and serene environment. Many customers are upset and struggling with life; therefore, a tranquil setting for an hour will help them unwind and relax.

Lighting scented candles and playing soft meditation music will help clear the energies in the room. Place some crystals nearby and a comfy chair for clients to sit on, too.

The Reading Table

Your table should be big enough to seat two people and allow you to lay out a spread of ten cards with an area for your chosen items. You might like to cover it with a cloth or a beautiful scarf. Many readers believe in the magical properties of color, so if you decide to use a tablecloth, go with spiritual shades like purple or turquoise. These hues will boost your powers and call forth good energies. However, if the table has a fine wood finish, you might prefer to leave it uncovered.

Protect Yourself

Everything on the planet gives out energy, and everyone that comes to see you will leave behind some of theirs. Because half the people you read for will probably shed a tear or two, and if you've been reading for someone that can't stop crying, the residual energy left in the room can sometimes be oppressive. Often, the clairvoyant will find the querent's hidden problems, and this can be overwhelming, especially if the querent hasn't addressed some of their deeply ingrained issues with anyone else. If you don't deal with the vibes after the reading, they are likely to hang in the air like a dark cloud, or, worse still, any negative energy might attach itself to you, leaving you drained and unhappy. An excellent way to combat this is to have a sizable chunk of black tourmaline on the table. The protective qualities of this magical crystal will keep any negativity at bay. The other gemstone we advise you to wear is fluorite, since it forms an invisible shield that deters unwanted energies from otherworldly visitors, such as ghosts and spirits. We have both experienced hauntings in our homes after reading for certain people. Often, a loved one that has passed will come through to give guidance but fail to leave once the person has gone home. It's no fun living in a house with a ghost,

especially if you are psychic. The spirit will immediately be drawn to you and wish to linger.

CASE STUDY: LEANNA
George

Early in my career, one particular woman in her late twenties had an appointment scheduled. When she arrived, she had a man with her who she said was her brother. She asked me if he could sit in on the reading because she was very nervous. I don't usually allow this because when the psychic energy is flowing, you can often get a prediction that isn't for the client but for whomever they bring along. However, on this occasion, and probably because I was still a bit of a newbie, I agreed.

As soon as she was seated next to him, the room became very cold, and a strange energy hung in the air. As she began shuffling the cards, I started to feel extremely uncomfortable; then, from behind me, to the left, I heard a gruff male voice that said, "That's not her brother; that's her fancy man!" I literally jumped out of the chair and looked behind me, but there was no one there. The client and her companion looked at me as if I was mad, so I sat sheepishly down again.

"You need to tell her to get rid of him," he said again, this time louder and more persistent. The blood drained from my face; no one could hear him but me. Worse still, how could I tell her to leave him when he was sitting in front of me? I gently broached the subject and said that a male spirit was here, and he was saying that the

man you are with is not your brother, but your partner. She looked embarrassed for a second and then admitted to it. She then asked me who the spirit man was, and before I could answer, the voice behind me bellowed, "George! I'm her dad, and that bastard is going to kill her!"

I have always been straightforward, having my feet firmly on the ground, but I was entirely out of my comfort zone and quite frightened. I told the woman that her father was trying to warn her, but she smirked as though I was making it all up.

"His name is George," I said, and before I could proceed, her father started reciting the address where she grew up, her mother's name, and the full names of her two siblings. As I relayed this information, she started to pay attention. The man sitting opposite me was getting agitated, and I suddenly realized he was the one who had brought the dark energy to my home. If George said he would kill her, what's to say he wouldn't attack me? I decided not to get involved or relay any more information about her father or her relationship.

It was probably the most challenging reading I have ever done in my life because the whole time I tried to read her cards, George was shouting in my ear. It reminded me of the movie Ghost with Patrick Swayze and Whoopi Goldberg. After the hour was up, I saw them both out and flopped into a chair with a cup of tea; my head was spinning.

"You need to phone her NOW!" George barked. "That man will bloody kill her; if he does, it'll be all your fault!" Being alone in the house,

I could finally respond to him, so I naively begged him to leave me alone. "I'm not going anywhere," he said. "Not until you pick up that bloody phone and CALL HER!"

I relented; anything to get rid of him and his bad language. All I wanted was my home and my sanity back. She answered the phone immediately, so I told her what her father had said and informed her that he was still with me and urged her to leave her partner. Her reaction wasn't what I expected at all. She was so blasé and unimpressed, replying that she couldn't possibly leave him because she loved him so much. If I had been conveying this information to any other person in the world, the thought of a parent returning from the grave to give such an important message would have been the biggest deal. I ended the call and said aloud, "Well, I tried."

All was quiet for two weeks, and the depressing energy finally lifted from the house.

One morning I was at the sink, washing the dishes, when that all too familiar gruff voice spoke again.

"He's gone and bloody done it," he said. "She's in the hospital." Later in the day I turned on the local news, and the man's picture was on the screen. He had been taken into custody for attacking his girlfriend so badly that he had been charged with attempted murder. He subsequently received a hefty sentence and spent many years behind bars.

George never revisited me, and I am happy to say that in the thirty-two years I have been a Tarot reader, this was the only time I've ever had such an encounter.

When a spirit enters your home, you might notice strong smells, sometimes of perfume or tobacco. Objects and other things will get moved, and cold spots will appear in areas of your house. Wearing a black obsidian crystal is also a powerful protector against psychic attacks; this stone will guard you against ghosts like George, and poltergeist entities who might make an uninvited appearance.

Salt also acts as a protective wall; many readers like having a small bowl on the table. Burning sage incense or essential oil will most definitely keep negativity at bay. If you want to make doubly sure your home is left spiritually spick-and-span, you can purchase some Tibetan bells and ring them around the room a few times. After consultations, we always like to open the window for ten minutes and let any unwelcome energy out.

We think twice about walking the streets alone at night and wouldn't ordinarily invite a strange man into our house. But, sadly, you must think of every eventuality. Attacks or inappropriate behaviors often come without warning; believe me, it's no fun. Many clairvoyants and psychics in the UK will only read for women, but that's such a shame for genuine men who seek spiritual counsel. Just arrange a time for the consultation when you know someone else is around. Perhaps ask a friend or partner to open the door to them so the client can see you are not alone in the house. Most psychics will read for people on a recommendation, which isn't so bad. A husband, friend, or son of a returning client will more than likely be a safe bet. The male gender is not necessarily the only one capable of bad behavior—aggressive female clients may also make you feel threatened.

How to Stay Safe

Here is the first rule of thumb for all female Tarot readers out there: It's not a good idea to read for a man if you are alone in your home or premises. In no way is this a general criticism of men. Many wonderful gentlemen in this world wouldn't harm a fly. Still, sadly, whether we like it or not, there are also some undesirable people.

CASE STUDY: LEANNA
Forgetting One's Manners

I had been reading for the same man every six months for three years and had never felt uncomfortable with him. He was always polite and gentle, and we would chat before and after the reading about family and spiritual things. When he called to make another appointment, I figured he was a safe bet and slotted him in for a reading when my husband was at work. The session went well, and everything was okay until he stood up to leave. Out of nowhere, he just pounced, and I found myself pinned to the wall. I might only be four feet eleven, but I am feisty, so I pushed him away in disgust. Thankfully, he realized that he had forgotten his manners and apologized. During our chat a few minutes before, I had mentioned my husband had recently started a new job, and when he asked about the hours he worked, I had no problem telling him it was a nine-to-five role. I was lucky things didn't take a more sinister twist that day.

Time Frames and Value for Money

In our opinion, a reading shouldn't last any longer than fifty minutes to an hour unless you are dealing with a client who is suicidal or suffering from loss or grief. In situations like these, you might like to give extra time because you'll never be able to turn things around for them in sixty minutes. If you're reading for three people in a day, it would be a good idea to group them together and have them come in on the hour, which is easy if you are reading in twos or threes. Every psychic is different; some will find they are burned out after two readings and want a break for an hour before seeing another customer. It isn't unusual to feel a

little foggy-headed and hungry (not sure why this happens), so try to have a rest. Most readers find that four readings a day is the maximum they can do. Any more than that could be problematic, especially if some people come in later. Their consultation might be lackluster because they need to psychically rest and restore their energy. Not only that, but their voice can be strained, becoming croaky, or they could lose it altogether after talking for four hours nonstop.

If you are working at an event or have been invited to read at a Tarot party, you might have five or six clients. In cases like this, you can do mini readings, giving each person around thirty minutes.

These kinds of events are perfect for business because you can arrange for the people to come for a more extended reading at a future time.

When a Client Doesn't Leave

Some people become very engrossed in their reading and enjoy it so much that they just don't take the hint when it's time to go home. Every psychic encounters this issue at some point, and knowing how to address it will help you avoid talking to the person for at least another half hour. Start gathering the cards and place them in their box; this makes it quite evident that the consultation is over. If that fails to work, take a business card and hand it to them. Perhaps reach for your calendar and ask them if they would like to book another sitting in six months. If that doesn't work, try standing up. Usually, the client will follow your lead and start to make their way out the door. If they are still lingering, tell them that you must go now because you need to prepare for your next client.

Pricing

Some individuals will shun a psychic or Tarot reader and criticize them for charging for their services because they think making money from their ability is unethical. These people fail to realize that just like providing any other service out there, you are spending a great deal of your time and energy. A masseuse may be skilled in the art of massage, or an artist may be gifted with creativity. Does this mean we can hang a beautiful painting in our home without paying for it? Like many other professions, Tarot readers have honed their skills, studied hard, and obtained the right to charge a fee for their time. We both gave up lucrative careers to pursue the psychic pathway. It's sad, but many readers charge far too much for their services. Others can charge too little, undercutting everyone else, so getting the balance right is imperative. An excellent way to gauge the price is to look at what the local hairdressers and beauticians charge for an hour's work. They will have products they need to buy, but you also have cards, crystals, incense, tea, and coffee, not to mention toilet rolls and an increased water and heating bill.

As a guideline, in 2023, the average psychic charges somewhere between $45 and $55 per sitting. When you start your Tarot journey, we advise you to lower your price to about $20. Explain to the client that you are a newbie to Tarot, and then gradually raise the cost to an amount that suits you when you are more confident with your predictions.

When a Client Forgets to Pay

Because the client has been concentrating so hard on the reading and the amount of information swirling about in their heads, it's possible that your client will forget to pay you. Usually, you can tell when it has slipped someone's mind because they will get up and walk toward the door while chatting about what you have just told them. One easy fix for this kind of situation, and to save any unnecessary embarrassment on the client's part, is to have a money tin somewhere near the exit with a small pile of business cards beside it. Before you open the door for them to leave, take your cash box in hand and pass them a business card. Just like if you were at the checkout in the local grocery store, give them the card and say, "That will be $45 today, thank you." As far as the client is concerned, this will look like the norm. You may want to invest in a card machine; they are relatively inexpensive and a preferred way for many clients to pay. You can ask the person, "Are you paying by cash or card?" to prompt them. In truth, most people will pay happily while you are sitting at the table, and some will place the cash down even before the reading commences.

When NOT to Charge

There will be times when you are faced with a client who is in the worst phase of their life. A child may have died, or the visitor could be suicidal or struggling with poverty but desperately in need of a reading. You will instinctively know when to waive the fee because your conscience will kick in, and you'll be uncomfortable asking for their money. This situation is particularly challenging because there have been numerous times when we have experienced financial hardship, and every penny has mattered.

As a rule of thumb, whatever circumstances we find ourselves in, it's best to be charitable. It's uncanny how the spirit world recompenses us at times like these; you might receive a phone call for a group booking, or the next client scheduled will leave a large tip. The money will always come back to you, one way or another. In a nutshell, our advice is to just listen to your conscience, and you shouldn't be out of pocket.

Charging Your Friends

As a Tarot reader, you will acquire many friends over the years. There are wonderful people out there, and most will be on the same spiritual wavelength as you. We have met nearly all our friends through our readings, and we feel so God-blessed to have these special people in our lives. The problem arises when one or two of them frequently want you to read their cards, and you will automatically feel awkward about charging them. If your friend is a hairdresser, a healer, a beautician, a manicurist, a reflexologist, or has some other profession you might like to use, swapping energies is very acceptable. You will probably never have to pay for a hair appointment because, after a few years, you will come to know at least ten stylists. A cut and blow dry for a reading is a fair trade. One of our friends who didn't have a skill to swap would pay for lunch once every six months in exchange for two readings a year. If you prefer not to do that, another good idea is to have a 50 percent discount for friends. If you don't set this rule and decide not to charge, you'll be amazed at how many people will want to *be your friend*. You'll also find yourself doing about three free readings a week, which means you'll be working at least one day of the week for nothing!

Appointments

When making an appointment for a client, decide what method of diary you want to use. Some prefer to use a calendar app on their phone, whereas others favor a proper hardback planner.

A more common way to communicate is via text. These days, your appointments will probably arrive via Instagram, X (formerly Twitter), WhatsApp, email, or Facebook. Very few people make a phone call to arrange a reading, so we must get used to checking every social media platform daily. When communication is underway, explain to the client what type of reading they can expect. Some psychics will be gifted with mediumistic skills and can converse with loved ones on the other side; others might want to include palmistry with their Tarot readings. Everyone is different. Also, inform them how long the reading will last and remember to take their phone number or email address when booking a date and time; this is important because something could crop up on your end and you might need to cancel. Also, you can send a confirmation text afterward and drop them a line a few days before the reading to remind them.

Once your consultation is over and the person is happy, it's good business to book them in again before they leave. This way, you are filling up your calendar, ensuring your money energy continues flowing. We have our business cards designed to have appointment dates on the reverse of the card, or they can be left blank to write the date and time of the next session.

Naturally, there will be those customers with whom you struggle to establish a connection, and you'll be relieved when the reading is over. Add a note to their phone number indicating that the reading was very challenging; if they call you again, you can make an excuse and decline them. We know this sounds harsh, but relating with your client on a spiritual level is a must, and being on a different vibration means they won't get the best out of you. Maybe another reader would be better suited for them.

Selecting Cards for a Client

If you have a regular clientele, you will instinctively know that certain decks won't work for everyone. The images may be too dramatic, so you would choose a gentler deck with perhaps softer colors and less graphic imagery. When reading for young adults or people who have never had a reading before, go for a pretty and optimistic pack to not alarm them. For those who have visited you regularly over the years, allow them to point to the pack they would like you to use. Often, their instincts will make certain it will be the right choice.

Long-Distance Readings

Some readers prefer not to open their doors to the general public and instead use platforms such as Zoom or Skype. These types of readings are just as good and will enable you to reach out to people overseas as well. Since both of us had spent many years doing international consultations when Covid arrived, we could still continue working; however, there are some slight differences when choosing the cards.

Card Selection

Since each Tarot card has a number association, your client will be requested to select thirty. Ask them to write down numbers 0 to 78 on separate pieces of paper, place them in a bowl or bag, and then randomly choose thirty. They can send these to you in the order they appear. For years we had our clients jot down the first numbers that came to mind, but doing it this way is not ideal because they can accidentally write the same number twice. It's also crucial that the querent avoids choosing numbers that are associated with their birthdays or anniversaries because these cards are likely to have no bearing on their reading. We have discovered that online number generators also fail to produce the required result. There needs to be more of a personal touch, like shuffling.

Some people interested in having readings often own at least one pack of Tarot cards, so they can bypass the number-choosing method altogether. If this is the case, ask them to shuffle their cards for around five minutes. Instruct them to cut the pack with their left hand into three stacks, then select one pile. Place the two remaining stacks back together, and rest the chosen pile on the top. Take thirty cards from the top, writing them down as they go.

For long-distance or virtual readings, you will need some further information from the client ahead of time.

* The client's name
* The client's birth sign (this helps if you know a little about astrology)
* The client's age (for timing)
* A recent photograph (for you to tune into ahead of the reading)
* Any outlining question they wish you to focus on
* Their Skype address or phone number

Also, ensure that you send them details of how to pay you; this can be either by bank transfer or other outlets, like PayPal. It's best if your fee is paid a few days beforehand, and as with all face-to-face appointments, send them a text reminder.

Once you have all the information and their chosen numbers or cards, you can use this to translate them into the relevant Tarot cards.

EXAMPLE: *Numbers: 6, 78, 45, 69, 51, 8, 14, 65, 39, 43*
(6) the Lovers, (78) King of Pentacles, (45) Nine of Cups, (69) Five of Pentacles, (51) Ace of Swords, (8) Strength, (14) Temperance, (65) Ace of Pentacles, (39) Three of Cups, (43) Seven of Cups

Repeat this twice more so you have thirty cards in three ten-card spreads. Next, lay out all three spreads before you, and then begin your reading.

You won't have the client sitting across a table, and if you're not a fan of FaceTime, you'll need to spend a little time before the reading meditating on their photograph; this will help you tune into their persona. When you first wake in the morning after a long sleep, you always find the psychic flow to be at its best. At this time, your soul is in an altered state of consciousness, which is the perfect time to meditate. Let your mind drift and focus on the person you are about to read for, paying attention to anything that pops into your mind. Because it's so easy to forget, immediately write down any psychic information you might receive.

Recording the Readings

Sometimes there is so much information in a reading that the client cannot remember it all, so the most sensible option is to record it; this is a personal choice, and while some readers like us don't mind recording, others will prefer not to. Often, the person will play it back to their friends and family, so be careful how you deliver the reading to avoid unwittingly criticizing someone.

The other issue with recording is when the seeker or someone close to them is having an affair. When this comes to light, press the pause button; this protects both yourself and the client.

someone in a reading; in that case, you must never say it while the session is being recorded. Hit the pause button and tell the client you have some sensitive information and don't feel comfortable recording it.

CASE STUDY: LEANNA
Be Careful When Recording

In my earlier years of being a Tarot reader, a woman arrived for her consultation, and I picked up on her husband being cruel and abusive. I was so frightened for her; I stressed that her husband wasn't good enough for her and that she needed to get rid of him straightaway, pack her bags, and leave. I even mentioned that he would probably be the type to cheat on her and she could do so much better. Later that day, I didn't think much more of it until my front door nearly fell off its hinges. I jumped out of the chair to see who was pounding when I came face to face with the woman's husband! Back then we used cassette tapes, and either he had got hold of it or she played it back to him, because he was furious. Thankfully, he didn't physically hurt me, but he did hurl a barrage of abuse at me, and when he finally turned to walk away, I was left feeling very scared.

CASE STUDY: BELETA
When Recordings Are in the Wrong Hands

Many years ago, I was conducting a reading for a young married woman, and in her cards, she was having a red-hot love affair with a man she was crazy about. I tentatively inquired whether the recording would be private, and she reassured me that it was for her ears only. I was still uncomfortable about the whole situation but took her at her word and continued. As she was leaving, I warned her to ensure that the reading didn't end up in the wrong hands. That very evening her husband became suspicious and found the tape. He was so upset, he overdosed on many pills and was hospitalized for a week. Fortunately, he survived the ordeal. It was a huge baptism of fire for me. I have since been extra cautious of allowing anything provocative to be recorded again.

If in doubt, leave it out.

There will be times when it's best to be forthright with the client. They might be with a controlling or abusive partner, or the client may be having an affair. Suppose you do need to say something derogatory about

Advertising

Getting your name out there is much easier today than it was when we first started out. For us, we relied totally on word of mouth and a small advertisement in a local newspaper. Nowadays, social media is the way to go, with platforms like Facebook, Instagram, and X (formerly Twitter). On their social media walls, many of our students just starting out in the world of Tarot will announce that they are taking appointments and need individuals to practice on. They might ask for the person to offer a small donation if they are happy with the reading. Depending on the size of your friends list, an advertisement like this should get you at least forty responses. Clients who enjoyed their reading will usually return yearly and pass your name to their family and friends. Once you're established, if the business is a little slow, you can re-post that you have availability. After a while, you won't have to drum up business like this; if anything, you'll book six months in advance and turn new business away.

Presenting Yourself

For some reason, most people expect a Tarot reader to be mysterious and a little bit glamorous, too. It's not necessary to go whole hog and have a string of coins around your forehead, but wearing something colorful and perhaps some unusual or beautiful jewelry really does help to create the right ambience. Often, your clients will ask to take a photograph with

you, so it's always nice to be looking your best.

CASE STUDY
Slumming It

Many years ago, we heard of a Tarot reader who was amazingly accurate with her predictions. She was well-known far and wide, but she was so rough and ready that if you wanted a reading, you had to slum it. When she opened the door to greet you, her hair would be scraped back, and she always had a cigarette shoved in her mouth. On entering her home, there would be an acrid smell of the cat's full litter tray, and her large German shepherd would jump up and sniff your private parts. She used the kitchen table to lay out her cards, but before she got down to the reading, she would swipe away the dirty plates from the meal the night before. She had even been known to eat a takeaway while performing the reading. It was the sort of place where you would wipe your feet on the way out and run home to take a shower! To her credit, although she swore like a trooper and had a raunchy sense of humor, she was one of the best in her field.

Some Advice

We have touched on this subject already in the book, but it does deserve another mention. If you become proficient in the art of Tarot, you will likely create a large following of people over time. Sometimes, every single word that leaves your mouth will be correct, leaving your clients astounded. These folks will put you high up on a pedestal, shouting from the rooftops how fantastic you are, and this can quickly inflate your ego and leave you feeling like the bee's knees. We have both experienced this in our careers and learned very quickly how important it is to keep one's feet firmly on the ground. We keep in mind that we work for spirit and aim to help as many people as possible using our guides and theirs and other spirit helpers. Without them connecting to our subconscious, we wouldn't be able to communicate any important information at all. Showing signs of arrogance, conceit, or overconfidence could temporarily take away the gift. Later, one might encounter a wave of challenging clients, and everything that is said will be wrong. All will be well if we predict with kindness and humility!

Client Types

We've added this section to the book to give the novice reader a glimpse of what to expect if they decide to have a career as a Tarot reader. Over time, you will meet an array of different and interesting people and learn a lot from them along the way. Some will be much easier to connect to, and others you will struggle with. Knowing how to handle the more complicated client will set you in good stead. The one thing to remember is that everything in life happens for a reason, and each person you meet along the way is sent to you because you might be able to help them on their path, or you can learn something from them.

THE CHATTERBOX

Now and again, you will encounter a client who will talk continually throughout the reading. No matter how hard you try to interrupt, they will chatter on and on, giving you a complete history of their life. People like this can leave a reader frustrated. When you get a chance to interject, gently tell them that you need a moment's silence to tune into the cards, and that their willingness to inform you about everything might cause you to be psychically biased; this usually does the trick.

THE ELDERLY

Often, the elderly in their eighties and nineties will come for a reading. Because they are in the latter phase of their life, their sons, daughters, and grandchildren might be the sole focus in the cards. The Tarot hardly ever covers incidents that happened years ago, so it's unlikely you will be able to get a clear look at their past unless you psychically channel it. However, these folks are often more concerned about health matters and how they can best enjoy the future. Never be fooled by thinking that just because they are elderly they don't have much of a future. We have read for many people of this generation that have gone on to marry, even in their eighties.

THE SICK AND DYING

Occasionally, you will have someone come for a reading that will soon die. Often, they seek reassurance that there is an afterlife and hope you can guide them as to what they can expect when they pass away. At times like these, it would be best to choose a gentle deck and steer the reading around the spiritual aspects. We have included some information in this book that might help you. (See chapter 7, "Situations You Might Face: Death," page 301.)

THE SKEPTICAL CLIENT

Now and again, you will come across someone skeptical or out to test you; they can often make it very clear from the onset that they are a nonbeliever and are just along for the ride. During the reading, some folks might smirk or make fun of you, saying things like, "You tell me, you're the psychic," or they'll remain stone-faced, giving nothing away. If you sense this at any point during the reading, there is really

no point continuing. They are clearly not ready to have a consultation, and you won't be able to tap into their energy if they have surrounded themselves with a brick wall. Kindly tell them that you are finding it hard to make a connection and that maybe another reader might do better for them. However long you have been struggling with the reading, it is best not to charge.

CASE STUDY: BELETA
The Attorney

Standing in the doorway was a tall, handsome, distinguished man called Robert. He scrutinized me from head to toe, and I could tell he was sussing me out. From the moment I saw him, I knew the reading would be tricky; it was obvious he didn't trust me. Silently, I called on the spirit realms for a little help. Once seated in the reading room, he stared at me again.

"So, how long have you been doing this job?" he inquired politely.

"Over forty years," I replied.

"And where do you get your so-called 'knowledge' from?"

Sighing, I pointed to the ceiling. "I get my messages from the spirit world, and I use the Tarot to predict future events." I signaled to him to shuffle the cards. He narrowed his eyes and stayed silent.

As the cards unfolded, I psychically felt he had a grandfather named Percy, and then I went on to tell him that he'd had an unhappy childhood. As I relayed this information, his face gave nothing away, so I pressed on. "By the way, Percy says Robert isn't your real name; he says you are called Oliver."

I continued. "Do you work in or around the court system?" He remained silent. ". . . Is that correct, Oliver?"

He nodded briefly and muttered under his breath that he was an attorney. I went on to tell him that someone at work had it in for him and that he needed to watch his back. He fidgeted in his chair, and I knew I'd hit a nerve and was right.

"Your marriage looks dysfunctional," I said. "Are you thinking of getting a divorce?"

His eyebrows shot to the heavens. "You tell me!" he snapped.

I carried on, trying not to get angry with him. "You need to pay close attention; your wife could really take you to the cleaners!"

He leaned back in his chair, trying to make me out. "Who's been telling you these things about me? How have you obtained this information?" he bit out. I reminded him he wasn't in the courtroom and told him I had done my very best, and then, deciding it wasn't worth the aggravation, I cut the reading short and showed him the door.

I received a call from him that evening, in which he apologized profusely for his behavior. He told me that he was overwhelmed by the reading, especially the part about Percy and his unhappy childhood, and that he would love to come back and have another consultation. I relented, and so he visited me every six months for many years. I am happy to say that he was always on his best behavior!

THE PROFESSIONAL PSYCHIC

Psychics will always want to check out other readers, so seeing other professionals is quite common. Some can be very nice, and you'll get on well, whereas others might have a big following and an ego to match. One of the most challenging things when reading for fellow psychics is that they are also deciphering the cards as you are interpreting them. They might say things like, "Where in the spread did you see that prediction?" or "I can't see how you came to that conclusion." If you know your cards well, you won't have a problem, but if you're starting out and still have a lot to learn, you might prefer to use the cards as a crutch and focus mainly on your psychic senses. They can't argue with that!

THE WISE SOULS

Once in a blue moon, someone very special will arrive for a reading, and you will instantly know they have been "sent by spirit." Some might classify them as earth angels or earth avatars; these are beings that don't need to reincarnate anymore because their soul has reached a state of near perfection. Instead, they choose to come back to earth to help people or give the reader information about their own lives regarding health and the way forward. It is a very uplifting experience, and you feel awestruck in meeting them.

THE SINISTER

You will occasionally meet a client who makes the hairs on your neck stand up. If this happens, you could be in the zone of a negative character, and you must immediately decide whether to continue. As we have mentioned before, whenever you do a reading, it's best to always wear a black obsidian crystal for protection and ask a spirit guide to encircle you in the light. Always try to have someone in the home you can call if you need them.

CASE STUDY: BELETA
The Dark Side

After reading for five individuals at a Tarot party, I was exhausted and waiting for my final client. A man came in, and I immediately noticed that one of his eyebrows was white and the other brown. He was in his late twenties and had a shock of wiry black hair. Straightaway, I felt disadvantaged and didn't want to read for him. A division went up between us, and for the first time in my life, I couldn't find anything to say. Everything I mentioned was wrong, and the Tarot cards were a chaotic mess.

"I thought you were supposed to be good," he sniped, "but really, you're a load of crap!"

"Are you dabbling with the dark forces?" I said quietly. "Because I sense a great deal of negativity around you." He stood up and glowered down at me, throwing his cash on the table. "Karma will come back to bite you," I reminded him

as he left the room. After he'd gone, I was shaking and certainly didn't want his money.

The hostess came in and inquired if I was alright. I asked her why she had invited him, and she looked sheepish. "He's my brother, Beleta, and he worships Satan. I prayed you would be able to turn him around because I despair of what will happen to him."

What could I do? My guides wouldn't even let me read for him!

The next day I went to the local animal rescue and donated the money he had given me. That night I lit a white candle and asked the archangel Michael to protect him.

THE NERVOUS CLIENT

Anxiety is a very common problem; probably half of the people you read for will feel very nervous before the reading begins. You'll spot it immediately because their hands will shake while shuffling the cards, or they will drop them, scattering them in all directions on the floor. All you can do in this instance is to reassure them and perhaps choose a gentle deck that is not too graphic to put them at ease. You can also give them a piece of amethyst to hold, which has a calming energy and should settle them down. Don't worry, though, because once they've returned to you a couple of times, they will lose the nerves altogether.

THE GRIEVING CLIENT

A grieving client is the most challenging of all, and as a rule, we would never charge for a reading that is heavily overcome with grief. It's best to choose a spiritual deck of Tarot and ask the client to hold a small piece of angelite crystal, which you can provide until the reading ends. The stone will calm them and help them to settle. With individuals who have lost someone, there are usually many tears and much heartache during the reading, so a gentle approach is necessary, as is a sympathetic ear. Sadly, death is not a popular topic for people to discuss, but the reading will be a good outlet to assuage their grief. Use some of the spiritual lessons in this book (see chapter 7: "Situations You Might Face") to give them an idea of where their loved ones might be. We are both firm believers that we will meet our cherished ones again on the other side, so tell them it's not goodbye; it's just farewell for now.

THE RACY CLIENT

Many clients will take a shine to a psychic, finding them enigmatic and mysterious. They usually ask you if you're single and offer to take you out on a date. Sometimes, the client will return for another reading later, laden with gifts of flowers or chocolates. It's great for the ego, but if the attention is unwanted, it can become quite problematic.

CASE STUDY: BELETA
The Meeting

I met my lovely husband, John, through a postal reading forty-three years ago. I studied the palm prints he had sent, and although his hand was spiritual, I could see he'd had dozens of affairs. He was such a "Jack the Lad"; I remember thinking that some poor woman would need a bucketful of luck if she got embroiled with him!

Over the year, I had done two postal readings for him, and back in those days, people rarely sent photos, so I had no idea how he looked. I was at an event sometime later when this younger, good-looking man walked over to me. I tuned in immediately and said, "Hello, John Greenaway!" He had made the five-hour journey just to meet me in person. We were married two years later, and he has been a loyal and wonderful husband. I did warn him, though, before we wed that if he strayed, my guides would be the first to tell me.

THE INTIMIDATING CLIENT

Most clients you see will be very nice, but you may face a downright scary one once or twice in your career. If anyone makes you uncomfortable, continuing the reading is a bad idea. As we have mentioned before, you will need to connect with the client to give them a decent reading, but some people are just so off the charts that it will be impossible to reach them.

CASE STUDY: LEANNA
Some Unsavory Characters

I decided to include this bizarre story in the book, and I apologize in advance for the profanity; I simply wanted to relay it exactly as it happened.

I was a young mother with an autistic baby, living in the backstreets of northern England, and money was so tight that my first husband and I struggled to make ends meet. Because I was only twenty-one, Mamma had dissuaded me from being a Tarot reader, believing I should have a little more life experience before I took on the responsibility of seeing paid clients. However, when things came to a head with my finances, we agreed I should do a few readings each week to help with the cash flow. "It'll be good practice for you," she said.

After placing an advertisement in the local paper, I received my very first call. The woman at the end of the telephone said she had four friends who wanted to have a reading and asked if I could do a party booking at my home. I agreed straightaway, feeling relieved that at least we would be able to feed ourselves that week. I had a long conversation with Mamma about what to wear and how to present the home, so I cleaned the house from top to bottom and lit candles to create the right ambience. I was so nervous; my heart was banging through my chest.

When the doorbell rang, I opened it to four of the most intimidating women I had ever seen in my life. They were around my age and very brash. One had a skull tattooed down the left side of her face, and two had piercings through their lips and

noses; all were chewing gum. I think they'd been smoking something strange, too, because a peculiar odor began to permeate the hall. I felt immediately threatened, especially when they strolled into my home, laughing with each other and saying the F-word in every other sentence. I stood there in a beautiful deep purple kaftan, adorned in Mamma's dynamic jewelry, my husband and baby upstairs in the bedroom. I had never felt more out of place in my whole life. They flopped down on my couch, and the blond one with the pierced lip pulled out a bottle of strong cider and proceeded to pass it around the group. I guided the first one toward the reading room, where I had set up my table.

"If ya no good, lass, you'll not get paid!" she said in a thick Yorkshire accent. I gulped as the other three laughed hysterically.

Since this was my first ever paid reading, I tried my best to be confident.

"I see here that you are in a relationship!" I said as I turned the cards over. "You might have one or two issues in the coming months, and you'll need to decide if he's the right man for you."

"Nah!" she said. "That's a load of crap! I love my Eddie. We've been together since I was fourteen. Ya not very good, are ya!" I raised my eyebrows, heart still beating fast, and swiftly moved on.

"I can see you'll have a little girl in the future. She's very sweet and might even be psychic," I said.

"What the fuck!" she replied loudly. "I ain't having no more fucking kids . . . for fuck's sake, deal some proper cards!" The reading was going south, and after thirty minutes, I guided her back into the lounge, where her friends were clearly getting very tipsy. One of them was even stubbing out a joint of cannabis in my potted ivy plant.

"She was fucking crap," I heard her say to her friend. "I ain't paying her!"

I politely asked the women not to smoke as I had a baby upstairs, and then led the second one into the dining room. As she was shuffling the cards, I silently prayed to my guide and asked him to make every word out of my mouth accurate so that I could get through this nightmare ordeal.

"Your mother is here in the cards," I said. "She has something wrong with her knee and will need surgery."

"That's right, lass," she said, smiling. "She's gotta have a new one. She's booked in for the op next week!"

"And your sister is with a horrible man. Do you dislike him?"

"Yeah, he's a right bastard, knocks her around from pillar to post. I hate him."

The reading continued to be correct, and I silently thanked my guide once it had ended. He answered my prayer, and everything I relayed to her was 100 percent right. I went back into the lounge to invite the next one in.

The third reading went very much like the second. I told her she had four children and that her father was an alcoholic. She was close to her grandmother, and she was also psychic. All pre-

dictions were spot-on—another happy customer. I breathed out a sigh of relief.

As I was finishing up with the fourth, I could hear the women in the other room, their voices getting louder and louder until they began shouting.

"You're full of crap!" one said to the other. "She got everything right; something must be wrong with you!"

"She's a fucking charlatan," the woman bit out. "She's not getting my money!"

"You WILL fucking pay her," the woman replied. "She's brilliant."

"And are you gonna fucking make me?" she screamed.

As I opened the door, two of the women were fighting on the ground, with one of them pounding the other in the face while the blond one with the lip piercing attempted to kick her away with her legs. I stood there stunned with my mouth wide open, hoping the ornaments would remain in one piece. It finally came to a head when the skull-faced woman straddled the difficult customer, grabbed the half-drunk bottle of cider, and hit her hard over the head. As I heard my baby crying upstairs, the fire rose in my belly, and I suddenly felt this great rage; enough was enough!

"Put your money on the table and get out of my house," I screamed. "You should all be ashamed of yourselves!" I couldn't quite believe it, but in their rough and ready way, three of the women immediately rose to their feet, apologized profusely, and then opened their purses to pay. The problematic woman rolled her eyes, and after "skull face" stared her down for a moment with a *clenched fist, she paid up. I pointed to the door, and they silently walked out. Locking it behind them, I glanced down at the 40 pounds I had just earned and wondered if it was all worth it. Talk about a baptism of fire! Thankfully, I never saw the group of women again, and I have never had a session like that since. I'm amazed it didn't put me off readings for life, but there you go; here I am over thirty years later, and still seeing clients.*

Dealing with Neighbors

Because most Tarot readers work from home, it can cause a lot of controversy with the people that live around you. You'll either be loved or hated, with some neighbors thinking that you are evil, giving you a wide berth. One of the main issues rests with parking. Folks can be very territorial about space, and sometimes a visiting client can cause backlash. Even those that park legally can come up against rudeness, with some neighbors thinking they own the avenue.

CASE STUDY: BELETA
Nosy Neighbors

I remember once a young woman who had just lost her five-year-old daughter to meningitis; as she was getting out of the car (legally parked), an irate neighbor charged out of her house and told her with a tirade of foul expletives to get away. Before we could even begin the reading, it took me ages to soothe her. I also had to calm myself down and focus hard on not being angry with the disgraceful neighbor.

Taking Responsibility

Some Tarot readers, especially those with little life experience, can be pretty flippant in their readings and harm the reputation of other readers. These so-called psychics or clairvoyants frequently disregard their clients' welfare and just blurt out anything they believe they have seen in a spread without considering how it will impact the client. Here are a few examples of the situations we've faced.

CASE STUDY: LEANNA
Choose Your Words Carefully

Some years ago, I welcomed a woman in for a reading who was clearly pregnant, and as soon as she sat down, she burst into tears. I passed her a handkerchief and asked if she was okay with me proceeding with the reading, and she nodded. She hadn't even finished shuffling the cards when she broke down again, so, instinctively, I held her hand and asked her what was wrong. She told me that she had visited a local clairvoyant a few months earlier and had been informed that her pregnancy would result in a miscarriage. The Tarot reader was flippant and shrugged off the prediction as though it were unimportant. I immediately dealt the cards and reassured her I couldn't see anything of the sort; the cards showed a healthy baby without complications. I tried to soothe her, but the damage had already been done, and no amount of comforting her made any difference. Six months later, she arrived for another reading, this time with her babe in her arms, and I noted she looked exhausted. I said kindly, "I told you the baby would be fine." She was still clearly distressed and said that she hadn't slept properly since the child was born. She was concerned that the Tarot reader might have misinterpreted the reading, and perhaps the infant might die of SIDS (sudden infant death syndrome). Again, I dealt the cards and told her in no uncertain terms that this would not happen. She came to see me every six months for ten years, and even when so much time had passed and the Tarot reader's predictions had failed to come true, the woman still felt her child might suddenly pass away because this irresponsible Tarot reader had predicted the death.

The impact of all this ruined the young woman's life. She didn't enjoy her pregnancy and suffered severe anxiety for years, thinking her child might suddenly be snatched from her. The youngster was never let out of her sight and was not allowed to stay overnight at friends' houses or participate in any school outings. In effect, both their lives were affected.

For the record, I did call this dreadful reader and gave her a piece of my mind. She couldn't even remember doing the reading.

CASE STUDY: BELETA
Too Much Information

Against my better judgement, I had fit in a few extra clients who were desperate for a reading. I was already tired and wondered how on earth I would get through it all as my psychic energy was depleted. Reluctantly, I escorted the last client into the conservatory, who seemed a nice enough young woman. She smiled brightly at me and said she had been looking forward to meeting me and was excited to have a reading. As the cards started to unfold, I saw that she was in a relationship and instinctively knew he was wrong for her. The Lovers and the Three of Swords were glaring up at me from the spread, and I knew straightaway he'd be the unfaithful type. I warned her not to continue the relationship because I felt another woman was in the background. Her face crumpled, and tears sprang into her eyes as she glared at me with hostility. "Well, thanks for that bit of information; you've just ruined everything," she spat out. "I'm marrying him tomorrow!"

This colossal blunder has stayed with me throughout my entire career. Whether my prediction was right or wrong, whichever way you look at it, I ruined that poor girl's wedding day. I still don't know if her marriage did stand the test of time or whether my prediction was, in fact, correct. Still, looking back on it, I should have chosen my words more carefully and stuck to my schedule of how many readings I do in one day.

It's important to realize that Tarot readers carry a great responsibility. Many clients will listen intently to whatever you say, and some may even base their entire life on the outcome of the cards. Most of the readings are recorded and played repeatedly, sometimes with a whole family or group of friends listening in. What we say can sometimes be taken out of context, with the client's imagination running away. You must choose your words carefully and never be afraid to avoid certain predictions. It's not your job to deliver bad news, and it's far better to skirt around a subject if you feel out of your depth. It's a Tarot reader's responsibility to ensure that when the client leaves their establishment, they are sent away in a better frame of mind, with hope in their heart and possibly a better understanding of spiritual matters.

Even if you decide to only study the cards for fun, you have a responsibility to whomever you are reading for to ensure that the message is delivered sensitively and without cause for concern. Prediction with cards is one thing, but you must also acquire some Tarot techniques. The last thing you want to do is frighten or scare someone with a prediction, so use the tips in this book, and choose your approach carefully.

How to Deliver a Reading

Most people are on the planet to learn hard lessons, and no matter who you are predicting for, everyone has their own troubles. As a Tarot reader, it's your job to help them with any difficulties and steer them in a positive direction. You can be an excellent flare path to many individuals and give them a deeper understanding of spiritual matters.

Suppose you are reading the cards and you see a terrible situation unfolding. In that case, however proficient your Tarot skills are, you may be unable to tell whether the problem has already happened or if it will happen in the future. Therefore, when you broach the subject, it's better to word it in the future tense. One of the most complex parts of reading Tarot is finding out the basics of a person's life. You will probably see court mentors in the reading and Knights and Pages popping up all over the place, but because you have limited knowledge of the client's life, you'll struggle to know who they are. Often, the cards will make much more sense if you know the client's marital status and whether they have children. Usually, acquiring this information can be considered fishing (asking clients direct questions). There are ways to determine whether the client is married or single or has children by making a statement before asking the question.

Example: "There is a relationship in the cards; I take it you are in one?" If the client says no, you can then determine that it's perhaps a new person she might meet. The cards will then make more sense, and you can give her a description of the man to come and his character. You can use the same method with children.

"There's a little girl here in the cards. Do you have her yet?" Or "I take it you're a mother because there's a little boy in the cards." If the person you are reading for is a more mature woman, you would say, "There's a little granddaughter here; has she arrived yet?" This method is perfectly acceptable. Without this basic information, a reading can be muddled and not make much sense. Of course, there will always be times when you can't place a particular court mentor in the client's life, and when this happens, it's best not to try to make it fit; just set it to one side.

Another example: "These cards are all about work; you should be employed, am I right?" (You are not fishing because you are telling her all the cards are related to her employment.) Once you've recognized she is employed, you can then word the rest of the reading in the future tense.

"Big changes are coming in with your work, a restructure could occur, and everyone will be up in arms!" She might agree with you and tell you it's happening right now. If not, you have worded it so that she might expect it in the future. Of course, she might say she doesn't work and is a stay-at-home mom, so the cards might relate not to her but to her partner.

A Few Tips

If you are giving a prediction for the future and the client tells you it's already happened, they will probably be impressed that you picked it up and will forgive you for getting the timing wrong. The way the world works is that wherever there is a problem, there is usually a solution. People tend to go through periods of drama that last for a while before things settle down. There's a balance between negative and positive in life, and one will always follow the other. We always teach our students that you must never deliver a pessimistic prediction without following up with something positive.

EXAMPLE 1: WHAT NOT TO SAY
"You are having a terrible time at the moment. Is your husband having an affair?"

To begin with, you could be correct, but your prediction might not happen for another six months, so it is wrong as far as the client is concerned. The second drawback is that if you hint that her husband might be having an affair, you will cast a shadow over her head. She will likely spend the rest of her marriage not trusting him because she thinks he'll run off with another woman. In effect, with just a few flippant words, you have ruined her marriage.

EXAMPLE 1: A BETTER WAY TO WORD IT
"You have a few cards in this spread that are slightly unsettled. Over the coming months, you'll face one or two challenges in your relationship. Still, it's nothing you can't deal with [positive follow-up]. Expect a time when the two of you are not in sync with each other. The cards advise you to keep communicating, and you'll be able to see things more clearly."

By wording it this way, you are telling the client she will go through an unsettled time, and the issue could be linked to her relationship. You are also telling her that it's nothing she can't deal with; this gives her a positive message after you have delivered the negative. If she does catch him cheating in the future, she will remember you have indicated a difficult time. On the other hand, she may well tell you that she's just left her husband. If this is the case, you could then ask her if he was unfaithful in the marriage.

EXAMPLE 2: WHAT NOT TO SAY
"Your daughter is ill, and she's in the hospital."

The client may not even have a daughter, so you are sticking your neck on the block by saying she does. If there is a daughter, you've implied that she's in the hospital. There might not be anything wrong with her yet, and the client will go away worried about her daughter's health!

EXAMPLE 2: A BETTER WAY TO WORD IT
"There's a young girl in the cards who might have to spend time in the hospital."

This way, the child might not necessarily be hers and could belong to someone she knows. She might come back and ask if you think it's her daughter. You could then say yes, but give her hope by saying everything should be fine.

Working with Your Spirit Guides

Even the most psychically gifted readers will not wake up clairvoyant every morning. They will often need to rely solely on the accuracy of the cards to help give the querent the answers they seek. Being psychic isn't something you can quickly turn off and on. It takes great patience and time to hone these skills. Some days you might not have slept well, so you will be tired, and other times, your soul might be willing, but your psychic juices aren't flowing. At times like these, the Tarot will do all the work for you, and you will still be able to predict confidently.

Of course, it is so much better when you can twin the accuracy of the cards with your psychic flow. To do this successfully, you will need to call upon the spirit helpers to work with you. Some readers will work closely with their guide, whereas others, like us, choose to channel the client's guide for information. It's a bit like having a telephone line to the spirit world, where you can dial up to obtain your messages. Learning how to tap into this phone line isn't always straightforward. Unless you have mediumistic tendencies, you will rarely see or hear a spirit. For most people tapping into the other side, you will experience an inner knowing, like a profound feeling within your very being, and you will be 100 percent confident that these feelings are for real.

Your guides and spirits will never want to frighten you, so instead of appearing in a puff of smoke and giving you a heart attack, they whisper to your subconscious, providing you the self-assurance to go on and relay the message. When a spirit is near, you might feel a cold sensation, or you could experience goosebumps. Other signs are candles flickering, lights dipping or turning on and off, and floorboards creaking or popping; this is all quite normal. You as the reader are inadvertently making yourself available to all kinds of spiritual activities, serving as the vehicle for information to be passed on. So, your first and most important lesson is to learn how to protect yourself and your home from unwanted visitors and to only attract benevolent spirits into your reading.

When a spirit comes into contact with a psychic person, imagine a light shining over the person's head. All spirits, good or bad, can see this light and, like a moth to a flame, will hone in. It's vital to eliminate undesirable spirits and draw in the good guys. To do this, you need to perform a short protection ceremony before any reading commences.

Sit quietly in a room and close your eyes. Imagine a purple light surrounding you. Cross both hands over your chest and lower your head. Take ten deep breaths and, at the same time, visualize positive vibes engulfing you.

Imagine yourself pushing away negative energies until you are completely enveloped in pure light.

You might like to do this exercise before the client arrives. It only takes about five minutes, but you can do it for longer if you feel inclined; it's a lovely and relaxing practice. We like to perform it every morning, even if we are not scheduled to work. It gives us peace of mind to know that we are protected for the rest of the day.

Once you have your protection in place and before the client turns up, you can draw in the guides by saying this short affirmation.

Spirits above, I call upon you, surround me
in your luminous light.
Pass your spiritual knowledge to me, guide
and protect me throughout.

Tarot Guidelines

TRY TO AVOID READINGS IF YOU ARE UNWELL OR EMOTIONAL.

A Tarot consultant's job is to tune into the energy of the querent, so it's best to be in tip-top condition. For the reader, it's impossible to have the correct psychic flow when feeling out of sorts. Concentrating can be difficult, but more important, it's not in the client's best interest.

DON'T MIX THE SPIRITS—AVOID ALCOHOL.

It's so easy, when at a party or gathering and alcohol has been consumed, to give in to the demands of others and take out the Tarot cards. It's widely known within clairvoyant circles that drinking when on duty doesn't augur well. Daring or inappropriate things may be said, increasing the risk that predictions you make could be entirely wrong.

DON'T DO READINGS FOR ANYONE UNDER EIGHTEEN.

We have a rule of thumb: never read for anyone under eighteen. There are two reasons for this. One is that a person must have a certain amount of maturity before allowing someone to read for them. Youngsters lack life skills and might take things out of context or even become fearful. If there is bad news in their reading, it can be awkward to pass that information on to them as they might become stressed, and you could have a worried parent banging on your door. A good point to remember is that, in reality, they are still children, and there is only so much you can tell them at such a tender age, so it's better to wait until they are in their twenties. The only time we have been known to break these rules is when a parent approaches us for help when their child is taking drugs or venturing down a criminal path. Many young people who suffer from substance abuse issues are walking a very thin line and could overdose or die at any given moment. Making them aware of this from a spiritual perspective is sometimes enough to stop them in their tracks and get them back on the right path.

NEVER READ FOR A CLIENT MORE THAN TWICE A YEAR.

Many people get hooked on having readings and will want their monthly fix. Having too many is a complete waste of your time and their money. A general Tarot reading will cover the recent past and a portion of the present, and will predict events within a six-to twelve-month time frame. When performing multiple readings for a client, every set of cards could be exactly the same as before. It's far better to have a rule that you only read for the same person on a biannual basis. This way, new information should be available to them.

DON'T READ FOR SOMEONE REPEATEDLY IF THEIR LIFE DOESN'T CHANGE.

This is a tricky scenario, but often, the spirit world will only open doors for clients when they have moved on from one stage of their life out of choice. An example might be a woman who is miserable in her abusive marriage. When she has a reading, you can foresee her being happy with someone else. For her to find this happiness, she must first summon the courage to leave her present partner and change her path in life. Until she does that, her circumstances won't alter, and the Tarot cards will predict a more or less identical reading. As harsh as it sounds, if you have a client like this, it's best to say that you will be glad to read for them again once their situation has changed.

DON'T ALLOW OTHERS TO SIT IN ON A READING.

People often request that their friend, mother, sister, etc., join them at their reading because they need moral support. This is not a good idea because you are likely to pick up on the spectators' problems, or perhaps someone in the spirit world will come in to speak to them. It can then become very complex and muddled.

> ## CASE STUDY: BELETA
> ### Evading the Truth
>
> *Once, the Lovers and the Three of Swords jumped out from the spread, and I asked a client if she was having an affair. She vehemently denied it, even though her face told a different story. Later the woman rang to apologize for lying and admitted she was having an affair with the husband of the friend she had brought along!*

MAKE SURE PETS ARE BANNED FROM THE ROOM.

Our little furry friends can be a big distraction when you allow them to sit in on a reading. Most Tarot readers are animal lovers and will have at least one cat or dog in their family. As lovely as it might be to have a dog under your feet or a cat curled up innocently in a chair, animals really do tap into the psychic energies and will wake up the minute you get into the swing of a reading. Cats are great ones for jumping up on the table and flicking the cards onto the floor.

HAVE A "NO BABIES OR CHILDREN" POLICY.

So many times we have allowed a nursing mother to bring her baby along when hav-ing a reading. Although it's delightful to see, the client is almost always distracted by her child and will not truly focus on what you are saying. This goes for toddlers as well. Very rarely will a two- or three-year-old sit still for an hour, so the mother's attention will again be drawn away from the reading. After a while, the reader will also become distracted, as the child could run around or touch or-naments. It's better for the client to get a babysitter for the hour they are with you.

OFFER A GLASS OF WATER FOR YOURSELF AND THE QUERENT.

It's a nice touch to have a glass of water ready for the client when they arrive for a reading, but more important, pour one for yourself. Remember, you will be talking nonstop for a whole hour and possibly more if you have two or three readings scheduled one after the other. Tarot readers often get what we call the "reader's croak" and can lose their voice altogether. Sometimes, you might even develop a tickly cough, so keep some lozenges nearby, just in case.

GIVE YOURSELF TEN MINUTES TO TALK TO THE CLIENT AFTERWARD.

Many clients like to discuss their reading once it is over, so it's best to allow a little time afterward to listen to them. They will often give you important feedback and tell you a little bit more about a particular situation you might have discovered in the reading. Taking time gives them a feeling of value, and they will be much more relaxed.

Always give hope and encouragement.

We do repeat this advice throughout the book. However dismal a person's reading might be, try to find a positive viewpoint on situations that will need working on, and send the person away feeling stronger than when they arrived.

Also, providing a spiritual alternative might give them some extra comfort.

Always be patient.

Remember, 80 percent of your predictions will be concerning relationships, sex, and unrequited love. This can be repetitious and mind-numbing, especially if it's your third consultation that day. After reading the cards for a few years, you could become frustrated with problems that you feel are trivial, but put your own feelings to one side and understand that, to the client, it's the center of their universe.

Tell the client about the timings beforehand.

Before you begin your consultation:

1. Inform the client that timings can be hit or miss in a reading.
2. Discuss how you can often see a situation unfold in the cards and that only twelve of the Major Arcana cards give you a rough idea of time scales.
3. Ask them to tell you if one of your predictions might have already happened.

This is handy and will help you determine what any results might be.

When the Cards Are Stubborn

Sometimes nothing will make sense with the reading, and confusion will be your worst enemy, especially if you are trying to read for someone who really wants answers. First, try another deck, and see if the new cards perform any better. At the same time, reassure the querent that this can be perfectly normal.

If the cards remain jumbled, there is only one thing to do: stop the session. For whatever reason, the client is not meant to have a reading. It can be because the person's guide doesn't want them to have the information at this time, or that you cannot connect to their energy. We always refuse their fee if this happens.

9

Tarot Magic

Many people mistakenly think that Tarot can only be used as a tool for divination. However, since Tarot cards are infused with magical power, they also can bring about wishes and desires if you use them in rituals and affirmations. We would first choose the appropriate card or cards related to our wish and place them on an altar, which can be a table or work surface where you can assemble magical items. These chosen cards would then be used in conjunction with other magical objects and incantations.

There are a few things to bear in mind before you try your hand at Tarot magic. Like any ritual prayer or spell, you must have the right intent.

When we invoke our desires, we must always ensure that we are not hurting or influencing anyone else. With any magical practice, the bounce-back effect will occur if rules are not met. Like attracts like, so if you send out a positive affirmation, you will receive a positive response. Should you decide to use Tarot magic in a negative way, hindering a person or influencing their free will, you are summoning the darker energies. If the energy is rejected by the receiver, it can turn around and return straight to its sender threefold! Still, one rule of thumb is that you must not interfere with another's karma. If you are working on a ritual for someone else, it's always best to ask their permission.

Many people will recite a mantra in an effort to win the lottery or achieve fame and wealth. This is not entirely realistic. Any form of magic has a peculiar way of providing you with only what you require. If your need is genuine, you might be fortunate and receive spiritual assistance; otherwise, the mantra will be completely ineffective. Sometimes the ritual will work in a roundabout way, only achieving part of the desire. This can happen for two reasons. First, when you speak the mantra, you could be distracted and let your mind wander, meaning that you are not truly focusing on the desire. The other reason is that you are not specific enough about your request. You might perform a ceremony for better health but forget to mention who is to receive it.

The Altar

Your altar can be a small table or a shelf in the home. You can really go to town and design it however you choose. Some people might like to have a Tarot altar set up all the time, whereas others will only assemble one when they want to perform a ritual. You can decorate it with a pretty cloth, or if you have a wooden table, you might like to keep it natural.

Candles

Burning candles alongside the rituals will give them more power. However, it's important to use the correct color candle that associates itself with the task at hand.

* White, Neutral (can be used for any ritual if you don't have the correct color): children, spiritual, protection, divination, healing, truth
* Red: strength, bravery, love, sex, passion, assertiveness, changes, removing obstacles
* Pink: love and romance, reconciliation, the end of abuse, friendships, fidelity and loyalty in relationships and marriage
* Green: money, business, work, prosperity, good luck, peace, environment, nature, achieving goals, passing exams and tests (driving tests)
* Yellow: self-confidence and self-esteem, inspiration, learning new things, happiness, travel, communication, healing
* Orange: discipline, addiction, ambition, strength, travel, creativity, better parenting, education, finding lost items
* Silver and Blue: pregnancy, motherhood, dreamwork, insomnia, spiritual connection, guide communication, trust, marriage, interviews, studies
* Purple: any form of protection, house blessings, removal of entities or spirits, new business, work, self-employment, new jobs, summoning angels or guides
* Brown: animals, nature, garden, work, grounding, anything material, stability in the family and at work

✶ Black: used as a vessel in rituals to draw away anything negative; banishing, facing challenges, rebirth, karma

Remember, if you are in any doubt as to which color to use, simply opt for a white candle.

With regular candle magic rituals, the practitioner would inscribe the candle with their desired wish. For example, if you needed more cash, with a small knife, you would scratch your full name and the words "money luck" or "more money" into the wax. If you have a specific amount of money you need, you can add that to the inscription. However, engraving your candle when using Tarot in rituals is not always necessary because, if chosen correctly, the cards you place on your altar will automatically represent your wish. It's your choice!

We like to carry out Tarot mantras before and after our readings. It puts us in the right frame of mind and allows us to control what happens to the energies in our homes. Here are some of our rituals that you might like to try.

Enhance Your Psychic Powers

This is a great one to perform an hour or so before you begin your readings and will, hopefully, open the psychic floodgates.

You will need the following:

FROM THE TAROT: THE MAGICIAN

✶ 4 white tealight candles
✶ A good pinch of dried mugwort (to enhance the psychic ability)
✶ A small piece of apatite or moldavite crystal

Set up a small altar and position the Magician card in the center. Sprinkle the mugwort over the card and rest the crystal on top.

Place the four tea light candles around the four corners of the card, two at the top and two at the bottom, and then light them. Stand in front of your altar and chant this mantra seven times:

Open my mind, let me receive all the visions I can perceive.
I channel my thoughts, I focus intent, I gather the messages you have sent.

After reciting the above seven times, close the ritual by saying, "And so it is."

Leave the candles burning for an hour before blowing them out.

Place the Magician back in the pack and use the same deck in your next reading.

Summon Your Guide

This is another ritual you might like to do before you begin the reading. Our guides, or the client's guide, will often work closely with us when we read the cards, especially if they have particular messages they need you to pass on. This will help establish a connection between you and the spirit helper.

You will need the following:

FROM THE TAROT, ONE OF THE FOLLOWING CARDS: THE STAR, THE HIEROPHANT, THE HIGH PRIESTESS, THE HERMIT, OR TEMPERANCE

* A King, Queen, or Knight card that represents you
* A purple candle (to invoke the guides and angels)
* A small bowl of dried mint (for spirit communication)

As with the mantra above, perform this a few hours ahead of your readings. Place your cards on the altar, and position the bowl of mint to the right and the lit candle to the left. Say this mantra seven times:

I summon positive spirits today, to relay to me what you need to say.

I open my mind, now it is free, I summon your light to shine unto me.

Close with the words "And so it is."

The spirits love the smell of any kind of mint, so while the candle is burning, rub a little of the mint between your fingers to release some of the scent. Let the candle burn for a few hours, then blow it out. Place the cards back in the deck, then take the mint bowl and rest it on your reading table so it can continue to work its magic throughout the consultation.

Protection from Unwanted Spirits

When we call on the spirits to assist us with our readings, we invite all types of otherworldly beings into our space and run the risk of allowing something malevolent in. Whether the spirits are good or bad, you may notice after the reading that the air is very thick in the reading room, or there will be cold spots; you might even sense a presence and a heaviness in your head.

At times like these, one must close the portal between the earth and spirit realms.

You will need the following:

FROM THE TAROT: THE DEVIL,
THE SUN, AND THE ACE OF CUPS

* A decent-size piece of black obsidian (for protection)
* 1 black candle (to trap negative energy) and 1 white candle (to purify), 4 to 5 inches tall
* 1 sage incense stick and a holder (to purify the space)
* A bell (to settle down the energies)
* 1 piece of black tourmaline to wear (to ground and protect you)

Place the three Tarot cards on the table with the Devil in the center and one of the other two cards on each side. Rest the black obsidian in front of them. Situate the black candle to the left and the white candle to the right and light them. Hold the incense in your left hand and ignite the tip with a match or lighter. After thirty seconds or so, blow out the flame, allowing the smoke to permeate throughout the room. In your right hand, ring the bell repeatedly for about thirty seconds. Place the bell on the altar, and rest the incense in its holder. Next, say this mantra twelve times:

I bind any evil to the wax of the black;
*   you shan't stay here; I send*
*   you back.*

I welcome the good with the wax of the
*   white to cleanse this space,*
*   in both day and night.*

This ritual calls for a little more power than usual, and so when you have recited it twelve times, close by saying, "And so it is." This time it's important that the candles and the incense burn down on their own, so don't extinguish them or the mantra won't work. Once the ritual is complete, place the cards back in the deck.

Other Mantra Examples

HEALING

When someone is unwell, without them realizing it, the illness can often manifest into negative energy. It will hang around for ages and take a while to dispel. This Tarot mantra can speed up the recovery process because it works toward changing those negative vibes into positive ones. If you are unwell or someone close to you is, give this a try.

You will need the following:

A COURT MENTOR CARD THAT
REPRESENTS THE PERSON WHO IS ILL

* Five of Pentacles (the illness)
* Ace of Cups (super positive card)

✳ Sun (a happy ending)
✳ A medium-sized piece of amethyst crystal (for healing)
✳ One yellow candle in a suitable holder (for recovery)

Place the significator card in the center of the altar, the Five of Pentacles below, the Ace of Cups to the left, and the Sun to the right. Light the candle and place it somewhere on the table where there is space.

Hold the crystal in your left hand. Say this mantra seven times:

I call upon the spirits to shower me [or name] with healing light.
Change the energy that surrounds me, from dark to brilliant bright.

After you have spoken the mantra seven times, close the ritual by saying, "And so it is."

Place the crystal on the altar next to the candle and leave everything where it is until the candle has burned all the way down. The person who is sick should sleep with the crystal under their pillow every night for a week.

Harmony in the Family
This mantra can work well for anyone who is quarreling with a family member. This can include sibling rivalry or problems in a marriage or partnership. It's even been known to work for dogs or cats that don't get along. Usually, the people or pets will have to live under the same roof.

You will need the following:

From the Tarot: the four Aces (collectively they hold great power)

✳ A paper and pen
✳ A white candle (for harmony)
✳ A piece of clear quartz (to amplify the magic)

On the first night of a new moon phase, place the four Aces in a horizontal line on the altar, starting with the Ace of Swords and followed by the Ace of Wands, the Ace of Pentacles, and, finally, the Ace of Cups. Light the white candle and place it at the back of the cards. On the piece of paper, write down the names of the people who are in dispute and the words below:

No more will you quarrel. You'll give each other space,
Harmony will occur with the mighty and magical Ace.

Place this on the altar and rest the quartz crystal on top.

Next, recite the words on the paper seven times, and once you have, close with the words, "And so it is." It is really important you don't disturb the candle. Allow it to burn down, and only then can you pack up the altar and place the cards back in their box. The piece of paper has to be burned, so if you have an open fire, you can throw it in.

If not, get a fireproof dish, take it outside, place the paper in it, and set fire to the paper. Please ensure you do this safely and keep away from children and pets.

FERTILITY

If you or someone close to you is having problems conceiving, you might like to try this mantra. For this ritual, you will need to perform the steps below for seven consecutive nights.

You will need the following:

FROM THE TAROT: THE EMPRESS, ANY PAGE CARD, AND THE STAR

* 1 small egg (whole with the shell) in a dish (represents fertility)
* A piece of carnelian crystal (for conception)
* A handful of torn basil leaves or one teaspoon of dried basil (the fertility herb)
* A blue candle (pale or dark—for children)

On the altar, place the Empress card upright in the center; next, rest the Page horizontally on top, and finally, situate the Star to the right. Light the candle and place this on the left. Take the carnelian and put it in the dish with the egg. Scatter the basil over the top of the items. Put this bowl on the table where there is a space.

A FERTILITY MANTRA FOR YOURSELF

Repeat these words seven times.

Let my stomach swell with an infant who is well.
Mother nature, bless me
She shall cushion and protect me.

A FERTILITY MANTRA FOR SOMEONE ELSE

I call upon the universe to grace [name] with a child,
No longer leave her barren; lift her face with a smile.

Let the candle burn and leave everything overnight on the altar. In the morning, you can place the cards back in the pack.

Take the egg, cook it however you like, and then eat it with the basil (or give it to the person wanting to get pregnant and tell her to do the same). The carnelian stone must be placed on a nightstand by the bed. And the best bit—make lots of love!

Creating Your Own Tarot Mantra

Sometimes, no matter how many books you search through, there won't be a ritual for your situation. It isn't difficult to invent your own. In most cases, it's better, because manifesting energy with passion comes directly from your heart and gives more desirable results.

Example: If you were stressed with work and wanted a new job, you would select the Ace of Wands from the deck, as this card symbolizes a new career, along with a King, Queen, or Knight that represents you. You might want to go whole hog and have the Ace of Pentacles present on the altar also; this will ensure more money will be coming in with the new job.

You would place these cards in the center of your altar and situate four green lit candles (the color for work) around the outside of the cards.

Next, you would write yourself an incantation, something like this:

I call upon the cosmos to bring new
opportunities my way,
New work awaits me, a new job today.

Say the mantra seven times; this is a magical number and will ensure your message is received by the universe. When you have recited it seven times, end the ritual by saying, "And so it is."

Your mantra does not have to rhyme; the most important thing is that it is heartfelt. You can also summon your own deity and say something like this if you wish:

[Name of deity], I ask you from the bottom
of my heart to bring a new job to me.
I am unhappy where I am and desire a
change.
I trust your judgement and await your
response.
And so it is.

Human beings are not all necessarily on the same vibration; therefore, it doesn't matter at all what faith you ascribe to. If your request is genuine, whoever you choose to worship should help you, and your mantra will be successful.

Another example: If you're single and want to attract a new love into your life, you might choose the Lovers card or the Two of Cups, as these are excellent relationship cards. If you are hoping for a particular kind of partner, you would have to find one of the Kings, Queens, or Knights in the deck representing the sort of person you want to meet.

The candle color for love is pink, so you would place this on the altar with your chosen cards. After lighting the candle, you would recite something like this:

I seek a nice companion to stand by my side,
Someone who will share my love, someone kind, sent from above.

Or perhaps you would like to ask your chosen deity in your own words:

[Name of deity], I ask your assistance this day. Please help me find a nice partner. Someone who I can share my love with. A partner who can support me and whom I can cherish.

With either scenario, like before, say the mantra seven times and close with the words, "And so it is."

Whatever your desire is, as long as it's realistic and genuine and created with love and kindness, you can always rely on your trusted Tarot to help you with your wish. You can use as many cards as you like, grouping them to tell a story, or you can use each card singularly to portray your desired results.

Good luck!

Epilogue

It takes bravery to do the things we do, and at times, we are sadly the recipients of others' bigotry. It helps that we come from psychic families and are fortunate enough to have a fantastic support network. Still, starting off solo can be a difficult and lonely journey, especially if you have a bad day or make a huge mistake. Natural readers have a calling in their hearts, so don't let others put you off, and know that you will be given spiritual help along the way. Most of our students in the past have made firm friendships with each other and kept the link going for many years. It's great to be with like-minded people where you know you can be yourself, so joining a Tarot course or an online group is always a good start. Even after all these years of reading the Tarot, we are both still discovering new things about the cards.

Do experiment with different spreads and decks and select the ones you feel would be best for certain clients. If you feel mortified at a reading that's gone terribly wrong, don't lose confidence; tomorrow is another day. You won't be able to solve everyone's problems, and there will be those clients you can't connect with. Someone once told us that if you can help make a difference in just one person's life, you have achieved great things. We like to think this is the case. It feels nice to know you might have helped someone along the way or that you've opened their mind to all things spiritual.

We hope this book has given you an insight into the joys, trials, and tribulations of our careers, and that you can learn from our mistakes and gain some wisdom from our words.

We wish you success along the way, and remember, the more readings you do, the greater your psychic skills will become.

Practice makes perfect!

Blessed be,
Beleta and Leanna Greenaway

Acknowledgments

We would like to take this opportunity to say a big thanks to all those people who gave their permission for us to use their stories in our case studies. By allowing us to share, we hope it goes on to help and inspire other readers in the future.